Making
a
Difference

Making a Difference

Strategies and tools for transforming your organization

Bruce Nixon

AMACOM
American Management Association
New York • Atlanta • Boston • Kansas City • San Francisco • Washington, D.C.
Brussels • Mexico City • Toronto

This book is available at a special
discount when ordered in bulk quantities.
For information, contact Special Sales Department,
AMACOM, a division of American Management Association,
1601 Broadway, New York, NY 10019.

This publication is designed to provide accurate and authoritative
information in regard to the subject matter covered. It is sold with
the understanding that the publisher is not engaged in rendering legal, accounting, or other professional service. If legal advice or other
expert assistance is required, the services of a competent professional person should be sought.

HD
58.8
.N58
1998

Library of Congress Cataloging-in-Publication Data

Nixon, Bruce.
    Making a difference : strategies and real time models to
transform your organization / Bruce Nixon.
        p. cm.
    Includes bibliographical references and index.
    ISBN 0-8144-0402-2
    1. Organizational change. 2. Organizational behavior.
3. Industrial management. 4. Strategic planning. I. Title
    HD58.8.N58 1998   98-22618
    658.4'063—dc21   CIP

Printing number

10 9 8 7 6 5 4 3 2 1

Contents

Forewords

I decided I wanted two forewords – one American and one British. In a way the book is transatlantic: I have been inspired by American thought and practice; the book will be published in both countries; my first proper job was in Los Angeles; later I was profoundly influenced by 5½ years working just south of the Atlantic in Jamaica; my wife is American and I have spent many lazy summers in New England with family and friends; my two youngest children are proudly half American. Therefore I invited two people whose work I admire – one on the Pacific Coast, the other from Yorkshire, England – to contribute the following forewords. Somehow, in a book which attempts to offer a global perspective, it seems fitting that the two forewords circle the world.

Roger Harrison writes...

Bruce Nixon's *Making a Difference* presents leading edge ideas of 'organization transformation' for HRD professionals and internal consultants in a way that strikes just the right balance of vision with common sense and practicality. Through his years of experience on the front lines of organizational change, he has achieved a deep and compassionate understanding of people and the systems in which they live and work. In this book he shares his undimmed hope in the redeemability of our society and its organizations, well tempered with the realism of a veteran of countless 'change campaigns.' The author eschews the vague enthusiasm with which transformational ideas are so often presented. Instead, *Making a Difference* offers a wealth of real-life stories of change and its pitfalls, together with principles and practices which will inform and enlighten even the most experienced among us.

I have been touched by the heart and commitment which shine through the experienced and practical treatment which characterizes the book. The person he is speaks eloquently through his prose, and I am truly glad to have encountered him. I am sure his book will touch the hearts and minds of many in our profession.

Mike Pedler writes...

This is a very personal book written from the heart of the author's beliefs and values. It offers the principles, tools and practice of what Bruce calls 'real-time management development' yet it is also in various ways the story of a consultant's journey. Perhaps all good practice is biographically rooted, which is why applying the prescriptions of the simple 'How to' books is invariably unsatisfactory, and it is clear from this account that what you do – as a consultant or trainer – is intimately bound up with who you are.

This truth is used to transform the old, slightly dog-eared and definitely male consultancy model (you know, begin with 'entry,' end with 'withdrawal') into a cycle which includes the consultant's own purposes and vision for the organization along with the usual bits. This departure from guaranteed success and relentless linearity is welcome and it also makes it clear that when – as a client – you engage a consultant, you are entering into a relationship with another person, with strengths, skills and energies, but also with quirks, failings and shadows.

Whatever the quirks, what shines through here are Bruce's sense of hard-won self-belief, his faith that all people and organizations can do better and the conviction that such transformations are a vital contribution to our emerging global society. The case studies in this book may make you feel pretty confident that with Bruce on your side you can make a difference, but they also illustrate and acknowledge failure. This seems entirely healthy, for some years now the organization development texts have been telling us that perhaps 70% of major organizational change efforts end in failure, yet on reading most consultancy books, you would be forgiven for thinking that you had somehow passed into a parallel universe. So, as well as models and methods, here are stories of heroism and failure, accounts of much pleasure and some pain, occasional innocence, plenty of goodwill but never any put-downs, cynicism or world weariness.

Bruce's philosophy rests on three main principles:

- *we are moving towards a world in which we are increasingly aware of how interconnected and interdependent we all are . . .* and, that this is a world in which...
- *we can all make a difference* because we all have so much more power than we think ... but only if we put...
- *our own personal development at the center of our practice*

To sum up – in his own words:

'*Whether we are fully aware of it or not, we are all part of a long march towards a more equitable and respectful global society, in which it is possible for everyone to be more truly human. And what we do in our organizations is an important part of this. Seen in this light, our work and learning together become part of something very inspiring and exciting.*'

To which, Amen.

Roger Harrison, PhD is a pioneer practitioner in the field of Organization Development, having participated in and contributed to nearly every phase of its growth from survey research and team building, to large system change and organization transformation. His many contributions to the professional literature include his *Collected Papers* and his professional autobiography, *Consultant's Journey, A Dance of Work and Spirit*, published by McGraw Hill Europe.

Mike Pedler, PhD is a writer, researcher and consultant. He is a partner in the Learning Company Project and Revans Professional Fellow in the Revans Center for Action Learning and Research at the University of Salford. Amongst his many publications are *Action Learning in Practice*, 3rd edition, Gower 1997; *The Learning Company: A Strategy for Sustainable Development*, 2nd edition, McGraw-Hill 1997; *Perfect plc?: The purpose and practice of organizational learning*, McGraw-Hill 1996.

Acknowledgments

Acknowledgments begin with Arthur Watts, Head Teacher at Kingsmead School in the Wirral, who rescued me from the effects of previous unhappy schooling at the age of ten and taught me lessons I have never forgotten about how to bring out individual potential. Then, Arthur Green, my history teacher at Birkenhead School inspired me with the idea of changing things for the better.

Colin Gill at Alcan Jamaica, in the sixties, gave me my first public speaking assignment in Kingston, Jamaica and introduced me to Douglas McGregor's classic *The Human Side of Enterprise*. Then Alan Marsh of Reed Paper and Elizabeth Sidney taught me about training managers. Elizabeth gave me my first taste of freelance work and work in a film including a part. Jim Wickens of Sun Alliance showed me how to use management development to work on real opportunities and issues. He also gave me the freedom and support to experiment and really learn about organization development. Like so many, I am greatly indebted to Professor Reg Revans whose revolutionary ideas about management development I first read in the early 1970s. Mel Berger taught me about project-based management development and a holistic approach. David Casey and, later, Michael Simmons introduced me to consulting. Chris Bull, Michael Simmons and Charlie Kreiner, a big American, taught me a great deal about counseling, leadership, race and gender issues and the ways in which men in particular are oppressed because of their gender conditioning. Chris Bull's Change Model influenced my Empowerment Model. Robin Coates and Neslyn Watson-Druce are two other loving friends and teachers. I learned a lot with colleagues at Sun Alliance, including Richard Allen, Don Hole, Brian Lawrence, Chris Nutt, John Seddon, Carmel Silverosa, John Thatcher, Mary Thompson and Jean Woollard. Professor Alan Mumford, an excellent editor, helped me write better articles about my work in those days.

I am indebted to many clients, including the anonymous ones who contributed to the case studies, who gave me opportunities for us to learn together. Several suggested I write a book and finally I accepted their advice! Mike Pedler, another helpful editor, first suggested I learn about large group interventions. Many people have since taught me more about them including Julie Beedon, Nancy Cebula, Paul Cox, Sandra Janoff, Martin Leith, Frank McKeown, Harrison Owen, Robert Rehm and Marvin Weisbord. Julia Cameron's *Artist's Way* was a tremendous support whilst writing the book – an example and a daily companion. I am indebted to Gilmour and Carole Drummond for their patient encouragement and creative contributions and for giving me the chance to publish; Stuart Macfarlane for his good work and production advice; Rita Yorston for all her painstaking word processing; my wife Suzanne for her support throughout the writing of this book and lots of suggestions for improving the text; and my five children, Mark, Guy, Charlie, Hannah and George, for teaching me such a lot about becoming a better person.

* * *

The author and publisher acknowledge the following sources of copyright material:

Words from *The Prophet* by Kahlil Gibran are used by permission from the National Committee of Gibran 1951, © all rights reserved.

Words from *Managing on the Edge* © Richard Pascale 1991. Reprinted by permission of ICM, International Creative Management, Inc.

Words from *Joyce Grenfell Requests the Pleasure*, copyright © Joyce Grenfell 1976. (Taken from the BBC Radio Collection tape of 1989 based on the book.)

About the Author

❖

Bruce Nixon has over 30 years' experience of helping organizations and people thrive and prosper in conditions of change and uncertainty. He believes we need to change the culture of our organizations and learn different attitudes and behavior so that we are better able to cope in these difficult times. He does long-term work with directors, managers and HR people in the private and public sectors. For several years he has led open programs for people interested in organization change and development.

He has worked both on the inside of organizations and as an external consultant. Before starting his own business ten years ago, Bruce was Training and Development Manager with Sun Alliance Insurance (now Royal & Sun Alliance Insurance) where he initiated a wide range of innovative and effective management and organization development programs. He has trained many developers and consultants both internal and external.

After graduating from Oxford University in Philosophy, Politics and Economics, his first job was in a department store in Los Angeles. He then worked in various HR roles in Peek Frean, Birds Eye Foods, Alcan Aluminium (in the UK and Jamaica) and Reed Paper.

Always interested in pioneering, he particularly enjoyed helping set up the personnel department in a new plant in Jamaica and helping transform the personnel function in Sun Alliance. He now enjoys the unpredictability, freedom and adventure of working for himself and the opportunities it offers for learning and development.

He has written many articles and papers about his work and has contributed to several books one of which he edited (now published in China). He is an active member of the Association for Management Education and Development (AMED) on whose executive he served for six years. Currently he is tutor for the Development Strategy module of the AMED 'Developing the Developers' Course leading to the Henley Management College Diploma in Management and Organization Development. He is a Fellow of the Institute of Personnel and Development. This is his first book.

Married to an American, he has three grown-up sons and two younger children. He lives in Berkhamsted, England, and often spends warm summers in New England.

Chapter Summaries

PART I **Seeing the Big Picture**

Chapter 1 Global Forces – the situation we are in
Global transformation; Consequences; Changing human aspirations; Benign and shadow side; Historical perspective.

Chapter 2 Tomorrow's Organizations – principles for surviving and thriving
Win the hearts and minds of all stakeholders; Empower and enable; Learn how to both value diversity and unite people in common cause; Be excellent in responding well to uncertainty, complexity and change; Love our work and love ourselves; Have an attitude of long-term stewardship.

Chapter 3 Tomorrow's Culture and Leadership
Adversarial culture; Partnership culture; Old leadership messages; Enabling leadership; A new culture for organizations; Key survival skills.

PART II **Principles, Strategies and Basic Tools**

Chapter 4 Principles and Tools for Transfformation – a new vision for learning and development
Principles; How to encourage cultural change; Tools for transformation.

Chapter 5 Taking a Strategic Approach – developing your own vision and strategy
The trouble with organizations; A fresh mind-set; A new model for internal consultants; Doing this work in teams; Some effective strategies.

PART III Taking Practical Steps

Chapter 6 Real Time Management Development – working with managers on their real opportunities
The way we develop managers lags far behind; But the truth is never that simple; A radically different approach; Principles; The overall structure of RTMD; Starting – building readiness and planning; Workshop I; Workshop II (two days); How does RTMD change attitudes and behavior?; Creating critical mass and embedding change; Key factors that make for success; Benefits to business.

Chapter 7 Using Real Time Management Development – to change the culture of an organization
Four case studies; Having realistic expectations; Case study 1: bottom up; Case study 2: working near the top; Case study 3: top down; Case study 4: stuck at the top.

Chapter 8 Getting the Whole System into the Room – gaining the commitment of the whole workforce to change
My journey; The case for getting the whole system into the room; Background history; Future search; Open space technology; Real time strategic change; Search conferences; Comparing the four approaches; Conclusions.

Chapter 9 Giving and Getting a Good Listening To – releasing individual potential
Listening is an important part of your strategy; Why one-to-one facilitating is so important; How we react to what is going on out there; Useful assumptions about people; How our potential gets blocked; Stereotypes; Cultural and organization norms that limit people; Practical implications; Giving people a good listening to; Continuous learning and improvement; Giving feedback.

Chapter 10 Transforming Teamwork – valuing diversity *and* fostering collaboration
What goes on in teams – the patterns; Breaking the patterns *and* creating a new vision of teamwork; Symbols; Starting; Ground rules; Core work; Task and process; Cross-cultural team building; Conclusion.

Chapter 11 Using Support Groups and Networking for Change
Why you need support; When it works and when it does not; Getting robust support; Call it whatever you like; Choosing mem-

bership; Avoiding the 'cosy club'; Basic processes for a support group; Self-love, self esteem; Trust your thinking – the principle of the first thought; Networking – creating one team.

Introduction

❖

'If there's one overriding lesson from our experience, I think it's that there are indeed great rewards for organizations that pay as much attention to the engineering going on in the so-called "soft" side of their business as the "hard" side.' Bob Lutz, President of Chrysler Corporation. Quoted in *Tomorrow's Company—The Role of Business in a Changing World,* Royal Society of Arts Inquiry, published by Gower, 1995.

'In 1993, Toyota set itself the goal of halving production costs – while continuing to improve performance – within seven years. It is on target.' *Tomorrow's Company – The Role of Business in a Changing World,* Royal Society of Arts Inquiry, published by Gower, 1995.

'We are a poor country but a rich people.' A Cuban.

The situation we are in

Organizations and people face a tidal wave of global economic, technological and social change. For many, the name of the game is survival. We are not going to survive in the global economy through technological innovation alone. If we are going to withstand relentless global competition, we need to radically change our way of doing business. Growing numbers at all levels believe that, to have a better chance of success, organizations need to engage the energy, creativity and intelligence of the whole workforce and involve other stakeholders, like customers, suppliers,

investors and the community. We have to give up the old hierarchical, adversarial approach which wastes individual talents
and saps energy in unproductive conflict. Instead we need to
build trust, drive out fear and create productive partnerships in
which everyone can offer their unique knowledge and talents,
otherwise we shall see continued decline in our businesses and
an increasingly impoverished society. People who know how to
help their organizations do this can make a decisive difference.

Most of us earn our livings by working in or supplying organizations of one sort or another. For many of us this work is our
chief means of self-expression and the main way in which we offer our gifts to the world. And yet our organizations and the drive
for economic survival and increasing prosperity are not everything. Appreciating how interconnected all the members and
stakeholders of an organization are is a step in the right direction. But we also need to encompass in our vision, our families
and friends, our communities, the community of people
throughout the world and the Earth on which all life depends.

Working in organizations is difficult. We face increasing uncertainty about the continued prosperity and survival of our organizations and our positions in them. There are great pressures
on the fewer people employed and the ways in which people in
organizations behave and treat each other are often painful and
dysfunctional. Many organizations have experienced traumatic
change and there is a need for healing. Sometimes we are aware
that the work we do or the work of the organization is not wholly
good work – it may be harmful to society in some respects or bad
for us. We face dilemmas because everyone needs to earn a living. Also it does not make sense to adopt a position of moral
superiority. We are all involved directly or indirectly.

The importance of organizations is huge. They provide the majority of the goods and services we need, a living for people in
paid work and much of the wealth upon which a civilized society depends. Without sufficient healthy, thriving organizations
and the employment they can provide, there is a real danger of
society disintegrating into disorder and chaos. Organizations are
the chief means through which human beings develop and express their capacity to form a community, co-operate and work
together in common cause. Together with the family, organizations provide one of the most important arenas in which we express ourselves, learn, develop and grow. Organizations have a

huge contribution to make in building a better world society. If society is to change for the better, it will happen, to a large extent, through the changes that take place within organizations, the responsibility they take and the influence they exert on the world outside. They are important places in which we can experiment and learn how to work together less exploitatively and with greater respect for each other. Just as organizations can be alienating and frustrating, they have the potential to be and often are exciting, rewarding and fulfilling. It is our choice. We can make them or our parts of them what we want them to be.

We human beings are engaged in a journey together, some would say a spiritual journey, in which we are learning, albeit erratically and with difficulty, to live together as sisters and brothers and with other forms of life on this planet. Increasingly we are appreciating the extent of our interdependence. Our progress is laborious, sometimes destructive and sometimes benign. We take some steps forward and then some back. History goes backwards as well as forwards. We try out one way, discover its inadequacies and try another. Sometimes we move from one extreme to another. In this way progress is 'dialectical.' Taking a long-term historical perspective, we have made great progress in many areas. It is as if we are constantly being confronted with the consequences of our actions and forced to learn, partly through the ever present prospect of loss of our living, chaos, pollution of the planet, or annihilation if we do not. Enlightenment and self-interest tend to conspire together in the long-term.

In a sense there is nothing new in the situation we face, and yet it is new. We have never been here before. We cannot know how to respond. We can only discover and in this sense we are all travellers. Many of us have learned not to trust people who claim to have the answers or speak with certainty. It is a time of major transition from one kind of society to another. The situation at once offers grave threats, rich opportunities and hope for a better world. Perhaps more people have more choice than ever before. It is an exciting time with huge potential for creativity, partnership and fulfillment, especially if we can learn to bring out everyone's potential and respect our differences.

Who the book is for

This book is for people who are passionate about wanting their organizations to flourish and become better places in which to work and who believe they can contribute. It is for people who share the view that we need to make a major shift in mind-set away from the hierarchical, adversarial approach towards an inclusive and empowering one that gets the best out of everyone. It is also for people who have a wider perspective and care about their communities, society as a whole, the world of nations and the Earth. If you have read thus far you are probably one of these people.

The book is primarily aimed at the human resource development (HRD) practitioner or developer – the company's 'internal consultant' or 'facilitator.' But you could be a CEO, director, manager or any other member of the company who wants to exert your influence on how your organization leads its people. There are many quiet revolutionaries all over the world working away at helping organizations adapt and transform themselves so as to survive and thrive and be good places to work in. If you are one of these, this book is for you.

The book is written for people who work in ordinary organizations which may not be particularly pioneering or innovative in the way people are led and managed but want to become more so. It is for those who want to work with the paradox of how to be ethical and responsible world citizens, make work in their organizations a better experience for everyone *and* survive and prosper in a world that is fiercely competitive and increasingly uncertain. It is for people who wish to see prosperity *and* sustainable development; who wish to be stewards rather than exploiters and use their skills to good purpose. It is for those who recognize they are travellers in a largely uncharted terrain. It is not for people who expect simple answers or certainty, nor those who believe they are entirely in control of their lives. It is for those who believe they can *make a difference* and want to exercise leadership at whatever level in their organizations in changing them for the better.

The purpose of the book

Challenging tradition is not easy especially when you are immersed in the pressures, opportunities and challenges of daily life in the typical organization. You and it are struggling to survive. My intention is to provide you with *both* inspiration and support for your own visionary ideas and efforts *and* practical, readily accessible ideas and tools that will help you make a decisive difference to your organization.

Themes of the book

'We have flown in the air like birds and swum the sea like fishes but we have yet to learn the simple act of walking the earth like brothers and sisters.' Martin Luther King.

Almost every chief executive I meet says in so many words:

'Technical innovation won't be enough. I want people to take individual responsibility based on an understanding of the whole picture. I also want people to work together as a team, realizing that we are all interdependent. We have to do this if we want to continuously improve and deliver constantly increasing quality at decreasing cost. That is the only way we will survive.'

There seem to be two big issues in organizations today. They have been around for a long time and we are still struggling with them after many decades:

- How can we bring out everyone's potential and enlist it in the service of the organization?
- How can we learn to respect and value every different person and work together to achieve common goals?

The two are of course interrelated – you cannot do one without the other. People will not develop or offer their full potential in an organization which does not value and respect difference or in which people do not work together. And for people to contribute without reservation they need to feel that there is a sufficient degree of fairness and equity in their treatment and rewards.

These are equally big issues on a national and global scale. A major theme of the book is learning how we can resolve these two issues and it offers practical ways and suggestions for doing so.

Real time development

A second major theme of the book is what I call *real time development*. By this I mean bringing about change and transformation *and* learning at the same time – not separating the two. 'Learning by doing' if you like. I believe the richest seam for learning is the *real* opportunities, issues, difficulties and successes that people have. There is no need to separate learning and doing. The didactic approach is first you learn and then you apply it or do it. It usually employs all sorts of contrived experiences like case studies, role plays, simulations and psychometric instruments. I don't believe we need to do this to learn. Sometimes it is certainly the most appropriate approach and then it is invaluable but in my opinion it is greatly overused. The more I listen to people in business, the more I am persuaded that much of the didactic training which companies spend their money on makes very little difference – particularly if it is not combined with real time development. My experience is that most people learn far more from working with their own reality, the 'here and now' and how they want to change things, although it can be very challenging. In comparison, the didactic approach is comfortable and, because of the lack of challenge, it is relatively boring. Also the didactic, contrived approach tends to be fundamentally *disempowering* as I shall enlarge on in the book.

I do not think we can afford the luxury of *old paradigm*, classroom development. We cannot afford to learn, then try to apply it and show, if we can, that it made a difference. What we have to do I believe is create *new paradigm* development experiences in which people work on transforming their business and learn in so doing at the same time.

Some people tell me that there is nothing new in all this, they are already doing it. But when I get closer and find out what they are actually doing, it is what we were doing 20 and more years ago – essentially classroom teaching. Despite their protests, they are stuck in the *old paradigm.* This is a form of complacency.

This then is another major theme of the book – how to transform development so that it means transforming the business whilst learning at the same time – *continuously improving and learning* and getting a business pay-off are integral parts of it. This means embedding development into how we do business and seeing it as part of doing business. The book aims to provide models for real time development.

However, the truth is never that simple. Everyone is different and people learn in a rich variety of ways. Barry Oshry's work, briefly mentioned in Chapter 6, is an example of simulations being used to powerful effect to stimulate learning and change.

How the book works – the rationale

The book is based on the Empowerment Model and its layout broadly follows that structure. Putting it simply this is *taking individual responsibility whilst seeing the whole picture.* Putting it another way it is *thinking global; acting local.* I believe that if we are going to make a decisive difference we need to have an accurate picture of the whole situation to which many people from the whole system have contributed, be clear about our values and purpose, have an inspiring and personal vision of the future we want, decide clear strategies to bring this about, understand and work on what may get in the way (out there, in our group and in ourselves) and, finally, make plans to act and get the support we need.

The design of the book reflects this model. *Part I Seeing the big picture* is about global forces, a vision for tomorrow's organization, principles for surviving and thriving and tomorrow's culture and leadership. This is very much a personal interpretation and vision and you will need to create your own. Part I is mine; you need to create yours. *Part II Strategies, principles and basic tools* describes your role as an 'internal consultant' or 'facilitator,' the contribution you can make, sets out some strategies you can adopt to make a difference, the underlying principles of real time development and some of the basic tools you can use. *Part III Taking practical steps* describes the strategies in practical de-

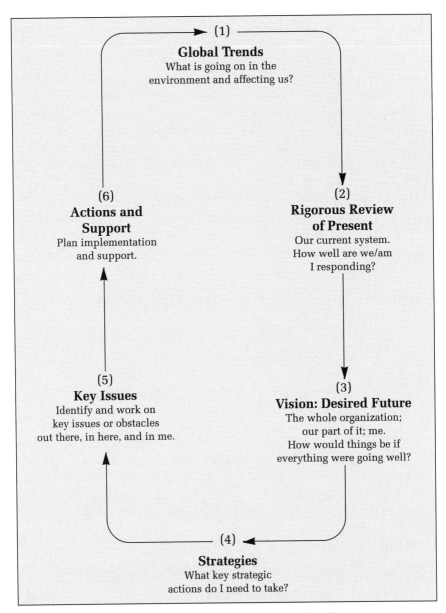

Figure I.1   Empowerment Model

tail. It also attempts to explain what gets in the way of releasing individual and team potential and suggests some things we can do about it. There are more detailed tools in the *Appendices: Tools for transformation.*

How to use the book

You need your own 'Big Picture' to give meaning, energy and passion to your work. Use Part I to stimulate your own thinking and then create your own Part I. You already have it deeply embedded within you and you just need to articulate it. But this book will help bring it out into the forefront of your mind.

'Having a picture of the cathedral as you mix the mortar.'

Use Part II and the 'Internal Consultant's Model' in Chapter 5 to develop your strategic vision. You can use the strategies described in Chapter 5 but most likely they will suggest others that come from your own creativity based on the situation you are in. Use Part III to help you to develop your strategies into practical work with your clients.

You can use the practical models in this book for your own work and to facilitate the work of others. No doubt you will want to change these models and create your own. Also you are welcome to use the figures in the text as a basis for flip charts or overheads. You can copy them, modify them and create your own. If you use the models or figures I should appreciate it if you tell people where they came from.

Making a difference

In the book I frequently use the phrase 'making a difference' because that is all I believe we can do. To claim more is to be immodest, grandiose and pretentious. It is to appeal to the ego. Yet making a difference is very worthwhile. We are all interconnected and it is by making our difference that we transform the situation.

Dialogue and feedback

I hope this book will help you make a difference in your organization. May you prosper with your endeavors. I should be delighted to hear from any reader who wishes to share with me how they have used this book and the effects this has had, or to exchange views, insights and experiences in doing this work. I offer a short open program for people interested in facilitating transformation and building partnerships in their organizations and can send you details of this. I may be contacted at:

Bruce Nixon Associates
'Hillway,' 2 Castle Hill Avenue
Berkhamsted
Herts HP4 1HJ
England, UK
e-mail:brucenixon@mcmail.com
Tel/Fax: +44 (0) 1442 864856
(only during office hours (local time))

Part I

❖

Seeing the
Big Picture

1
❖
Global Forces
The situation
we are in

'When you look at a massive problem it is good to remember about eating an elephant. There is only one way to eat it: one piece at a time. The sea is vast but the sea is just drops of water and each drop counts.' Desmond Tutu.

Global transformation

We live in a time of transformation. It is at once exciting, liberating, developmental, full of opportunity and promise and also threatening, frightening, daunting, painful and exhausting. It is a time of difficulty, complexity, uncertainty and huge pressures for those in or out of organizations. It is a world in which there can be no more illusions of security, predictability or simple solutions. It is a world for which many of us feel ill prepared. We search for new paradigms to understand and help us with what is happening and new survival skills.

It is widely believed that we are in the midst of a transition from one form of society to another comparable to the agricultural and industrial revolutions – a shift from industrial to post-industrial society. But the changes are happening faster than ever before.

The main forces in this transformation are the widespread human desire for a higher material standard of living, technological revolution and globalization of the economy, itself aided by tech-

nological development. At the same time there are other powerful trends. There is a worldwide desire for greater involvement, participation and democracy both in societies and in organizations.
Many people want to break out from dictatorship in their countries
or authoritarian control in their organizations. Different societies
are trying to discover how to encourage individual enterprise and
create prosperity without unleashing greed and sleaze, how to provide equality of opportunity, fairness and social justice and, at the
same time, offer individual freedom and choice. Many people are
still struggling to break out from exploitation and economic imperi-
alism, particularly in the Third World. And how can we solve all
these problems *and* protect the Earth? In our different ways we are
all looking for answers.

Amongst the key advances are those in manufacturing, information technology, telecommunications, medicine, transportation and
agriculture. In the future, wealth in the so called First World is
likely to be based on knowledge and high technology which require
highly educated and trained workforces. Globalization of markets is
resulting in a steady shift of manufacturing and economic energy
away from Europe and North America to the economies of Eastern
Asia and to a lesser extent Latin America. A major global readjustment is taking place which has the potential to redistribute material
prosperity more equitably between nations and is already doing so.
Often, but not always, economic development goes hand in hand
with political democracy.

These developments have the potential ultimately to offer all of
us on the planet a better and more secure life, particularly if wise
rather than greedy choices are made, cultural diversity is fully valued and respected and we pursue sustainable economic development. However the picture, as it develops, is very mixed and a process of major readjustment is often painful. We cannot predict or
control the outcome but we can exert an influence.

Consequences

Many of the effects of economic and technological change on
Western society have been benign. For most people today work is
physically much less hard both in the workplace and in the home.
In response to the pressure of global competition, much ineffi-
ciency, waste, complacency and bureaucracy have been eliminated.

In many instances quality, value and service have dramatically improved. A breath of fresh air has blown through many organizations, much of it inspired by Japanese influence on manufacturing and by American ideas. In some organizations people at every level have become far more involved in decision making and problem solving.

There has been much restructuring in both the private and public sectors, some of which has been clearly beneficial, some less certainly so, and more is to come. Some large organizations have been broken up into more manageable parts and others have been flattened, providing more scope for enterprise, initiative and flexibility. To some degree hierarchies are breaking down and more democratic and more chaotic forms of organizations are emerging. Networked organizations are unfolding, corporate centers are being drastically reduced and whole functions sub-contracted. New technology is making information much more widely available in organizations. Some enlightened business leaders are keen to use e-mail to get feedback from any employee who wants to give it straight to the top, instead of through intermediaries. The notion of stakeholders and partnership is increasingly important, including partnership within organizations, with customers, with suppliers, with investors, with the community and even with competitors. As all but core work is contracted out there are new opportunities for self-employment and entrepreneurship. More people are becoming home workers.

More radical changes, aided by exciting advances in telecoms and information technology, are on the way. Some predict that we are on the edge of a revolution in education based on internationally linked multi-media interactive technologies. There are likely to be more and more interconnected small businesses which constitute major players in the global scene. These developments conspire to break down hierarchies, teams in the traditional sense and large scale organizations. Old concepts of leadership are being rendered obsolete and the concept of partnership becomes more relevant. It is as if technology and human aspirations for greater autonomy and equality conspire to throw the existing state into turmoil and chaos.

For some this is an exciting picture but the down side is the disenfranchising of people in our societies who have difficulty swimming in this sea. Whilst for some it means opportunities for a new and more independent life, for others it means lower pay and benefits, heightened insecurity or unemployment. People who are insufficiently educated or trained will not get a look in. The hopes of some self-employed have ended in a debt, repossession and family break-up. An interesting development is that many men are finding it harder to get work whilst women are more employable and the proportion of women in the UK workforce is set to exceed 50% by the end of the century.

Restructuring and down-sizing in organizations can have traumatic effects both on those who have left and, sometimes worse, on those who remain employed. As a result there is a great need for healing in many organizations. Even those who continue to enjoy the material benefits of employment find the pace gruelling as fewer and fewer remain to carry the load. While some people don't have enough work, others have too much. Many discover that the talk of empowerment and reduction of hierarchy has a hollow ring. The command and control model still prevails. Under the skin, their organizations are just as controlling and oppressive and many people live in a state of fear. This is not to say that there are not many genuine and benign initiatives in democratizing the workplace. It is that old habits die hard, particularly in difficult times, and we find it easier to talk about mission, vision, values and beliefs than to put them into daily and consistent practice. Of course it has to be added that some leaders are, to put it bluntly, primarily motivated by the attractions of power, control and money and don't want to change. Some engage in the double talk of saying one thing and quite plainly doing something else, perhaps not aware that they are doing this.

As many industries in Europe and North America die or struggle to survive, unemployment grows. Once again there is an increasing gap between rich and poor. We are almost back to the situation existing at the end of the 1930s. Similarly, the gap between rich and some poor nations, particularly in Africa, is widening. Although it benefits people in the West, concentration on growing cash crops for export has had adverse effects on the ability of people in the so-called Third World to feed themselves. The effects of World Bank and IMF policies on the poor in the Third World have been harsh. Amongst the results are an absolute deterioration in education, health and welfare services in many of these nations. (Paradoxically, Cuba has in some respects a better health service, better education, and more local participation than many developed democracies.) Poor people in such countries have most often borne the brunt of the effects of arms sales mainly emanating from Europe and North America. Indirectly we are all implicated in what happens in the Third World and are likely to be affected by it.

In the so-called developed nations, increasing burdens are placed on the smaller numbers in work by growing unemployment and aging populations. The provision of education, health, other public services and welfare is under increasing strain. The level of unemployment, particularly amongst the young and black people, and the growing gap between rich and poor present a real threat to civilized society, order and stability, not only in Western countries. It is becoming clear that it is not sensible to pursue limitless economic growth as the answer to unemployment whilst ignoring the effects on the ecology of the Earth and the quality of life upon it. Limitless consumption cannot provide a satisfactory solution.

We already have enormous ecological problems owing to modern agriculture, industrial processes, growing use of motor transport and other sources of atmospheric pollution. These problems are likely to worsen dramatically as economic development and Western style prosperity spread throughout the world. It is not only the ecological consequences that threaten the quality of our lives but also the noise, stress and destruction of beautiful natural and man made environments.

Changing human aspirations

So far what I have written has largely been about the consequences of technological change and globalization of the economy. At the same time there seem to be changes in human consciousness running parallel with, and partly as a reaction to, technological and economic development, despite or perhaps because of the harsh realities many people face.

It is not only that material expectations are rising. In other respects our horizons and expectations are growing. Membership of, and maybe the influence of, single issue groups or non-governmental organizations (NGOs) is growing and far exceeds that of political parties. In the UK, there are signs of a growing impatience with the egotism and adversarialism of party politics and its domination by men. The newly elected House of Commons has over 100 women members. Trust in politicians is at an all time low and in the UK a significant minority want radical constitutional reform including proportional representation, devolution, a Bill of Rights and freedom of information. The newly elected government is trying to respond to these trends in public opinion. People are much better informed and more aware. Inconsistencies and abuses are 'outed' very quickly by alert and inquisitive media. The mass of people are far more critical and questioning. New technology is making it harder to suppress information even in oppressive regimes. Not only does an image conscious organization have to offer genuine quality and value; it has also to show evidence of being a responsible member of the community and a world citizen.

People are far more ecologically aware. More and more people care about pollution in all its forms and the future of the planet as an environment for human and other life forms. There is growing concern about the adverse effects of increasing use of the motor car and transportation of food over vast distances. The public are better informed about health issues and the importance of diet. More people care about the treatment of other species and their survival and are aware of the importance of bio-diversity. More people are becoming vegetarian and want organic food. They care about how food is produced and are not impressed by those who talk only of cost effectiveness and efficiency in its production as if that justified the adverse consequences.

There is growing awareness, as people travel more, of the value and importance of cultural diversity and reaction against businesses which are out of step with this. In some ways we are all growing more alike as we learn from each other and enjoy the richness of our cultural diversity. For example, people in the West are enjoying a huge variety of food and cuisine from all over the world. Nations are collaborating more, forming regional economic unions and giving up some sovereignty. Sovereignty is being eroded by the power of multi-national organizations. Yet in other respects we cherish our differences and uniqueness. The large Nation State concept of the nineteenth century which ignored regional differences is being challenged in many parts of the world where people are struggling for independence or devolution.

People care about fairness and justice and the effect of Western economic policies on the so-called Third World. They can see the inadequacy of an uncritical belief in market forces and capitalism. They care about equal opportunities and fairness and are more aware of and attuned to issues of gender, race, age, disability and other differences. They recognize the need for a better balance between ying and yang, masculine and feminine and the left and right sides of the brain. They are disenchanted with the blatant greed of the 1980s and leaders who are preoccupied with building empires of money and power. There is considerable public disquiet about alleged boardroom greed and sleaze in public life. As long as they can survive economically, many people want to do something that is 'worthwhile' and contributes to society and feel the product they make or the service they offer is 'good.' They want to do good work rather than be hugely compensated for work which is not good. There is growing realization that unemployment is no longer a cyclical problem and growing concern about the widening gap between rich and poor. Consequently enlightenment is becoming good business and, at a more superficial level, good marketing.

People are far more cynical or skeptical and quicker to spot or suspect insincerity, inconsistency or a lack of integrity. We have an increasingly sophisticated and educated public. Many people are looking for meaning and quality in their lives and recognize that they are spiritual beings. I see a growing interest in various forms of spirituality and healing perhaps as a response to the uncertainty, pressures and pain involved in working in organizations or surviving outside them. Many people have come to the conclusion that Cartesian thinking and total belief in science and the machine are not adequate. They see the universe as mysterious and wonderful and not wholly in the control of human beings. They see the interconnectedness of all things – in a global economy it is easier to see just how interconnected we are – understanding the importance of paradox in their lives, realizing there are no simple solutions or answers, attractive as they might be. The pursuit of power and money for its own sake does not impress or inspire such people and, given a choice, they look for work, employers, products and services, customers and investments that accord with their values. They also realize that not all progress can be measured in terms of Gross National Product. They do not believe that unrestrained capitalism, consumerism and free market forces provide the basis for a healthy society. Trickle-down theories of

- Globalization of the economy and global readjustment.
- Technological revolution.
- Desire for a higher material standard of living.
- Desire for democracy and independence.
- Decline, downsizing, restructuring and unemployment.
- The ecological crisis.
- Growing gap between rich and poor within and between nations.
- Demographic change – aging populations.
- Higher expectations of quality of work and life.
- Growing appreciation of our interconnectedness.
- The decline of deference and desire for respect for difference and partnership.
- Growing concern about the Third World.
- The search for meaning, healing and spirituality.

Figure 1.1   Global forces

wealth creation have been shown not to fulfill what was hoped for them.

There is a growing desire among growing numbers of people in the world of work for autonomy, interdependence and democracy. They want to see a move away from patriarchy, control and compliance. If deference in organizations is not dead it is certainly in decline. An increasing number of organizations are pioneering new and enlightened ways of doing business which are far more inclusive – see Lewis & Lytton, 1995; Murata, 1991; Roddick, 1992; Semler, 1993.

Many business leaders acknowledge that responding to these trends is fundamental to business success. The Royal Society of Arts inquiry, *Tomorrow's Company – The Role of Business in a Changing World* makes interesting reading. It is based on the views of 48 company leaders. They see the major obstacles preventing UK companies from becoming globally competitive as: complacency and ignorance of world standards, over reliance on financial measures of performance and our national adversarial culture. Confronted with the UK's long-term competitive decline, its low productivity and low quality, the inquiry participants see a way ahead that places emphasis on partnership and inclusive relationships with all key stakeholders, including employees at all levels, suppliers, customers, investors and the community as a whole. The inquiry found widespread agreement that sustainable success depends on the management of all key relationships. Companies that do so, as opposed to setting profits as their primary goal, show above average long-term financial returns.

This is the benign side. There is also the shadow side – not everyone sees the world in this way or would support these aspirations. These are benign forces which can be supported or resisted. On the whole benign forces seem to prevail. From a historical perspective, perhaps nothing in this respect is new (except the possibility of complete and total annihilation). There always has been such a conflict, but this is the form it takes today.

Less than 500 years ago William Tyndale was burned at the stake for translating the Bible into English. I think this helps put things into perspective. In the past hundred years we have seen huge steps forward in many aspects of life, for example, the living conditions of ordinary people in Western countries have improved enormously; work whether at home or in the workplace is much less arduous; the position and influence of women in society and in organizations have advanced greatly; relationships between many fathers and their children have softened and become more intimate; and the situation of black people in our societies has improved, whilst there is a long way to go. Advances in medicine have wiped out some diseases and much increased life expectancy; we have the means to provide a decent life for everyone on the planet; and a more equitable distribution of prosperity on the planet does seem to be gradually emerging. These are just a few examples which illustrate that whilst history goes backwards and forwards, we are making progress. A study of history also shows that many of these themes have been a human preoccupation for a very long time (Zeldin, 1995).

Figure 1.1 summarizes the trends and forces outlined in this chapter.

References and suggested further reading

Aberdene, P. and Naisbitt, J. (1992) *Megatrends for Women – From Liberation to Leadership*, Fawcett Columbine, New York, USA.

Castro, F. (1993) *Tomorrow is Too Late*, Ocean Press, Melbourne, Australia.

Fox, M. (1994) *The Re-invention of Work*, Harper, San Francisco, USA.

Handy, C. (1997) *The Hungry Spirit, Beyond Capitalism – A Quest for Purpose in the Modern World*, Hutchinson, London, UK.

Harman, W. and Hormann, J. (1990) *Creative Work*, Knowledge Systems Inc., Indianapolis, USA.

Hawken, P. (1993) *The Ecology of Commerce*, Harper Business, New York, USA.

Henderson, H. (1993) *Paradigms in Progress – Life Beyond Economics*, Admantine Press, London, UK.

Korten, D. (1995) *When Corporations Rule the World*, Earthscan Books, London, UK and Berrett-Koehler, USA.

Lewis, K. and Lytton, S. (1995) *How to Transform your Company and Enjoy it!*, Management Books 2000, Chalford, Glos., UK.

Manley, M. (1990) *The Politics of Change*, Harvard University Press, Washington DC, USA.

Murata, K. (1991) *How to Make Japanese Management Methods Work in the West*, Gower, London, UK.

Naisbitt, J. (1994) *The Global Paradox*, Nicholas Brealey, London, UK.

Roddick, A. (1992) *Body and Soul*, Vermillion, London, UK.

Rodney, W. (1972, 1989) *How Europe Underdeveloped Africa*, East African Educational Publishers, Nairobi, Kenya. (Available from Africa Book Center, Covent Garden, London, UK (Tel: 44(0)171-240-6649).)

Royal Society of Arts *RSA Inquiry, Tomorrow's Company – The Role of Business in a Changing World* (1996), Gower, London, UK.

Semler, R. (1993) *Maverick, The Success Story Behind the World's Most Unusual Workplace*, Warner Books, USA.

Schumacher, E. F. (1973) *Small is Beautiful*, Abacus, London, UK.

Zeldin, T. (1995), *An Intimate History of Humanity*, Minerva, London, UK

2

Tomorrow's
Organizations
Principles for surviving
and thriving

'The world has enough for everyone's need, but not for anyone's greed.' Mahatma Gandhi.

'Convincing people is a form of violence.' quoted in Theodore Zeldin's *An Intimate History of Humanity.*

'The "Made in Europe" study showed that 70.0 per cent of UK companies thought they performed at world-class levels, whereas only 2.3 per cent were found to do so.' Tomorrow's Company, Royal Society of Arts Inquiry, published by Gower, 1995.

A fresh view seems to be emerging amongst some business leaders today. It is that the traditional focus of Anglo-Saxon companies on short-term financial performance needs to be replaced by attention to long-term strategic health. Strategic health depends on being fully aware of all the major forces affecting the business and having inclusive rather than adversarial relationships with all stakeholders. This viewpoint is expressed in the RSA's inquiry,

Tomorrow's Company – The Role in Business in a Changing World, already referred to in the previous chapter. It is also supported by Will Hutton in his *The State We Are In* (Hutton, 1995).

In some ways the successful functioning of an organization is like that of an individual. Words like grace, synchronicity, serendipity or fortunate coincidence come to mind (Chopra, 1994; Coelho, 1993; Redfield, 1994). We engage in a constructive relationship with the forces within ourselves and those around us in the universe, going with, learning from, rather than ignoring or fighting against, and mysteriously what we desire takes place. This, it seems to me, can apply as much to an organization which works constructively with its own system and its environment (see Figure 2.1).

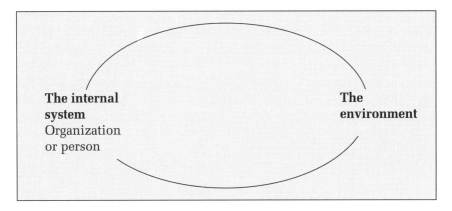

The internal
system
Organization
or person

The
environment

Figure 2.1   The relationships between the system and the environment and within the system itself

1. Win the hearts and minds of all stakeholders.

2. Empower and enable.

3. Learn how to both value diversity and unite people in common cause.

4. Be excellent in responding well to uncertainty, complexity and change.

5. Love our work and love ourselves.

6. Have an attitude of long-term stewardship.

Figure 2.2   Six principles

I suggest six principles reflecting the idea in Figure 2.1 that may help a business (profit-making or otherwise) survive and thrive. As is often the case, they form an interrelated system. They seem simple – almost too simple or obvious – and yet the implications are enormous and difficult. I shall discuss the principles in turn (see Figure 2.2).

Win the hearts and minds of all stakeholders

Stakeholders include employees, suppliers, customers, investors and the community. No one can be perfect at winning over the stakeholders but some organizations do it better than others or do it for a time. (Success can so easily turn into arrogance or complacency.) UK examples include ABB, British Airways, the Body Shop, FI, ICI, IKEA, John Lewis Partnership, Marks & Spencer, Unipart, Virgin and others you will think of. Businesses are more likely to survive and grow when they have the enthusiastic support and challenge of all their stakeholders. They are most likely to attract the ablest and most strongly motivated people and inspire them to offer their full energies and talents. People need to be proud to be involved as stakeholders. For people to be excited and proud to be involved today means that the organization has to be good at a lot of different things. Not only does the organization have to offer genuine quality and value, it also has to show evidence of being a responsible member of the community and a world citizen. It has to respond to the enhanced awareness, concerns and aspirations of people today.

My guess is that an evident and sincere appreciation of the issues and trends outlined in the previous chapter, most likely to emerge from a healthy dialogue with all stakeholders, will be increasingly important to business *survival* and a stable society in which business can prosper.

This has radical implications. Leaders of business who are primarily good at working with power, manipulation, competitive strategy, marketing and money will not have all the necessary requirements. They will seem blinkered if not disabled. Successful leaders will be more balanced. They will be highly responsible citizens of the community and of the world. Guided by a sense of purpose and principles they will understand the importance of struggling to practice the values they espouse and will be acutely aware of the cynicism that is created by not doing so. They will try to 'walk the talk.' They too will be informed about global and ecological issues and see the importance of meaning and spirituality. They will show integrity, honesty and humility and admit that they are fallible and learning all the time. A learning company requires learning leaders. Because they are mature people in this sense they will be able to inspire people and win hearts and minds, no matter how humble the service or product they offer. They will conduct their business in a way that others can respect and admire.

Empower and enable

In an unstable, uncertain and highly competitive world, the excellence a business offers its customers and its creativity, flexibility and resourcefulness in responding to changing needs, markets and competition are vital. In this constant quest for excellence *all* its employees and suppliers matter enormously.

Most of the people I meet have far more to offer than they believe they are capable of. Many demonstrate their unused leadership potential outside their workplace. Smart business leaders will know how to release and nurture these creative talents and energies. They will know how to create conditions which people experience as empowering – which liberate their talents in achieving the interests of the organization and its stakeholders.

Empowerment involves valuing and respecting everyone who works for or supplies the organization. It also means clear goals, guidelines and limits and needed resources. It involves seeing their potential, seeing the good in them and fostering it. People give their best and learn most readily when they are valued, encouraged, supported through difficulties and given honest yet thoughtful feedback when they want or need it. People value being treated with complete honesty and being told the truth, however difficult. This builds trust and respect, partly because it is so astonishingly rare, as long as it is done with sensitivity and consideration. It is more common for leaders to calculate, in a paternalistic or patronizing way, how much of the truth they will tell. Most often this is transparent. 'Nobody tells us anything' is a common complaint. Generally people need to be appreciated much more and criticized much less. Whilst it is essential to choose people well and an organization cannot carry people who don't, can't or won't measure up, far too often when difficulties arise people are got rid of rather than honestly working through their problems.

A key skill in bringing out the talents and brilliance of both ordinary and extraordinary people is the art of listening and asking empowering and interesting questions (see Chapter 9). Yet our first inclination is to tell them, rather than ask them, what to do. We need to practice the art of inviting people to find their own unique solutions, believing that they are their own authorities on the unique job they do – or can become so. They need to look inside themselves for answers. (This is not to say that others cannot give them feedback, insights and inspiration.)

For an organization to be successful today, it needs to go further than merely bringing out the talents of individuals. It also needs to acquire the art of fostering innovation and creativity not only in individuals but also in groups and across the whole organization. This entails many things but in particular recognizing the importance of intuition, synergy, of people trusting their thinking, saying what they really think, challenging without attacking, not laughing *at* others, valuing difference, facing conflict however difficult, learning how to facilitate large groups of people with diverse and conflicting views, really listening to each other, encouraging risk taking and mistake-making, widespread networking and creating a culture that liberates people rather than encouraging caution, fear, compliance and collusion. It could be summed up as a partnership (Block, 1993). Scott Peck talks about creating genuine civility (not superficial politeness) and community in business, ie, really honest talk (Scott Peck, 1994). The best CEOs want people to care enough to really tell them what they think. This is what I believe is needed.

None of this is easy. Empowerment requires people to change the behavior and attitudes of a lifetime and overcome the habits of centuries. We need to break away from the myths and generations of conditioning that affect our collective consciousness. Furthermore, empowerment is a dynamic between two parties. It requires a robust, experimenting relationship without punishment if mistakes are made. It is not just a question of leaders changing their behavior. Those they lead have to change too. Leaders have to struggle against their own expectations and the expectations of others that they know best, make no mistakes, have to be in control and must be seen to be in control. Instead they need to judiciously trust and let go. 'The only way to regain control is by sharing it' is a wise paradox. People they lead need to give up compliance and dependency and not act on their fears, fantasies and feelings of inadequacy. They need to give up unrealistic expectations that leaders be charismatic, infallible and all knowing as opposed to ordinary – indeed, that if they are ordinary, then they are not fit for the job. We all have to acknowledge our engrained discomfort with chaos, uncertainty, mistake-making and not knowing what to do. That's often how it is and needs to be.

These are difficult things to do consistently, under stress and in the heat of the moment. It is easier to be a paragon when things are going well. We often revert to old ways in times of crisis. Yet organizations and people are coping with difficulty, if not crisis, most of the time.

Learn how to both value diversity and unite people in common cause

My experience is that most organizations are extremely uncomfortable with diversity and their selection and socialization procedures are designed to avoid it and suppress it respectively. Also it is ridiculous that most of us waste so much of our working lives and our energy strenuously pretending not to be different. Yet the world outside, the markets, customers, potential employees and suppliers – stakeholders – are increasingly diverse especially as we become one world, one global economy. It is well established too that creativity and innovation spring from diversity and working productively with difference and conflict.

Organizations struggle with uniting people in common cause and purpose. Most teams and organizations are bedeviled by internal competition, adversarial conflict, power-politics and divisions that get in the way of the teamwork needed to resolve problems and create well informed and astute strategies. These are the problems of the enlarged and sensitive ego. This creates an atmosphere which demotivates, causes severe stress, saps energy, wastes talents and drives people out. Adversarial conflict is usually worst amongst the people whose purpose should be to serve those doing the core tasks of the organization. This is only too apparent to the workforce who just wish they would get their act together.

It is not that we should give up our individualism and slavishly imitate some of our Far-Eastern sisters and brothers who are so brilliant at being team players. However within organizations we do need to give up the adversarial habits that over the centuries helped us establish order out of chaos, won wars and won us empires. We need to learn how to both value our individual flair *and* be good team players. We are being taught a lot about this by Japanese and other Asian companies who have set up in the West.

Instead of being frightened of difference and conflict, instead of pursuing power, wanting to be right, wanting to win arguments, wanting to be better than, we need to learn to welcome difference and conflict, let go, acknowledge that we don't know, that we are travelling and learning, that we will succeed better when everyone wins, that there are, most often, win-win solutions. We need to learn to listen with interest and with open minds and engage in dialogue. We need honesty, rigor and challenge. This will encourage learning, flexibility of response and creativity and help in solving problems and deciding the most appropriate ways forward.

This attitude will help us welcome women, people of different racial origins, cultures, ages, levels and skills into key decision-making and problem-solving roles. It will encourage us to develop partnerships with people and examine rigorously what partnership implies in terms of performance appraisal, hierarchy, status, rewards, company ownership and re-examine a host of other current policies and practices (Block, 1993). We cannot create partnership and a sense of involvement and ownership if all our policies and practices imply patriarchy, dominance, compliance and dependency. Nor can we do so when there are gross and apparently unjustifiable differences in rewards. A lot of harm has been done recently by what looks like boardroom greed. People see the double talk, fudging and hypocrisy immediately – even if they remain silent. And this implies another step. That is inviting feedback from many *different* people and really taking it seriously.

Be excellent in responding well to uncertainty, complexity and change

No matter how inspiring and enlightened an organization may be, the bottom line for all its stakeholders is that it survives and thrives in tough times. Aspirations are not enough. There has to be a happy partnership between enlightenment and shrewdness, toughness, astuteness, decisiveness, entrepreneurship, being streetwise and sometimes ruthlessness. We all have to be able to pay our bills. There is no virtue in enlightened failure.

Yet many of the skills, attitudes and practices described in the first three principles make it more likely that an organization will develop appropriate strategies and innovations that will lead to its continuing to survive and thrive. By valuing difference and understanding how to work with conflict, it is more likely that strategies will be based on a thoroughly realistic and accurate appreciation (to which all stakeholders have contributed) of the whole situation. If people are valued and supported well, it is more likely that they will survive and thrive in a situation of change, uncertainty and pressure. People will cope better with uncertainty if they are well informed about the situation, have confidence in themselves, have the skills they need to survive and have contributed to key decisions affecting their future. With this kind of culture, the organization is more likely to learn and adapt – especially if there is enough honest challenge to any form of complacency or unawareness of the severity of the situation. We can no longer afford a situation where a few like-minded people make the decisions and decide the way ahead and the rest withhold their contribution. In general, command and control (appropriate in some situations) needs to be replaced by far more liberating new forms.

We require a culture that welcomes rather than fears change, encourages the attitude that uncertainty is interesting, exciting and full of promise, that acknowledges that in this situation everyone is bound to have all kinds of feelings such as fear, feelings of inadequacy, anger, grief about the passing of the old order, confusion and being at sea.

We need a big shift in our culture *away from* denying the importance or existence of feelings in the workplace *towards* recognizing that feelings are normal, inevitable, not left at home and that they have to be acknowledged and worked with if we are to find our creativity, energy, excitement, optimism, commitment and goodwill towards one another. We need to struggle out of our emotional illiteracy in organizations.

Love our work and love ourselves

'Work is love made visible.' The Prophet, Kahlil Gibran.

'Doing what you most like doing and getting paid for it.'
Joyce Grenfell, entertainer.

I have not yet mentioned 'love.' It is a word we shy away from in the workplace, yet it is fundamental. Surprisingly, it is a word used by some of the most hard-headed entrepreneurs. Many people in talking about their work are lucky enough to say 'I love my work.' We sometimes hear 'He loves his work.' Such phrases go with quality and excellence. Roger Harrison has been stressing its importance in organizations for years (Harrison, 1995). Work is how we offer our gifts to the world and one key way in which we express our goodness and our love (Fox, 1994). Without work we love, we are deeply deprived, as those who are without work or in jobs they dislike can testify. If we are to give our best and flourish, we need to be doing work we love and love our work. (It can take many years to find our true vocation.) This does not mean that some of the time we won't hate it too. Passion and excellence are inextricably linked. We also need to love our workmates or most of them most of the time. This is linked to what I said about being honest with people who work with us. Real honesty requires love and vice versa. This is not to say that we will not experience frustration, anger and hostility some of the time. We surely need to love our customers though the same caveats apply. This is love in the sense of caring a lot, our hearts being in it and being willing to go out of our way to help, support, do our very best and go that extra mile that will make all the difference. This is principle but it is also business acumen.

To do this we have to feel good about ourselves and get the support of colleagues when we do not. We need to nurture, ie, love ourselves, meet our needs and sometimes take time out in whatever way is needed to restore ourselves. It is also true that sometimes we cannot afford to do this until later. But work can become an addictive habit or compulsion. It is no use going on and on, burning ourselves out and neglecting what and who matters most to us for the sake of our job. Nor can we honestly justify doing this indefinitely for the sake of the family or some other external purpose. This wisdom is becoming increasingly widespread and we shall have to become more unconventional and daring in bringing it into the workplace to create more harmony and balance, especially when life at work is at its most stressful and difficult. Perhaps it will not be so unusual for there to be exercise, games, silliness, relaxation, sitting in silence and meditation in the typical organization in the future – particularly when we are 'stuck' or in a crisis!

Have an attitude of long-term stewardship

I believe this principle underpins the others. It is not possible to win the hearts and minds of all stakeholders, empower and enable, respect and unite people in common cause, respond well to change and love our work and ourselves *and* be essentially exploitative.

In the past 20 years or so many good companies have failed, been taken over or seriously damaged themselves because of over-emphasis on short-term financial returns to the detriment of investing in the future. The RSA's inquiry provides evidence of a shift in the minds of directors away from short-term exploitation of assets, towards creating conditions for sustainable success and recognition that this in part depends upon a thriving business community and long-term trust relationships. This also means an ability to hold collaboration and competition in our heads at the same time.

A company that demonstrates concern for long-term success in the best interests of all stakeholders (not merely directors or shareholders) is most likely to win the respect of everyone involved in supporting it including employees, customers and suppliers. Most human beings have a strong sense of values and purpose and like to be associated with stewardship – something of which we can be proud – rather than exploitation. We prefer to be builders, creators of something that will endure, that offers secure livelihood, enduring quality, something that can be handed on to the next generation.

Not only are we learning that we need an attitude of long-term stewardship towards our companies but also we are being forced to learn how important it is to have an attitude of stewardship towards the Earth.

In reaching forward into this new world of work, which is also partly very old, directors, managers, developers and other stakeholders need to work in partnership to develop new and exciting forms in which people can work together more effectively (Semler, 1993; Weisbord, 1987). The rest of the book will offer some ideas and ways forward. However it will be a very incomplete picture as we are travelling together on a journey of discovery and we do not know where it will lead.

I should like to end this chapter with a quote from a visionary leader's speech made in the 1940s. Harry Ferguson was the English co-founder of the Anglo-Canadian company, Massey Ferguson Tractors, now part of U.S. based AGCO Corporation. Here was a creative, far-sighted business man with a global vision and a strong sense of purpose and responsibility.

Gentlemen, we have not asked you to come here primarily to see a tractor and a new system of implements. That is a secondary reason for the invitation we sent you. Before I go any further, I want to impress most deeply upon you that it is the Plan, the idea behind this new System, which is of primary importance.

The abolition of poverty is our first problem. What is poverty? What is want? Poverty and want can best be described as the inability to purchase the bare necessities of life. Any man who cannot obtain the necessities of life is definitely in poverty. Any man who can purchase them is not in poverty. He may be poor, but he is not in poverty.

Many plans have been presented for meeting the problem of poverty and destitution. But none of them can possibly succeed unless something be done to create the wealth with which to put those plans into effect.

Our Plan for prosperity, security and peace can be stated in two simple propositions.

1. *Make the good earth produce more than enough to keep its whole population in comfort and contentment.*

2. *And, what is equally vital, produce that 'more than enough' at prices which the people of the world can afford to pay.*

To put that Plan into effect, machinery must be designed fitted to that Plan. If the Plan be good and the machinery be good, then we have the greatest and best news that you have ever heard. We have a new hope for mankind.

That is our ambition. That is the course to which I am wholly dedicated.

'The Vision' from the Speeches of Harry Ferguson.

References and suggested further reading

Block, P. (1993) *Stewardship – Choosing Service Over Self-interest*, Berrett Keohler, San Francisco, USA.

Chopra, D. (1994) *The Seven Spiritual Laws of Success*, Amber-Allen/New World Library, San Rafael, USA.

Coelho, P. (1993) *The Alchemist – A Fable about Following Your Dream*, Harper, San Francisco, USA.

Fox, M. (1994) *The Re-invention of Work*, Harper, San Francisco, USA.

Gibran, K. (1991) *The Prophet*, Pan Books, London, UK.

Grenfell, J. (1976) *Joyce Grenfell Requests the Pleasure*, Macmillan, London, UK.

Harrison, R. (1995) *Consultant's Journey – A Professional and Personal Odyssey*, McGraw-Hill, Maidenhead, UK.

Hutton, W. (1995) *The State We Are In*, Jonathan Cape, London, UK.

Hutton, W. (1997) *The State to Come*, Vintage, London, UK.

Redfield, J. (1994) *The Celestine Prophesy*, Bantam Books, London, UK.

Scott Peck, M. (1994) *A World Waiting to Be Born: The Search for Civility*, Rider, London, UK.

Semler, R. (1993) *Maverick, the Success Story Behind the World's Most Unusual Workplace*, Warner Books, USA.

Weisbord, M. (1987) *Productive Workplaces*, Jossey-Bass, San Francisco, USA.

The last book on this list is the best management book I have read thus far.

3

❖

Tomorrow's Culture and Leadership

'Never doubt that a small group of committed citizens can change the world; indeed it is the only thing that ever has.' Margaret Mead.

'This is the third year since I proposed innovation in the following three domains: products, processes and our own minds. Of these, I would like to place particular emphasis on innovation of the mind, since it propels our challenging spirit towards the 21st century.' Satoshi Iue, Chairman, Sanyo Electric.

'Leaders create an irresistible invitation.' Anon.

Adversarial culture

In a really effective organization we need empowered people at every level who both contribute individual excellence and work as a community to deliver quality and value to customers. It is a refreshing experience when we deal with an organization that works in that way. But it is not very common.

There is something about the culture of the typical organization that discourages individual initiative, makes it hard for people to flourish and encourages division and conflict. These difficulties are rooted in the adversarial and manipulative way many leaders exercise power. Individuals and groups compete as if there is not enough to go round. The same difficulties are acted out in national and international politics. We see much the same in the microcosm of the family which usually provides our first experience of patriarchy and the assumption that we need to compete. But families are also places where fathers try not to be autocrats and learn from their kids, mums and dads work as good partners and children support each other and learn to take responsibility. It is a great place to learn.

I have learned more from listening to hundreds of people in organizations than any single source. When I start work in an organization, I invariably ask people what gets in the way of the organization functioning as well as it could. The same answers emerge again and again and I have listed them in Figure 3.1. This

---

- People at every level blaming and complaining instead of taking personal responsibility and initiative. Feeling powerless.
- A punishing, sometimes bullying climate which discourages risk-taking or frankness – worse when people are afraid of losing their jobs.
- A tendency to 'trash' or criticize colleagues.
- Too little appreciation and encouragement; too much criticism.
- Competition, playing politics and difficulty working collaboratively or corporately.
- Difficulty handling conflict openly and lack of respect for difference.
- Widespread distrust.
- Isolation and lack of support.
- Lack of honest two-way communication.
- Unwillingness to acknowledge mistakes, uncertainty, difficulties, feelings or need for help.
- Over-control and reluctance to involve others.
- Manipulation rather than direct dealing.
- A tendency to gross overworking leading to 'burn out' and undermining fitness for the job and life at home.
- Reluctance to take space to think or manage strategically.
- Difficulty bringing out the energy, initiative and talents of people at all levels.

Figure 3.1 What gets in the way

is an interactive system in which the various elements re-enforce each other.

I am shocked by the hostile climate I have described. Can it really be as bad as that? The answer is 'yes, sometimes it is just as bad as that.' Underneath a thin veneer of humor, politeness or professionalism, a substantial amount of this exists in the typical organization. It is part of the prevailing culture. Most of us learn to live with it unless it becomes too blatant or intolerable. Many able and independent people dislike it so much that they get out and start their own businesses. Many women, in my experience, dislike it particularly which may help to explain recent reports of a decline in the number of women at the top of organizations. The picture describes how power is commonly exercised, how competition is expressed and the largely damaging effects this has on our capacity to excel, co-operate and adapt. Despite the evidence to the contrary, we seem stuck in the belief that power has to be exercised in a manipulative covert way and that we are inevitably in a win-lose situation within the organization. Most of us can survive in an adversarial culture but individually and collectively we are not likely to offer our full potential. This is a hindrance.

We see the same drama of adversarialism, blaming, trashing, economy with the truth, lack of intellectual honesty and, often, powerlessness acted out daily on the floor of the British House of Commons and when politicians speak or write in the media. Why do we behave like this? Where does it all come from? Is it inherent in our nature? Would most of us act in an instrumental and exploitative way if we could get away with it? Did we learn to behave like this to survive in earlier times? Is it primarily the result of male conditioning? Whatever the explanation, it is a far cry from the culture we need to build in our organizations even if this behavior served to get us where we are today. Habits are difficult to change but we do have a choice about the kind of culture we can create, one that we believe will be more appropriate to our time.

Partnership culture

When I facilitate management workshops, I ask managers at the start, what kind of culture they want to create in the workplace that will enable them to work best and learn most. Subsequently we all struggle to put this into practice. A very different picture emerges (see Figure 3.2) from the one I described in Figure 3.1.

- Honesty and frankness.
- Encouragement and challenge.
- Trust and confidentiality.
- Appreciation and constructive criticism.
- Real listening.
- Respect for difference, tolerance, okay to be yourself.
- Consideration for feelings of others without tiptoeing.
- Acceptable to express feelings.
- Giving and receiving in balance.
- Excitement, fun, humor (not at another's expense).
- Not afraid to tackle disagreements or difficulties.
- Balance and time to reflect, exercise, relax and keep well.
- Everyone taking responsibility for outcomes.

Figure 3.2   The conditions in which people work best and learn most

It seems that a desire is being expressed to move through what Scott Peck describes as 'pseudo community' (ie, politeness, not being really authentic) and 'chaos,' in which organizations spend most of their time, into the 'community' needed to learn and solve important problems (Scott Peck, 1993).

I always point out that they are also describing the culture they want in order to function best in the organization. It is the reverse side of what they say that gets in the way of real effectiveness. Theirs may not be a very radical picture but it is brave in what is a risky and political environment. It expresses the yearning of many people who are trying to cope with difficult and demanding situations for a more truthful and supportive community. Perhaps the euphoria experienced on many workshops occurs because people get a glimpse of what is possible and the benefits it gives.

In my experience there is widespread desire to change the culture of organizations though varying degrees of awareness of the implications. There is recognition of the connection between quality of life within an organization and its ability to deliver quality and value to its customers. This is often expressed in admirable statements of mission, values and beliefs. Typically these are prepared by top management and handed down to a somewhat skeptical workforce who have not been involved in the process and feel no sense of ownership. Commonly there is a conflict between the espoused culture and actual behavior. Despite our best intentions, we struggle to act in ways that empower and unite people and we have difficulty learning to do so, perhaps partly because we have experienced so few good models. Giving up habits is simply difficult.

Old leadership messages

At the root of these difficulties, as Michael Simmons has shown (see Figure 3.3), are old messages about how to lead which limit both leaders and those they lead. These messages have been handed down through the example and experiences of male leaders because until now most organizations have been led by men. It is a patriarchal image of leadership. Although many of us dislike being led or leading in this way, it is difficult to break away from something so deeply rooted. Just as we swear not to repeat the mistakes our parents made in rearing us, we do so with our own children. We are not helped by the fact that some

- How I see things is correct.
- Keep separate from those you lead.
- Never show weakness, confusion or admit mistakes.
- Be consistent to the point of rigidity.
- Overwork and sacrifice self (becoming unfit and unfit to lead as a result).
- Criticize, manipulate and coerce.
- There is a basic win-lose conflict between groups.
- A leader pursues power rather than purpose.

Figure 3.3 Old leadership messages

women decide to beat men at their own game rather than develop their own way of leading.

> '*Someone said that a female executive has to be more macho than a man. I hope not. I hope as women come into their own they are able to develop a wide variety of personalities, like men. I like having a few laughs, like anyone else.*' Marjorie Scardino, Chief Executive of Pearson (Independent *on Sunday*, 20 October 1996).

Enabling leadership

An alternative model of leadership, designed to create a more enabling and adaptive culture is shown in Figure 3.4. This model is based on the thinking of Michael Simmons (Simmons, 1993 & 1996) who, in 1986, started the Network for a New Men's Leadership. This was established to help men work together to understand the effects of male gender conditioning on the way they lead and live their lives and to develop a more appropriate and

- Offer an inspiring vision of how the organization can be and encourage everyone to develop their own exciting visions.

- Learn to love change and uncertainty.

- Appreciate the whole situation and make sure everything goes well – implies listening to a wide range of people.

- Become a leader of leaders, not followers.

- Encourage leadership everywhere.

- Create an environment of appreciation, high expectations and support.

- See yourself as a life-long apprentice.

- Give up pretense and admit mistakes.

- Learn to ask empowering and interesting questions and listen with complete respect.

- Encourage taking responsibility instead of complaining and blaming.

Figure 3.4   Empowering leadership model

balanced way of leading both at work and at home. His work-shops had a big effect on me and many men I know.

It would be interesting to see how a model developed by women would differ. However the model above represents a better balance between ying and yang. I believe men and women will benefit greatly from working in partnership to develop new forms of leadership which are a better balance between what is characterized as masculine and feminine. Already women MPs and a woman Speaker are starting to exercise their influence on the adversarialism of the UK House of Commons. Men vary enormously and many of them do not like the hostile and adversarial climate of their organizations although it may be difficult for them to say so. The vast majority of managers (not all) I talk with recognize the 'old messages' as reflecting their own painful experience and welcome the alternative model.

I believe that fear of difference (including gender, sexual preference, class, race, ethnicity, religion, physical disabilities and age) is at the root of many of our difficulties in organizations and in global society. It starts at school where, after the first few years, children become absolutely terrified of being different. Currently, the culture of most organizations is determined by white, middle class men. If men and women develop a genuine and robust partnership, a different culture will emerge and we shall all benefit from the greater balance and creativity that will result. If we can succeed with gender – it's the closest to home – we may tackle other aspects of difference more easily. Home is a great place to start.

Although the culture of an organization is determined by the behavior and attitudes of large numbers of people at all levels, it only requires the leadership of a few people to start changing it. There is a myth that change has to start at the top. This is not how most change has taken place in history. It can help if the initiative comes from the top in an organization but sometimes there is very little likelihood of that in the short term. Often the most conservative people are at the top though sometimes they are the most radical. When change is initiated from the top, it requires a dynamic interaction between the leader and led. The leader needs to give up dominance but the led have to give up dependency and compliance.

Sometimes leadership, the catalytic challenge, comes from 'below' or outside.

I recently heard the story of the working class mother of a severely disabled child who could no longer stand the arrogance, insensitivity and bullying of a senior surgeon. Her angry outrage gave her the strength to challenge him in front of other hospital staff who had hitherto stood by powerlessly. Later they told her that it was the first time they had ever seen him apologize and that her action had given them courage to confront him in future.

It is not possible to empower people. As we have seen in this example, people choose to empower themselves. Not everyone wants to be empowered. However it is possible to remove or reduce obstacles to empowerment and create conditions in which people are encouraged to empower themselves. Empowerment means transferring power and control from the leader alone to the whole team. It means putting power in the hands of people, especially those closest to customers and other stakeholders, so that they can pursue the interests of the organization and in so doing fulfill their own needs. Empowerment fits well with the notion of encouraging leadership everywhere in the organization. This amounts to re-defining leadership and defining its

---

- Working for continuous improvement and learning.

- Engaging the creative energy, intelligence and initiative of the *whole system*.

- Valuing difference and working for common ground.

- Tapping into the huge energy to improve things – often expressed as complaint or criticism.

- Creating an atmosphere of excitement, appreciation, high expectations and opportunity to grow.

- Leading in a way that is inspiring, inclusive, enabling and shares power and control.

- Accepting the importance of feelings ('positive' and 'negative') and learning to work with them.

- Working with paradox (ie, both right and left brain) and seeking balance.

- Having an attitude of stewardship rather than exploitation.

Figure 3.5   Tomorrow's culture

essence as seeing that everything goes well. For this to work well, the goals of the organization and limits to people's authority need to be clear to everyone and the necessary support provided so they are able to use their knowledge and exercise their intelligence, creativity and judgment within a framework. In these conditions, management fears of losing control are not likely to be realized.

- Accepting and enjoying uncertainty, unpredictability, complexity and sometimes confusion.

- Developing a vision for the whole organization, your part in it and yourself.

- Learning to trust intuition especially in dealing with complexity and confusion – integrating right and left brain.

- Learning to trust yourself, look inside yourself for answers.

- Influencing from any level and building a network.

- Asking interesting and empowering questions.

- Giving and getting a good listening to.

- Developing support for yourself.

- Supporting people in expressing 'positive' and dealing with 'negative' feelings (emotional literacy).

- Seeking and giving honest, thoughtful feedback.

- Being prepared to tackle what is most difficult, especially challenging complacency or collusion.

- Working with conflict, resistance, diversity and difference.

- Facilitating groups and very large groups representing the whole system.

- Understanding what happens in groups.

- Learning to relax, nurture yourself, and be at peace in a sea of chaos – self-love.

- Focusing on what will make a decisive difference.

- Recognizing that empowerment is a dynamic between two, ie, the leader and the led.

Figure 3.6 Key survival skills

A new culture for organizations

Figure 3.5 describes the kind of organization culture which I believe is needed, based upon my experience. You may wish to help the people in your organization build a picture of the culture it needs and help them develop the behavior that goes with it.

Key survival skills

In order to function well in conditions of uncertainty, complexity and huge pressures, not only do people need an empowering culture; they also need key survival skills. Most only require a different mind-set and experimentation to acquire them. Some may need training or coaching. It is important not to view any of them as the exclusive province of people at the top of the hierarchy or specialists. These skills need to be widespread. See Figure 3.6 for what my list includes. Later chapters will elaborate on how some of these skills can be practiced.

In the next part, I shall describe some ideas and approaches which offer promise in bringing about real as opposed to cosmetic change in the culture of organizations.

References and suggested further reading

Morton, A. L. (1992), *A People's History of England*, Laurence and Wishart, London, UK.

Scott Peck, M. (1993), *A World Waiting to Be Born – the Search for Civility*, Rider, London, UK.

Simmons, M. 'Creating a New Leadership Initiative' *Management Development Review*, Vol. 6, No. 5, 1993.

Simmons, M. (1996), *Leadership and Gender*, Gower, London, UK.

Zinn, H. (1980), *A People's History of the United States*, Harper Perennial, New York, USA.

Part II
❖
Principles, Strategies and Basic Tools

4

Principles and Tools for Transformation
A new vision for learning and development

'It is easier to act ourselves into a better mode of thinking than to think ourselves into a better mode of acting.' Richard Pascale.

'You are all learners, doers and teachers.' Richard Bach.

'There is an Indian (Asian) proverb or axiom that says that everyone is in a house with four rooms, a physical, a mental, an emotional and a spiritual. Most of us tend to live in one room most of the time but, unless we go into every room every day, even if only to keep it aired we are not a complete person.' Rumer Godden.

In this chapter I offer some principles and tools for transformation. As often seems to be the case, the principles form an interrelated system.

Principles

Congruence

We all stand to gain from a flourishing society in which everyone is encouraged to offer their gifts and prosper as a result. We can contribute to this by helping to create inclusive workplaces that are enabling and encourage widespread leadership. By leadership I mean taking individual responsibility within the framework of understanding the whole situation.

If we want to create a new workplace we need a whole new vision of learning and development. We need to work with people, from the start, in ways that are fully 'congruent' with the kind of workplace we are trying to create. Put simply this means practicing what we preach. This is not easy! Nevertheless perhaps this is the underlying principle on which all the others are based.

Simplicity, unpretentiousness and rigor

For a start we need to offer ideas and methods that are inspiring, accessible, memorable and easily used by working people at every level in the organization – not just by an intellectual middle class. Only in that way can we be inclusive. Yet I am struck with how complex and élitist much of what I read and listen to is. Sometimes I am seduced by it and then I ask myself, 'What does all this boil down to?' Often something pretty simple. Is this a carry over from a class society adept at creating barriers that make it harder for everyone to realize their potential? Is it part of the silly idea that you have to show you are clever and present something new, complicated or arcane? My experience is that the very best and wisest practitioners in our field make things simple, are unpretentious and often funny. There is beauty, elegance and utility in simplicity and it is usually harder to achieve than complexity. I have an acid test: if I cannot explain to anyone without using jargon, in simple, ordinary language what I am doing and how, is it fit for the purpose? Furthermore, if it is clever and beguiling, does it stand up to the test of common sense? Rigor and simplicity seem to go together. Our job as facilitators is to provide rigorous structures, processes and practical tools that enable people to learn and work together successfully. It is not our job to give advice on what to do. In my experience the simplest structures are the most rigorous.

Encourage people to find their authority inside

If we want to empower, we need to encourage people to find their main source of strength and inspiration within themselves rather than in external authorities. We need to learn to trust our own thinking. Of course we can learn a lot from colleagues and the rare gifts and insights some people offer. It is also true that it can be difficult to express simply ideas that are new and represent a paradigm shift. We need these new ways of seeing the world. They are landmarks in human perception. But we can misuse people by treating them as gurus, putting them on pedestals and under-estimating ourselves. We can follow the latest fad or recipe. There is a paradox here. I learn an enormous amount from books, talks and workshops. There is a stream of exciting new ideas and insights. We need this as part of our broad connection with other human beings. It is part of how we support ourselves and draw inspiration. Authors are our facilitators or catalysts. But, at the end of the day, we need to cherish our own inner resources most of all. Maturity means seeing heroes realistically and recognizing that they represent what we most value in ourselves. Amongst my heroes are Henry Bessemer, Isambard Kingdom Brunel, Winston Churchill, William Morris, Martin Luther King, Helena Kennedy, Michael Manley, Nelson Mandela, Mahatma Gandhi, Marvin Weisbord, Michael Tippett and Franklin D. Roosevelt. It is really important to know who our heroes are and why. They give us a powerful sense of who we are.

Work with the real opportunities and issues people have

Using the Empowerment Model (described in the Introduction) enables people to work together to take individual responsibility within a shared view of the overall situation and the future they want to bring about. Through it people can learn to value every-one's contribution to understanding the current situation and building a picture of where they want to be. In this way it helps people practice inclusiveness. The model also provides a basis for *real time development*. By this I mean *learning by doing* – learning in events, retreats, workshops or one-to-one meetings by successfully working on the real opportunities and issues facing us. This is the richest source of learning. We do not need to teach or create contrived situations like role plays, case studies or use psychometric instruments to learn. This is didactic learning. It puts the teacher in charge. It easily disempowers. Our job as facilitators is to provide simple, rigorous structures that empower people to transform their workplace, make their business successful and learn in so doing. It is also to help them create and experiment with the kind of culture they want, find out that it works and transfer it to their workplace.

Practical business focus

Development needs to have a thoroughly practical focus in the uncertain and competitive global economy. Can we really afford to separate learning and working as we do in traditional development? To do so seems like an indulgence to me – almost 'fiddling while Rome burns.' The traditional didactic approach gives us the problem of transferring learning to the workplace and evaluating its benefits. If *we bring work into the learning event* or *bring learning into the working event* there is no transfer problem. *We learn as we work and work as we learn.* We learn as we plan and bring about changes the business needs to survive and thrive. We demonstrate that development is part of doing business and that having a clear business purpose and achieving a business pay off is an integral part of it. This is more credible to people at any level who are preoccupied with: 'How do we make this business survive and succeed in a highly competitive and uncertain world?' or 'How do I keep my job?' The real time approach gives facilitators and developers credibility and shows the relevance of what we have to offer. I shall describe it in more detail in Chapter 6.

At the start of any development initiative we need to ask two questions: 'What is the business purpose of this piece of work?' and 'If it succeeds, what will be the practical business pay-off against which we can measure its success?'

Partnership and ownership

To encourage partnership in our organizations, we need to model partnership in the way we work with our clients. This generally means not doing things for (or to) them but *with* them. It means planning and designing events with our customers or clients and, where appropriate, including them in the team of facilitators. This leads to more effective work because it is the result of sharing their knowledge (especially of the organization and its needs) and skills and ours. The work will have higher credibility too. This way we build our credibility and relationships with our clients. This approach empowers our clients to do it for themselves as we hand over our skills to them thus making development skills widely available as part of every manager's toolkit. This is usually more economical but also makes possible another key advantage – not only *transferring our skills* but also *transferring ownership*. Transferring ownership to our clients helps embed changes in attitudes and behavior into the fabric of the business. Whatever is created has to be theirs not ours or at least theirs and ours, if it is to have a good chance of lasting and continuing.

Trust and honesty

Partnership means a lot of things. Chief amongst these is trust. It means honestly admitting that what we are trying to do is difficult and will require long-term persistence; that sometimes we won't know what to do and we will make mistakes and need to learn from them; that there are no magic answers and no quick fixes; not claiming too much for what we can offer; being up front from the start that we all have to share responsibility for the outcomes and not even think about scapegoats if things go wrong. It means challenging the executives to involve themselves as equal partners and show they mean to change too. It means that we facilitators need the courage to be authentic with people without being judgmental. To do that effectively we may have to contain what is happening inside and not let our emotions spill out. Usually they spill out because we feel our 'ego' is under threat or we are in a panic. We have to be prepared to work with resistance, take on pathological, destructive behavior and expect and welcome the unexpected. We also have to be prepared to challenge and not collude with our clients in staying where they are. This takes both calmness and courage.

> *'If you always do what you always did, you'll always get what you always got.'*

Strategy needs to emerge

Another key principle comes in here. The strategy for change needs to emerge and be discovered by those involved – not imposed by you or pre-conceived by a few people in advance. The 'grand plan,' cascade down approach rarely works in my experience. A long-term initiative that is developed *with* people as it unfolds is more likely to be owned and also more likely to be appropriate and to work. The most we should plan for in a development or change initiative is the beginning, whilst having a lightly held vision of what is possible. This is most likely to be a 'pilot' developed with our partners to make a good start and find out what works. It is wisest to build together a vision of the desired future but to hang very loose about the details and how it all comes about. If people are given the freedom they have a way of gathering round an inspiring vision and making it happen in unexpected ways. We have to make this possible. Firmness about purpose but creative flexibility around strategy seems to work best.

However, an effective strategy for learning and transformation has to include ways of embedding change and making it long term. This is part of providing rigorous structures to support change. Whilst these need to emerge flexibly, we need to hold this issue in our minds and challenge our clients not to overlook it. Embedding change involves creating 'critical mass' (a term borrowed from nuclear science) (the minimum involvement of people after which the change will be self-sustaining.) You will have to judge when that point has been reached. But even then continuing support may be needed because of the cumulative effect of setbacks, fatigue, the tendency to slip back and the need to learn. Often this support comes best from someone who is less involved or is outside the system.

Think whole system: practice inclusiveness

This makes huge sense if we want to get the business strategy right. We need the input of the whole system – perhaps all stakeholders – in creating a common data base and in developing the desired future of the business and the strategy to get there. Facilitators who believe this need to model this principle in the way they approach their work and guide their clients. If our work does not embrace everyone in the organization, especially the core workers and if it focuses on top and middle people and leaves out or insufficiently engages the 'bottom,' it is not likely to bring about the practical 'pay-off.'

If we do this, we have got it all wrong, upside down, and we are practicing exclusiveness, leaving out the majority. Similarly if it leaves out other stakeholders such as suppliers and customers it may be flawed. We need to *think whole system*. Ultimately we have to find ways to *get the whole system into the room* if we are to benefit from the synergy of all the stakeholders and capitalize on the organizational learning that can take place (see Chapter 8). Connected with *thinking whole system* is inclusiveness. We need to model inclusiveness all the time we are working with people, demonstrating respect for the contribution of everyone in the room.

Work with the whole person

Just as we need to think whole system I believe we developers and facilitators need to be able to work with the whole person. We don't leave our feelings and our humanity at the door when we come to work. When we are working with people at work it is appropriate to help them think about the whole of their lives – it is all connected. People aren't just analytical, rational left brains. We are an interconnected system. How we feel, the state our bodies are in, our intuition, our energy and its rhythms, our spirituality, how we are affected by our environment, what inspires and moves us – all these things matter and affect how we are able to contribute and particularly affect our creativity.

> For example, a fine black woman leader came on a program I ran. Later she went on to lead career development programs for black nurses in the British National Health Service which are having a profound effect on the status of black nurses and challenging both racism and sexism. In 1997 she won a regional National Training Award from the Department of Education and Employment for her work with nurses and allied professions (minority ethnic groups) in the UK National Health Service. She also won Business Excellence and Consultancy and Training Awards from the National Federation of Black Women Business Owners. She told me that what made the difference was that she was able to cry for a couple of days on my program.

> At a simpler level, I find I get a lot of my best ideas doing the free style in the swimming pool. The energy flowing through my body gives me ideas. Sometimes, when I first wake up in the morning, I find suddenly that intractable problem is solved. My subconscious has solved it in the night.

> I remember during a particularly frustrating period at work I was a member of a bioenergetic running group (bioenergetics is a form of therapy that believes our body is the key to our difficulties). We ran round a large room for an hour or so each week screaming and ranting harmlessly at each other. (I was screaming at a general manager.) To add to the drama, the local teenagers peered in at us and pounded on the perspex windows. It was a lifeline for me. Next day I felt terrific.

Often I find that when I don't know what to do, or there seems to be a
crisis or the situation looks impossible, the best thing I can do is go for
a walk round the block. It's paradoxical: faced with a big problem the
best thing to do is stop and take a break.

To be up to the job we need to learn all we can about how to work
with individuals and groups in all sorts of different ways. If the
workplace is to be really different it has to be fit for the whole person. That is why we need to give people a fresh and exciting experience of how work can be which they will want to carry back into
the workplace. It is also why the physical setting matters. Formal
arrangements of tables and chairs suggest the tone of the school-
room or the boardroom and rigidity; an informal circle of chairs
without tables suggests a community of equal contributors. It also
symbolizes flexibility as everything can be moved quickly and easily
to enable people to work in whatever ways or groups they need.

Have a long-term perspective

This means recognizing that changing attitudes, behavior and
culture is a long-term job and requires a long-term strategy. People,
including you, change unpredictably, often gradually, sometimes
suddenly. But it also means being prepared for major difficulties
and set-backs along the way. You may decide you have given all
you can to your current organization and go elsewhere. You gave
your best even if you didn't fulfill all your hopes. When you look
back almost certainly you will know that you *made a difference*
– perhaps to many people – some of whom may later lead the
organization or lead other organizations. They won't at first take
on board all you offered. Sometimes they will amaze you in the
long-term. And you will have learned a lot and be better prepared
for the next opportunity. The most we can reasonably hope to do
in this world is make a difference and 'put our brick in the wall,'
I find it helpful to remind myself of this wise reflection, valuable
if not always true:

> *'Things that really work start at the ground roots and are not
> imposed from the top.'* Woman delegate to the Real World Rally,
> 9 November 1996, Friends Meeting House, London. (Real World
> is a coalition of nearly 40 NGOs dedicated to environmental sus-
> tainability, social justice, eradication of poverty and democratic
> renewal.)

- Be 'congruent' throughout.

- Use simple, rigorous structures and tools.

- Encourage people to find their authority inside – empower.

- Learn by doing – real time, not contrived.

- Create, experiment, try out an empowering culture – positive experiences convince better than words.

- Establish a clear business purpose and focus minds on the 'business pay-off.'

- Establish *partnership* with your 'customers' from the start. Have the attitude they are the 'stars,' not you.

- *Ownership* is crucial – hand over steadily and transfer your skills.

- Acknowledge it's difficult: no quick fixes or miracles; we all resist, make mistakes; it takes time and needs long-term persistence and support.

- Be up front that everyone shares responsibility for success.

- Challenge the executives to participate, model, support and show they mean to change too!

- Be authentic yet contain what's happening inside you.

- Be prepared for resistance (work with), 'pathology' (take on) and the unpredictable.

- Our job is to challenge not collude—'If you always do what you always did, you'll always get what you always got.'

- Start with a small pilot and let the strategy emerge.

- Think about how to embed change, make it long term.

- Think 'whole system,' Practice inclusiveness.

- Work with the whole person.

- Have a long-term perspective.

- Openness to synchronicity.

Figure 4.1   Principles to maximize the chances of success

Openness to synchronicity

I have become increasingly aware of something called synchronicity. (Sorry about this word!) It's when there are fortunate coincidences; events seem to conspire to support me in my efforts; something or someone I need turns up. I think this happens when I am following the right path, feeling relaxed and good about myself, I am unafraid and flexible, have an optimistic and generous attitude and I am open to these possibilities. You tend to get what you expect. This seems to be an extremely important principle in bringing about transformation: be open to synchronicity, serendipity, fortunate coincidence.

> '*Learn to accept the possibility that the universe is helping you with what you are doing.*' Julia Cameron.

These principles will be demonstrated in practical terms in the rest of the book. I did not start by conjuring them up and then applying them. I gradually realized what the principles were when I reflected on what I had done and what seemed to make it work – and sometimes what didn't work! These principles are summarized in Figure 4.1.

- Raise people's awareness of how they want things to be different by inviting them to express their views. Encourage them to speak from their hearts.

- Work with their energy to change things often expressed as complaints.

- Offer inspiring, visionary leadership which responds to their desire for things to be different.

- Provide different experiences of how work *can* be that model a new culture and enable people to work successfully on their opportunities and the issues they present.

- Provide new empowering tools and processes.

Figure 4.2 How to encourage cultural change

How to encourage cultural change

I am left with the question in my mind: 'But how, simply, can you encourage cultural change?' Figure 4.2 summarizes what has helped in my experience. I shall expand on this in succeeding chapters.

Tools for transformation

Finally, I have put together in the Appendices a number of tools I use. I think they adhere to the principle of simplicity and rigor. They are uncomplicated and easy to understand and used widely. Also, if persisted with, they push you through thinking rigorously, visioning, working on how you might block yourself or stop yourself from acting effectively. They all have in common that they can help people move from where they are to where they want to be. Take a brief look at them now. I will elaborate on how to use them later in the book.

References and suggested further reading

Bach, R. (1995) *Illusions – The Adventures of a Reluctant Messiah*, Mandarin Paperbacks, Random House, London, UK.

Cameron, J. (1994) *The Artist's Way – A Spiritual Path to Higher Creativity*, Souvenir Press, London, UK.

Chopra, D. (1994) *The Seven Spiritual Laws of Success*, Amber-Allen/New World Library, San Rafael, USA.

Godden, R. (1990) *A House with Four Rooms*, Corgi Books, London, UK.

Pascale, R. (1991) *Managing on the Edge*, Penguin Books, London, UK.

5

Taking a Strategic Approach

Developing your own vision and strategy

'We are all of us descended from slaves, or almost slaves. All
our biographies, if they went back far enough, would begin by
explaining how our ancestors came to be more, or less enslaved,
and to what degree we have become free of this inheritance.'
Theodore Zeldin.

'The world is still full of people who, though they have no
recognized slave masters, see themselves as having little
freedom, as being at the mercy of uncontrollable, anonymous
economic and social forces, or of their circumstances, or of their
own stupidity, and whose personal ambitions are permanently
blunted thereby.' Theodore Zeldin.

The trouble with organizations

These two quotations sum up a significant part of the problem
with organizations. We are acting out the dramas of hundreds of
years of history. Below the surface we are still in an ancient,
patriarchal and adversarial mind-set when a new, collaborative
one is needed. Despite the surface friendliness that characterizes
relationships in the typical organization and the material comforts

most offer, there is an underlying culture of fear and, consequently, powerlessness, distrust, adversarialism and inability to work collaboratively. And people in leadership roles, not the outright bullies but the ordinary mass of well intentioned leaders, have it in them to use fear and division as a means of imposing their will. There is an unspoken collusion between leaders and led that diminishes the capacity of people to take responsibility, take risks and speak their truth fearlessly. It diminishes the capacity of organizations to be excellent. It affects HRD people as much as any, limits their contribution and makes it harder for them to trust their own thinking or take bold initiatives.

> There are powerful symbols of patriarchy in organizations, for example, the size and location of offices, furnishings, arrangement of meeting rooms, eating facilities, cars and car parking. At one of my workplaces the directors' (they were a bit like barons, at times warring barons) offices were all on one floor and had ceilings twice as high as any others as in a country house. There were seven levels of eating facilities. Meeting room tables were long and narrow so there could be little interaction except with the leader at the top and everyone had to look up to him. Panic broke out when it was discovered that my new office was one meter larger than my rank permitted, never mind the number of people who needed to fit into it when we had a meeting.

> And I remember one astonishing incident. A member of my team left. He had a chair with arms, the others did not. After he had gone there was a scramble for that chair, as it represented a little extra status.

One consequence is that we, in HRD, restrict ourselves to relatively safe activities. These can include administering knowledge and skill training based on a systematic analysis of needs; introducing relatively bureaucratic measures such as performance management systems, succession planning schemes or defining competencies; pursuing professionalism, 'state of the art' and 'leading edge' as ends rather than means; using safe, conservative, large consultancies, management colleges and business schools rather than independent consultants as sources of help; acting as 'gatekeepers' or 'impresarios' rather than getting on stage ourselves; introducing and contracting consultants to do the work rather than doing the key work ourselves or in partnership with consultants; adopting a posture of responding to rather than being boldly proactive; and becoming submerged under the demands of others. This is not to say that activities like these are not some-times useful and appropriate, but they can amount to *avoidance* of taking bold leadership in helping the organization tackle its most fundamental issues. Also, they tend to disempower the HRD function and place it at the periphery rather than in the heart of the business. At worst the function can be seen as a cost and an obstacle, rather than a source of valued help. In tough times this makes us expendable.

A fresh mind-set

There is a completely different mind-set which places HRD people closer to the center of the business. It offers an altogether more rewarding and central role. It is the role of internal consultant. This is to be 'midwife' (Harrison, 1995) to change and sometimes healing. It is to facilitate the transformation of the organization by bringing out and encouraging the forces for change that are already there. This involves getting alongside and supporting the chief executive in transforming the organization. It involves helping people appreciate the current situation, articulate new visions and take the steps needed to bring about their desired future. In essence this is a leadership role but transformational, facilitating leadership of an informal kind that is likely to be increasingly needed in organizations in the future – leadership exercised from personal rather than positional power.

Some time ago I was involved in an empowerment conference in a London borough. Delegates were sharing their empowerment projects and what they had learned from their experiences to encourage others to take similar initiatives. One delegate gave us a wise saw: 'If you wish to empower others, first empower yourself.'

People in HRD are in a unique position to help their organizations. Frequently they have widespread contacts in the organization. This gives them both the source of data to make an accurate, whole-system diagnosis and the network needed to influence it. They also have the potential to develop and offer a unique set of skills and understanding which is required to help transform the organization, empower its people and create productive partnership between them. But to fulfill this role, they may first need to empower themselves.

A new model for internal consultants

The Consulting Model shown in Figure 5.1 is well known in various forms and provides an excellent basis for planning and conducting an intervention. It is now an old classic. I always hold it in my mind when doing consulting work.

- Gaining entry.

- Developing a clear agreement.

- Collecting data.

- Making a diagnosis.

- Planning change.

- Implementing change.

- Evaluating, monitoring, reviewing.

- Withdrawing.

Note: Ownership will be strongest when the key stages of bringing about change are carried out by the client with the support of the consultant.

Figure 5.1 Consulting model

I want to offer a different model – the Internal Consultant's Model (see Figure 5.2). It is based on the Empowerment Model but adapted to the internal consultant's role. This model is useful, not in planning a particular intervention, but in following that delegate's advice: 'First empower yourself.' It will help you to empower yourself and develop your *intervention strategy* to be midwife to your organization's transformation. For several reasons I believe it is important that *before* you facilitate your clients, you first get someone to facilitate you with the very same work you need to do with them.

One reason for this is that you may need to empower yourself. An empowered consultant will be more credible and better able to facilitate. Perceptive clients sense whether their consultant is a good model and are put off by any incongruence. To empower yourself you need to have your own views about the issues the organization faces; make your own diagnosis; be clear about your

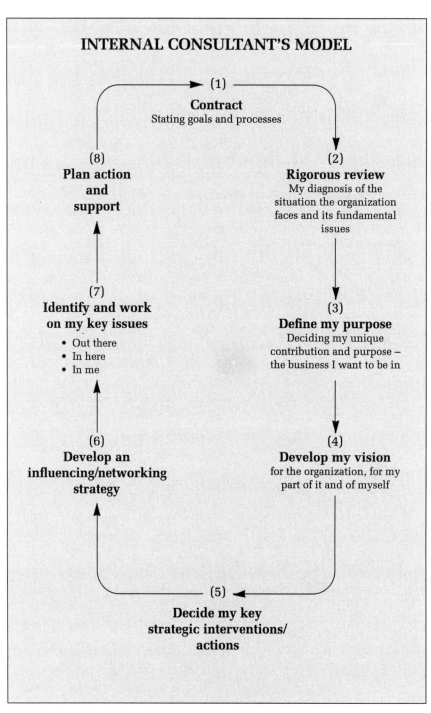

Figure 5.2   **Internal Consultant's Model**

mission and purpose; be clear about how you think the organization needs to change; have your own vision for it and your part in it; be clear about how you need to prioritize your efforts to assist and how you can make the best contribution; and understand where you will struggle in doing the work and what support or development you will need. This does not mean that you will not come to the work with an open mind or that you will impose your views. It means that you are well prepared as a facilitator and you are being proactive.

There is another reason why you need to get a skilled helper from inside or, preferably, outside the organization to facilitate you. (Someone outside the system can support you differently.) You will be better able to facilitate others in your organization, using this model, if you have experienced it from the inside as a client. If you are not employing a consultant, it is a good idea for two of you in partnership to co-facilitate each other so that you both gain skill and insight from working in client and helper role respectively. You learn to be a better consultant by learning to be a better client. You learn so much about yourself and the real world by listening to people talking about their struggles. It increases our awareness and we realize we are not alone or unusual. We are all in the same boat despite how it may appear on the surface.

Also, the better client you are, the better consultant you can be. There is something seriously incongruent about a consultant who is a reluctant or blocked client. Usually we are limited in helping others by how far we have travelled ourselves. Conversely, the more work we have done ourselves, the more we can help others.

The process is summarized in Figure 5.2. It is shown as a cycle because the work is never finished. Everything is changing constantly and you need to keep redoing the work at appropriate intervals. I will now summarize the various stages of the cycle in the form of questions that may need to be answered.

Contracting

What outcomes do you, the client, want from the meeting? What is the purpose of our meeting? What processes shall we use? How do you, the client, want to work? What works best for you? What behavior on the part of client and facilitator will lead to the best work and most learning? How do you want to be supported to achieve the best outcomes? What do you, the client, want from me, the facilitator? How much time is agreed for the meeting? Where do we want it to be held to provide the best conditions?

Rigorous review: making an organization diagnosis

What are the major external trends, changes or forces in the environment which affect the business? What is happening in the market place? What is the competition doing? How is the technology changing? How is the business responding? How good is the service we provide? What differentiates us from our competitors and gives us the advantage? What are our chances of survival if we continue like this? In what respects are we responding or functioning healthily? In what respects are we struggling or responding in ways which seem unhealthy? How is this affecting our ability to survive and thrive? What effect is this having on employees, customers, suppliers and other stakeholders? Where is the pain? What data is lacking and needs to be sought? What is it like for different people to work in the organization at the present time? What is the prevailing culture? Is it different in different parts? What stage of development is the organization at: entrepreneurial, bureaucratic, integrated? What is your diagnosis? What does all your data boil down to? What are the fundamental issues of the organization, those few that, if addressed, would make a fundamental difference, ie, what is your organization diagnosis?

Defining your purpose – the business you are in

If you are to offer all that you are capable of, it is important that you have defined your purpose. There needs to be alignment between what you most want to do and what the organization needs. This needs to be a purpose to which you are deeply committed. Your heart has to be in it. Another way of putting it is defining the business you are in. Useful questions are: What contribution is most needed here? What is the unique contribution I can offer? What is it in my heart and soul to do? What is my life's purpose? These questions seem to fit well after the rigorous review and are a prelude to the next stage which is to develop a vision of the desired future.

It helps some people do this work if they play some special piece of music, read a quotation or piece of poetry that means a lot to them, think of who they most admire, go for a walk in a special place perhaps with a close colleague. You should do whatever helps you get deeply in touch with who you are, and what are your values and beliefs.

Defining the business you are in is fundamental work. Upon it the rest of the work you do may depend. Get this right and the rest of the work will follow easily. But this work may be difficult. If your organization is trying to transform itself you may have to transform yourself and your team too. You may need a new mind-set. You are not exempt from the struggle of doing this.

Recently I was working with the management education and training unit of a large global company. The new chief executive said that the company needed to transform itself if it was to compete successfully and survive. This unit was having an away day to produce new strategies to support the chief executive's vision. The part they most struggled with was defining what business they needed to be in. They had been in the business of *delivering programs*. Now they needed to be in the business of *facilitating transformation*. They didn't find this shift in mind-set easy. They struggled with change just like the rest of the organization – a good experience for them to have before trying to help others. I spotted their difficulty at 8.00 a.m. while I struggled with getting a structured classroom rearranged as a flexible open space for their meeting.

Developing your vision

Is it presumptuous or irresponsible to develop your own vision for the organization? In my view it is not. Doing so is taking responsibility. Assuming that you (like most other employees) care deeply about the organization and have tried to reach a realistic, accurate and comprehensive appreciation of the current situation by listening to a wide range of people, it is highly responsible to develop a vision of the desired state. This is a crucial step in bringing about beneficial change that will inspire you as a leader and enable you to inspire and support others.

It is important that you develop a vision for the organization as a whole, for your part of it and for those other aspects of your life that are deeply important to you. The three need to be integrated, aligned. Otherwise there will be unresolved conflicts that will sap your energy. You are a whole person, not just a worker. We cannot for long live an unbalanced life or deny needs which are of deep importance. The essential question is: 'How would things be if everything were going well?' or 'What is the desired state?' Different people will want to express this in different ways. For some it works best if it is a picture or symbol. Others want a few words that sum it all up. I prefer a set of short descriptions that I find quite tangible so that I can recognize with satisfaction when I have got there and also see, in the fullness of time, what is now an inappropriate vision and needs to be changed. I carry my current vision statement for my life around with me in my briefcase and keep another copy beside my bed.

Deciding your key strategic interventions

'Intervention' is a useful word for a consultant or facilitator. It differs from a strategy in that it implies action which supports or facilitates others. In the past I found myself overwhelmed with plans and lists of things I needed to do that exhausted me and detracted from my capacity to act powerfully and make a real difference. Often I was unconsciously blocking myself in this way to avoid the fear I'd feel if I acted powerfully! (Cameron, 1995). This still happens to me at times. In my experience it helps enormously to think in terms of martial arts. What will require the least energy on your part and utilize the energy of the client or the client system? What is it that you can do that will represent the best use of your skills and time that will have the greatest effect and make a decisive difference? What represents working *with* the forces in the organization? What represents going with the energy in the organization and not pushing fruitlessly against *resistance*? In general a strategy should not consist of more than six statements, otherwise it is becoming an action plan.

Developing an influencing/networking strategy

If you are trying to facilitate transformation and sometimes healing (the healing may have to come before transformation) this means getting alongside people and staying close to them. It means making friends and allies and developing relationships of support and trust. Widespread relationships are vital as a source of accurate, whole-system data about the organization. They are also vital if you wish to facilitate the energy for change in the organization. You need to get alongside opinion leaders at all levels, people who understand the system and have credibility and influence. These are people to influence if you need their help in bringing about your own vision. It is vital that you are politically aware and sensitive but also astute enough not to get involved in the politics or take sides if you want to be trusted. Being trusted by everyone is one of your most valuable assets. You will be trusted if you show your integrity and are seen as an 'honest broker.' It is dangerous to align yourself with only certain kinds of people. You need to listen to and show respect for the full diversity of viewpoint, including cynics, and not just those at or near the top.

Somehow though, you need to prioritize how you spend your time with people. Some relationships will be more productive than others in fostering transformation. Some relationships will be valuable in providing you with the support and nurturing you need so that you do not become drained and exhausted. Some people give you energy – others 'drain' you. Ration your time with the latter. In your network you need two kinds of people: people who are benign and powerful leaders of transformation; people who provide you with support. Often, but not always, they will be the same people.

In building your network and getting alongside other leaders I have found it helpful to ask questions about how they see the organization, how they would like to change it and what most gets in the way of excellence. The sort of questions that work well in my experience are given in Appendix 3. I call them 'useful questions.'

Perhaps the most useful final question you can ask after you have listened for a while is 'How can I help?' (which is similar to 'How can I serve?'). I have this question on the top of my desk to remind me to ask it often and to remind me what I am here for. There is a useful exercise in Appendix 8 which will help you review your existing network and decide what you need to do to make it more effective.

Identifying and working on your key issues

Essentially this is about identifying and working with obstacles or issues that could get in the way of your strategy. There are three kinds: those out in the organization, 'the client system'; those in the team to which you belong or which you lead which may manifest themselves 'in here' when you get together; and, perhaps the most important of all, those in you. The latter are those over which you have most control but which are often, at least initially, the most difficult to admit to. Sometimes they are difficult to see or understand. Here you come up against your own resistance. I often start, irrationally, blaming problems out there, or in here before finally realizing that essentially they are in me – the way I behave, my rigidities, my emotional reactions, my fear, anger or panic, my unconscious negative expectations or the critical judgments I make which people sense, the subtle ways in which I project myself or simple deficiencies in my knowledge or skill. If I am to take responsibility, learn and be a good model for my clients it is essential that I acknowledge these issues, decide to act differently and actually make changes. This is true for everyone. We need to model being open about this. It is no use pretending.

Planning action and support

This is the final, relatively simple but absolutely essential step. As Joel Barker said:

> 'Vision without action is merely a dream. Action without vision just passes the time. Vision with action can change the world.'

The simple question is what then do you commit yourself to doing to make the strategy a reality? What are the steps that need to be taken and when? And, most important, what support will you get for yourself because inevitably there will be set-backs and situations you find difficult to cope with? Who are the very best people to help you sustain your vision and energy, act flexibly and wisely, particularly in dealing with situations you find difficult or do not easily understand?

Doing this work in teams

It is equally important to do this work in teams. An HRD team, or HRD people from different parts of the business should meet to share your data; make a common diagnosis; get behind a shared purpose and vision; decide how both collectively and individually you can make the biggest impact in supporting the leadership in transforming the organization; and plan how you will support each other. This is a good investment. Once a team has done this they need far less management and far fewer meetings. Basically they are 'all set' and mainly require good quality meetings to share success, review and give each other support. There is also a tremendous amount of learning to be gained – learning about how to do this work with a team that you can turn to good use in facilitating your clients. You will find out what the difficulties are and how to tackle them. Regard it as your laboratory in which to discover what works best and what does not. You will need at least a day – preferably away from the distractions of your site. It will help to have a facilitator from outside the system – someone who can see things it is hard for you to see because you are part of the system, or who can see where you are having difficulty in transforming yourselves, getting into a different mind-set.

Some effective strategies

Some elements of strategy are likely to be effective in a wide variety of situations. Amongst these are those listed in Figure 5.3.

* Redefine the business you are in as *consulting* or facilitating transformation.
* Push training and development resources out into the business.
* Get out into the business, develop widespread friendships and ask empowering questions.
* Be aware of, but stay outside, the politics.
* Enable people to work together to address the real opportunities and key issues of the organization.
* Work towards getting the *whole system* into the room.
* Train managers and other leaders in helping and facilitation – create a network of facilitators/champions.
* Encourage people to form support groups and to network.
* Help people in the organization value difference and work constructively with conflict. (Get gender, race, age and disabilities on the agenda.)
* Work where the energy is.
* Develop support for yourself – find a partner.

Figure 5.3   Strategies to facilitate transformation

Redefine the business you are in as consulting or facilitating transformation

Change the focus of your own team or HRD colleagues away from providing training and instead towards consulting. This will enable you to empower others to take ownership of training and development and see it as part of their job. You will move away from doing things *for* clients to doing things *with* clients or encouraging and equipping them to do things for themselves. It will mean you can achieve far more with fewer resources. You can then focus on the more difficult role of the internal consultant.

Push training and development resources out into the business

Get the resources out into the business, close to where they are needed. Get the work done locally. This follows the principles of empowerment and ownership but it is also where the job is usually done best as long as training skills are transferred and adequate support is provided. You may have a new role in inspiring and supporting these people. It is also astute at a time when centralized resources are vulnerable. A lot of HQ teams or company colleges have been closed recently. A small corporate resource may be needed for a clearly defined purpose.

Get out into the business, develop widespread friendships and ask empowering questions

Get alongside the CEO if you can but, if that is not possible, get alongside other key leaders you have access to. Ask leaders about their part of the business. Paradoxically, asking people questions is one of the most effective ways of influencing them. Talk with them about the business *not* training needs if you want to be seen as a consultant/facilitator. Ask: What is going well? What is difficult? How would they like things to be different? What gets in the way? What do they need to do? How could you help? This is probably one of the most powerful things you can do. By asking these questions you are helping to release the forces for change. These are empowering and supportive questions. Many leaders welcome being listened to. Leading can be a lonely job. Almost certainly you will find a considerable degree of agreement about how things need to change and what the obstacles are. Many people probably want to change things in the same way as you do and would value your efforts to assist. Not only are you supporting people, you are also creating support for yourself, and you are building your understanding of the total situation. Both the 'Empowerment Model' and 'Useful Questions Model' (see Appendices 1 and 3) provide a useful basis for one-to-one meetings with clients (see also Chapter 9).

Be aware of but stay outside politics

Your success as a facilitator depends on your being *trusted* by all your potential clients. If you are perceived as 'playing politics,' or taking sides in power politics, you will not be trusted. It is important that you are seen as having complete integrity.

Enable people to work together to address the real opportunities and key issues of the organization

You can offer management development workshops that focus on real opportunities and issues (see Real Time Management Development in Chapter 6) and bring people together from different parts of the organization. Alternatively, you can facilitate teams or groups (see Chapter 10). The opportunity to do this work may well flow from the one-to-one work you do with individual leaders described above. As a result of those meetings you will be in a better position to make attractive proposals that will enlist support.

Work towards getting the whole system into the room

People are discovering that top down approaches are less than satisfactory. They do not enlist the intelligence and energy of all stakeholders, particularly not those closest to the product, process or customer, in developing new strategies or redesigning the workplace. Also a few senior people do not have enough data about the whole system, therefore strategies or solutions originating from the top or from groups of experts are not fully effective. Nor do they attract the necessary commitment of the whole workforce. Top-down approaches also take far too long, and messages get distorted both on the way down and on the way up. Alternative approaches such as Future Search Conferences, Search Conferences, Open Space Technology and Real Time Strategic Change are emerging. A key aspect of these approaches is to get representatives of the whole system into one room. The internal consultant can play a useful part by encouraging leaders who see inadequacies in top-down approaches and want to look at alternatives. As the opportunities emerge, we need to equip ourselves to facilitate very large groups and develop our skills and expertise in this area. I am trying to find out about and get expertise in these methods as fast as I can because I think they will be increasingly needed in the future. (There will be more about this in Chapter 8.)

Train managers and other members of the workforce in the skills of one-to-one helping and group facilitation

These skills are crucial for the kind of leadership, formal or informal, needed in the modern workplace. They are also necessary if you are to adopt a strategy of empowering and encouraging ownership of development throughout the workforce. Managers and others can then support each other one-to-one and co-facilitate team events or real time development workshops with each other. In this way you are creating an army of people, a network of champions who can facilitate transformation, thus enabling you to focus your energies where they are most needed, for example, on work which requires your skills and experience or where someone who can stand outside the situation is needed. (There will be more about this in Chapter 12.)

Encourage people to form support groups and to network

One of the benefits of training managers in helping skills is that they see the value of support and often realize how isolated they were. They discover the value of giving and receiving support with people they trust. Encouraging support groups and networking can be a valuable part of your strategy to encourage transformation (see Chapter 11).

Help people in the organization value difference and work constructively with conflict

We need to help people move away from old-fashioned adversarialism and create an inclusive workplace. We need to help people into a different mind-set and see difference as valuable and indeed essential and help them see that it does not mean wasting energy in conflict if they look for common ground. It is not only about fairness; it is equally about creating a more robust, rigorous, creative and successful culture. It is also about using all the potential in the organization and addressing the waste that results from women and black or colored people feeling marginalized and not taking their place in the senior and leadership positions of the organization. It does not help a modern organization if its culture and policies are determined almost exclusively by white, middle class men of a certain age. For many companies this is a major issue although it may not be fully recognized. If we equip ourselves we can play a major part in helping our organizations with these issues. But first we have to deal with our own racism, sexism, ageism, classism, etc. We all have it in us. The first step is to admit it. (For more on this see Chapters 9 and 10.)

Work where the energy is

I have already argued that it is most fruitful to work where the energy is – with leaders who are most receptive to the forces of change and are working with them. Given that you have limited resources and need to prioritize, there is little to be gained from battling with resistance. It is unrewarding and draining for everyone to focus on difficulties and problems. It is more fruitful to concentrate energies on creating common ground about the desired future. It seems wise to work with clients who are themselves empowered and can exercise imaginative and empowering leadership – clients who are able to make good use of the skills and opportunities you offer.

Develop support for yourself – find a partner

I have also already argued that it is important that you develop support for yourself so that you can deal with set-backs more flexibly, learn from difficulties and sustain your energy. Providing yourself with good quality support needs to be a crucial part of your strategy. This equally applies to others but to understand its value and how to provide it you need first to get it for yourself.

It is probably a good idea to set up support for yourself not only within the organization but also outside it. The former enables you to form working alliances. The latter gives you the support of someone outside the system who is not subject to its influences, can sometimes better understand what is going on and can challenge you as only an outsider can.

> In my last job as an employee the situation got politically very difficult. I made two wise decisions. One was to fix regular half-day support meetings, off-site every two months, with a good colleague in another division. Basically we split the time, gave each other a good listening to and looked at how we could act boldly and collaborate. It was a brave decision on his part as he was being encouraged not to collaborate with me. In effect we became partners. As a result of this not only did we do better in our own areas, we also pulled off a long-term major intervention together which was greatly valued – a development program for top managers from across the divisions of the company. The other smart decision we made was to get ourselves support from an external 'shadow consultant' who was able to help us where we were getting stuck. As a result of this the two of us were able to achieve far more for the company than we could have done alone. We were also able to get our teams to collaborate instead of compete.

There will be more about support, internal and external, in Chapters 11 and 13.

The strategies which I have outlined in this chapter will be elaborated on in succeeding chapters.

References and suggested further reading

Cameron, J. (1995) *The Artist's Way – A Spiritual Path to Higher Creativity*, Pan Books, London, UK.

Harrison, R. (1995) *Consultant's Journey – A Professional and Personal Odyssey*, McGraw-Hill, Maidenhead, UK.

Zeldin, T. (1995) *An Intimate History of Humanity*, Minerva, London, UK.

Part III

❖

Taking Practical Steps

6

Real Time Management Development

Working with managers on their real opportunities

'The teacher ... If he is indeed wise he does not bid you enter the house of his wisdom, but rather leads you to the threshold of your own mind.' The Prophet, Kahlil Gibran.

The way we develop managers lags far behind

This chapter describes one key way in which you can help your organization transform itself. It is an approach to management development which enables people to work on their real opportunities and issues, bring a practical pay-off to the business and learn and develop in so doing. It provides a model for widespread use in empowering people at all levels in the organization.

Organizations face challenges of enormous proportions in the competitive global economy. To survive and thrive they need to provide quality and value through continuous improvement. I find growing recognition amongst leaders that hierarchical, top-down approaches don't work well enough and to achieve this they need to engage the energy, intelligence and co-operation of every-one involved, especially those closest to the customer, product or service. We need to involve the whole workforce and other stakeholders (for example, customers and suppliers) in developing vision and strategy for the business as well as in its implementation. The most progressive organizations are learning how to do this.

Yet, I believe the way we develop managers lags far behind these aspirations. They are not congruent with empowering people. For the most part we are still locked into top-down, didactic, classroom *teaching* when what is needed in times of chaos and uncertainty is learning, experiment and *discovery*. Managers are often offered development programs over which they have little control. They are confronted with the incongruity of being urged to create empowered workforces whilst their own development typically consists of being taught predetermined competencies (what entrepreneur or free spirit would put up with this?); listening to experts, top managers or gurus; the use of a variety of contrived experiences and various psychometric instruments. Whilst these elements can be appropriate, the downside is that all this can encourage dependency and detract from the idea of finding authority within and using the intelligence of the whole workforce to transform the enterprise. The classroom or lecture theater symbolizes a mind-set that is opposite to the one we need to create. And none of this can be shown to have a direct pay-off for the business at a time when the name of the game is *survival*. Reg Revans saw this many years ago when he invented Action Learning (Revans, 1971). Instead we need to create approaches to management development which are empowering and provide a model for managers to use in tapping the energy and creativity of their own workforces.

But the truth is never that simple

Extreme positions are rarely helpful and are usually flawed. There is a great danger in either/or polarizations. Both/and is usually the way. Most of us learn in a rich variety of ways. Presentations of fresh thinking, orally or in books or papers, can play a major part in challenging current mind-sets and creating a whole new way of seeing things. Role plays and simulations can give people new insights. Psychometric instruments, focus groups and surveys are sometimes useful.

However their use needs to be weighed against the question: 'Given where we are now, what is likely to be the most effective way of engaging and empowering the whole system of this organization in transforming itself?' In my experience, these methods have often not been very successful in transforming an organization, winning hearts and minds, empowering people or in encouraging them to trust their immense individual and collective resources.

Transformation is inevitable and will take place whatever we do but if we want to facilitate and ease its happening, I believe that real time approaches need to play a much greater, if not the major part. There is a saying that children learn what they live. Funnily enough the same seems to be true of adults. This is what real time methods offer. In practice, it is difficult to 'mix modes,' ie, to use a combination of what I call 'didactic and contrived' *and* 'real time' approaches, together, in the same event or intervention, without creating confusion, dependency and counter-dependency. This is because mixing modes can send out confusing messages like 'trust yourself but I know better than you' or 'we are partners, I respect you and I am going to share power with you but I know better than you, am above you in some way and I am going to stay in control.' To some degree this reflects the complexity of organizational life. But my current thinking is that it is better not to mix modes but instead to keep them well separated. If they are used together in the same event or intervention it must be with great care, awareness and understanding (be on the alert for the hazards I have mentioned too).

An example of successful use of simulations is Barry Oshry's highly creative work (see references in Chapters 9, 10 and 11). His brilliant insights and discoveries are based on simulations (whereas I have learned mainly from listening to people, witnessing what happens or experiencing it myself). Recently he wrote to me as follows:

> *'I am ... focused on unravelling system dynamics – how things fall into going wrong and how, with system sight, we can put them right.'*

> *... 'organizational and ... societal exercises are ... at the heart of my work – both in terms of my own learning about systems and for the contributions they make to others ... there is a special*

contribution that comes from system exercises, from taking people out of *their day-to-day worlds. Good system exercises enable people to see that problems which seem so personal and so specific to their organization and its conditions are not personal and not specific to them. This fundamental insight –* **It's not personal** *– releases energy, it depersonalizes situations, breaks down WE/THEM myths, redirects energy into the right places and enables people to turn their attention to their real time issues and make these more manageable. Our work focuses on giving people system sight and system exercises play a big part in making that happen.'*

I was so pleased to receive this addition to my own under-standing before going to print. Seldom have I witnessed or heard of simulations used with such insight, clarity of purpose and to such good effect. Now back to the main stream of this chapter.

A radically different approach

I have tried to create a radically different approach to management development. I call it business-led management development or real time management development (RTMD) because the learning comes from working on the real opportunities and issues each manager faces – this is the richest seam for learning. It is learning from life. It brings work into the learning place or learning into the workplace.

I believe it goes further than Action Learning (Action Learning represented a sea change when it started) in a number of ways. The focus of Action Learning as a process is on the learning of the individual manager not the system. RTMD enables larger groups of managers to get together, develop common ground and work together in transforming the company system or part of it. It gets part of the system into the room. Managers are also involved in its design and facilitation. It is flexible and demonstrates how one workshop can meet diverse needs. It provides a model for widespread use in empowering people and helping them work

Conventional Management Development	Real Time Management Development (RTMD)
• The subject matter is predetermined competencies and a neat and tidy body of knowledge.	• The subject is each manager's business and her or his exciting ideas and vision decisions.
• Learning has to be transferred to the business afterwards.	• Learning comes out of working on the business.
• The trainer is entertainer, guru, magician (and potential 'scapegoat,' even charlatan).	• The stars and heroes are the managers.
• Managers are passive.	• Managers are active and creative.
• Trainers are in charge and held responsible for outcomes.	• Managers are in charge and responsible for outcomes.
• Everyone's needs are similar (assumption).	• Everyone's needs are similar *and* different.
• Preplanned, prepared and predictable program or curriculum.	• Apart from a core method little is planned, everything's spontaneous, exciting, energizing.
• Unlike the real world.	• Like the real world.
• Under control and inflexible.	• Flexible and gets out of control.
• Trainers are teachers and experts.	• Trainers are facilitators and co-explorers in learning and discovery, responsible for structure and process.
• Methods disempower.	• Methods empower and provide models and tools managers can use.
• Encourages dependency on outside authorities.	• Encourage interdependence and belief in authority within.
• Business benefit is indirect and speculative.	• Benefit to the business is direct and observable.
• Trainers evaluate.	• Managers evaluate themselves.

Figure 6.1 Conventional Management Development vs. RTMD

- The **subject matter is the exciting opportunities**, visions, strategies, issues, plans, struggles, reflections and learning of the participants.
- **Learning will be largely from visioning, planning, acting, reviewing, reflecting** and **learning from each other.**
- We **facilitators will try to be congruent** with our vision and walk our talk about empowerment.
- We will give only short talks or briefings to introduce the work that needs to be done. **Our role is to offer structures, processes and methods; to facilitate;** provide good conditions to work and learn in; avoid creating dependency or 'counter dependency,' be a presence and a resource to individuals and groups; 'speak out' on major issues, say things that aren't being said and encourage others to do so.
- We will **use a wide variety of empowering processes** to maintain energy and excitement, respond to different needs and avoid monotony or boredom.
- There will be **no contrived exercises** such as simulations, role-plays, case studies, business games or other instruments.
- On the basis that there will be about 12 well-informed participants from a wide variety of backgrounds, we will not invite any expert speakers. Similarly, top managers will not be invited in, except as participants. People have access to both experts, benchmark companies and top management before or after the workshops. Such inputs would create a distraction from the work of the workshops. **All the resources we need for the workshop are 'in the room.'**
- The **unique needs of each participant will be provided for** by the broad core structure and the 'flexible program.'
- We will create a **new experience of working life** – challenge but not frighten off or alienate.
- **A long-term structure and long-term support** will be provided – ie, over many months because participants are making long-term strategic changes. Also they often need time to make fundamental shifts in mind-set and change the habits of a lifetime.
- We will **never allow ourselves to forget the business purpose** of what we are doing and the need for a practical pay-off for all stakeholders. Customers, jobs at all levels, suppliers, shareholders, the company and the community are at stake.

Figure 6.2   Key principles for RTMD

constructively together to achieve a common purpose. It helps participants adopt and practice the different attitudes and behaviors and create the different culture needed in business today. It also enables managers to understand how to release energy and excitement in their businesses. It helps them learn the importance of working with the whole person – not just their knowledge and skill but attitudes, energy, emotions, spirit, intuition, left and right brain – and achieve balance in planning and implementing change. It brings all these things into play. It differs from conventional management development (see Figure 6.1).

I acknowledge that these are two ends of a continuum but I believe we have to push our efforts over to the right-hand side. If our goal is to create an empowered workforce then our methods of developing people must be congruent with that aim, not methods which encourage dependence. Developers must walk their talk in this sense. The rest of this chapter describes what I have learned about how to do this.

Principles

Let us start with principles. I have come to the conclusion that principles are everything, well almost everything. Figure 6.2 sets out the principles of Real Time Management Development.

The overall structure of RTMD

The core process is based on the Empowerment Model (see Figure 6.3) and the overall structure of a typical RTMD program is set out in Figure 6.4.

Put very simply the stages are:

- Individual consultations with participants and other stakeholders.

- A half-day meeting in which participants and facilitators get together to validate the diagnosis, business purpose, objectives and design and start building a community.

- A first workshop to develop vision and strategy and start work on issues.

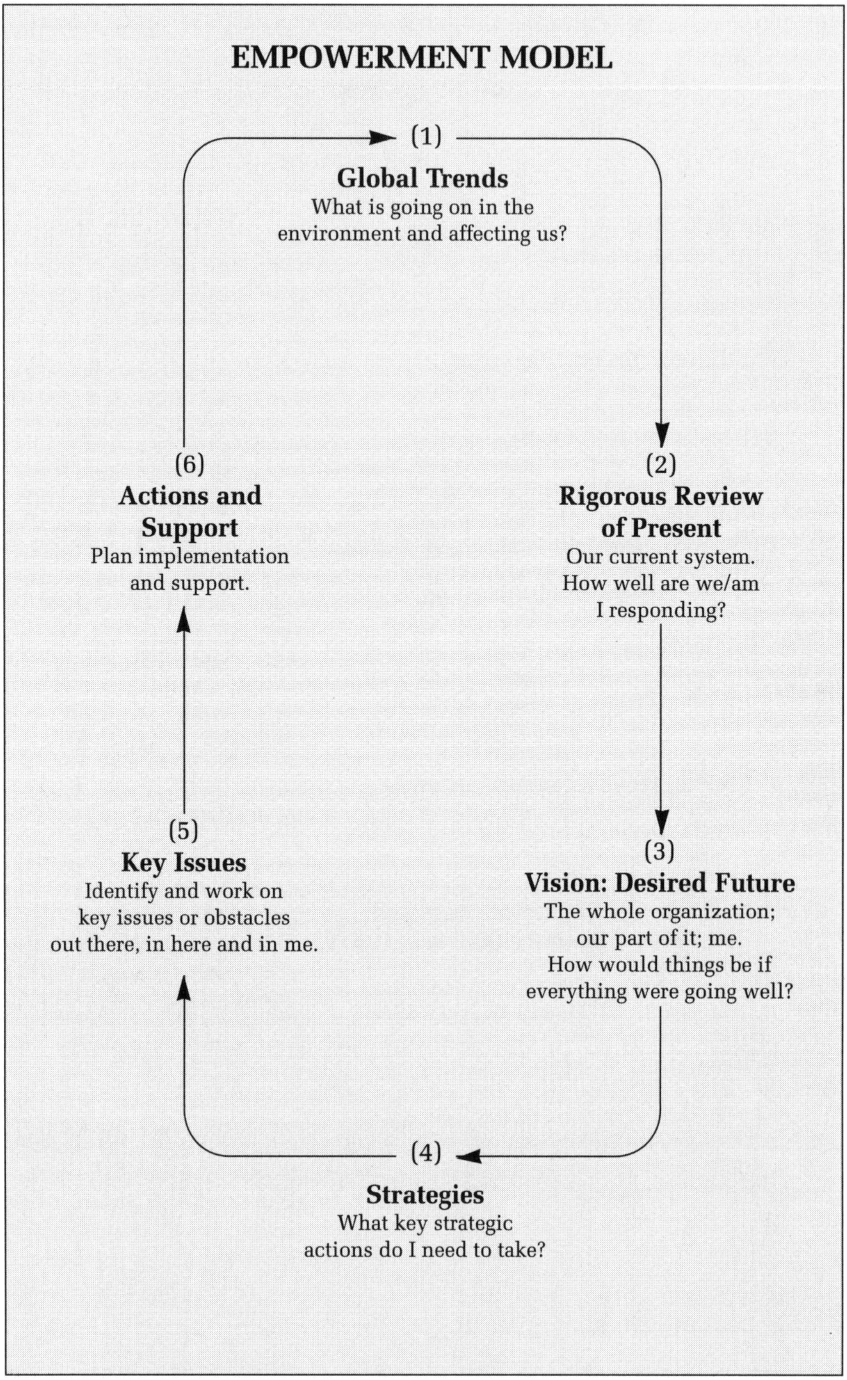

EMPOWERMENT MODEL

(1)
Global Trends
What is going on in the
environment and affecting us?

(6)
Actions and
Support
Plan implementation
and support.

(2)
Rigorous Review
of Present
Our current system.
How well are we/am
I responding?

(5)
Key Issues
Identify and work on
key issues or obstacles
out there, in here and in me.

(3)
Vision: Desired Future
The whole organization;
our part of it; me.
How would things be if
everything were going well?

(4)
Strategies
What key strategic
actions do I need to take?

Figure 6.3

- An initial period of implementation in which members network and meet in support groups.
- A second workshop to review progress, learn from what has happened, work on key issues, plan further changes and propose how the program should evolve to transform the organization.
- Continuing networking, support group meetings and implementation.
- An emerging strategy to extend the work throughout the whole system of the organization.

The Empowerment Model (Figure 6.3) provides a basis for all these activities; Figure 6.4 provides an overview.

Building readiness and planning

- Forming a partnership with the internal consultant.
- Contracting with the CEO and the executive.
- Deciding where to start.
- Forming a facilitator team.
- Individual consultations with participants.
- Involving participants and other stakeholders in data, diagnosis, objectives and outline design.
- Re-contracting with the CEO and the executive.
- Tutor team meet to design Workshop I and skill up.

Workshop I

- Contracting and building a working and learning community.
- Identifying global trends affecting our business – our environment.
- Rigorously reviewing how we are responding – our system.
- Building a picture of our desired future.
- Deciding strategies to get there.
- Working on key issues in the 'flexible program' (open space).
- Making commitments to action and support.
- Review.

Figure 6.4   Overview of typical RTMD program

Implementation and further planning

- Implementing change.
- Networking.
- Support groups meet.
- Facilitators consult participants.
- Designing second workshop.

Workshop II

- Rebuilding the climate; re-contracting.
- Sharing successes, difficulties and new key issues.
- Using flexible programs to work on key issues.
- Making new commitments to further change.
- Review and determine the way ahead for the RTMD program.

Building critical mass and sustaining change

- Involving participants and other stakeholders in deciding the way ahead.
- Working upwards.
- Running similar workshops at the same level.
- Cascading down.
- Training directors and managers as facilitators.
- Working with teams.
- Holding 'alumni' events to build networks.
- Holding whole system events.

Figure 6.4 *continued*   Overview of typical RTMD program

Starting – building readiness and planning

It is wise to start with a pilot initiative to be followed by an emerging long-term strategy to transform the organization. Where and how you start is important. You need to start an RTMD program where there is the greatest probability of a pay-off. That means targeting potential participants who are ready for change – potential champions, opinion leaders and people who will make the best use of the opportunity – drawn from as many different parts of the organization as possible, but include some cynics and skeptics as their views are important. Stakeholders at various levels need to be involved in planning the RTMD program, especially the chief executive officer (CEO) or top manager of that part of the organization, and her or his team. Rigorous contracting with the CEO (however defined) and the executive or top management team is crucial in most cases. It is particularly

- **Planning meeting with internal partner**
  Her/his diagnosis, vision, strategy, planning of initial intervention including where to start, participants to target and who else to invite to join the facilitator team.

- **Contracting with the CEO**
  Her/his diagnosis, vision, expectations, goals, *business purpose*.
  Is she/he willing to stick with a long-term intervention?
  How willing to be open and have others be open with her/him?
  Her/his views about stakeholders to be involved, facilitators and target participants.
  How the CEO needs to support the program and her/his responsibility for its success. Does she/he want to participate?
  Does she/he really want an empowered workforce?
  Is she/he willing to change too? How, specifically?

- **Planning meeting with design/facilitator team**
  Diagnosis, visions, strategy, 'charter' on how we will work together, team building, initial plans, selection of participants.

- **Individual consultations with participants**
  Their diagnosis, what they want to change, key issues, expectations and their advice.

- **Design of Workshop I by facilitator team**
  Based on diagnosis of key issues of participants; may involve other stakeholders in diagnosis later.
  Skilling of facilitator team.

- **Presentation to CEO and her/his team**

- **Presentation and further consultation with participants as a group**
  Their diagnosis, the workshop and how the team designed it, *purpose*, objectives, approach and methods, their advice to facilitators.
  Do they want to consult other stakeholders and, if so, how?

- **Possible consultation meeting with other stakeholders**
  Their diagnosis and advice to facilitators on what is proposed.

Figure 6.5 Building readiness and planning

important to contract with the CEO and executive about their responsibility for the success of the initiative and how they need to support it. Perhaps they will be participants. The program needs to be linked to a key business goal from the start so that everyone can clearly see the program's relevance to business survival and prosperity. The *business purpose* or goal of the work is a key part of contracting with the CEO. Also she or he needs to be satisfied that the intervention will support the transformation she or he is trying to bring about.

The initial phase of the intervention – building readiness and planning – is summarized in Figure 6.5.

As an external consultant I nearly always start by forming a partnership with the 'internal' consultant or whoever is responsible for management development. We have an initial planning meeting to talk through her or his organizational diagnosis, vision and goals. We try to model the processes and use the tools from the start. We decide what participants we should target initially and who from that target group we should invite to join us in designing and facilitating the program. Usually three facilitators are enough for a group of 12 participants (or four for a group of 16), assuming that small groups of 3-4, each with a facilitator, will be needed. You may think this is overly staff intensive but it pays dividends in terms of the results that come out of the small groups and in training directors and managers to facilitate. The latter see its value and they love doing it. It opens their eyes to a new and very satisfying role: *facilitator*. I have always found it helps enormously to invite a respected and skilled member of the target group to join us as a facilitator. (Others, including other stakeholders, may need to come in to help our organizational diagnosis later.) Not only does it give credibility to our work, but also helps make sure we come up with a design that will work well for the participants. This combination of an internal consultant, a director or manager and an external consultant provides an excellent blend of knowledge and skills for a team to design and facilitate a program that really fits and challenges the participants. In most organizations gender is an issue and so it is important that both genders are represented in this team.

One of the first things the internal consultant and I do together is meet and contract with the CEO along the lines described in Figure 6.5. Next, the internal consultant, director or manager and I spend half a day together to build ourselves into a team, share data about the organization, start making a diagnosis and develop our vision and goals for the intervention we are embarking on. Again we try to model and practice the processes and behavior we will adopt with participants. We try to create an empowering climate within our team. We are training ourselves. We talk about who we will target as participants and also whether, and if so how, we would like to involve other stakeholders.

Before we can design the program, we need to go out and consult the participants, collect data, and start helping them diagnose their key issues and opportunities and think about how they will use the program. Figure 6.6, 'Individual consultations,' describes some questions that are useful for this purpose. In my experience it is very important to ask early in the meeting what is going well. It implies you make positive assumptions and are not there to criticize. Really at this stage we are offering the participants some individual consultancy. Also what we are doing is building trust, commitment and readiness for change and making sure we get the objectives and design as right as we can. We are also starting to model partnership and empowerment in the way we initiate a program by involving participants – often after years of imposing courses upon them. It is important to explain that the program will probably be unlike anything they have experienced before! It won't be a course. It will be a place

---

- What is your thinking about key trends in the business environment?
- How well is the organization responding? What is going well? What are you not happy with? What gets in the way? What are the difficulties?
- What is your vision? How would things be if everything were going well?
- What will get in the way if you don't tackle it?
- What will you do and what support do you need?
- How could this program help? What would be the pay-off if it were highly successful? Its *business purpose*?
- What advice do you have for us?

(adapted from Useful Questions Model, Appendix 3)

Figure 6.6 Individual consultations

where they can do strategic work with their colleagues and three facilitators.

We then come back and spend a day or so designing the first workshop and our presentations to the CEO, her or his team and, probably afterwards, the participants. Because of the way we have consulted all of them, their endorsement is most probable but they may have invaluable suggestions. It is usually persuasive first to reflect back to people what they have said; then to present our diagnosis and our proposals. Anything unpalatable needs to be handled sensitively – there should be no shocks for the CEO in front of her or his colleagues!

The broad structure of the workshop follows the Empowerment Model (Figure 6.3) but the detailed design within the broad structure is critically important. It needs to reflect our organizational diagnosis based on what the participants have told us. It helps if a title for the program is chosen which reflects the key issues. We also need to build our own exciting vision for the event so that we can be inspired and inspiring facilitators.

The presentation of our diagnosis and proposals to the participants, based on an evidently sound understanding of their needs and issues, is crucial. We have built relationships with individuals, now we have the harder task of building readiness in the group. Dynamics start coming into play. It is the beginning of

---

By the end of the program you will have:

- Built a comprehensive picture of the global environment affecting your business.
- Rigorously appraised how the organization is responding to its environment.
- Developed a clear vision of the desired future for the organization, your part of it and yourself.
- Developed strategies, including key people you need to influence, to bring about the desired future.
- Identified key issues (including your own attitudes, blocks and skill deficiencies) that will get in the way and started to tackle them.
- Made plans including a support system for yourself.

Figure 6.7   Typical objectives of a RTMD program

facilitating the group. Also we are starting to introduce them to what the experience will be like and to us as a team of facilitators. We need to stress that everyone takes responsibility for the program. At the end of the presentation they should be as well prepared for a new experience as is possible and should be willing to trust us. Usually most of them, whilst apprehensive, are excited to be involved in developing an initiative that has the potential to be of enormous benefit. Anyone should feel free to opt-out if it is not for them.

Typically, to explain the program we use flip charts or overhead transparencies based on Figures 6.8 – 6.12.

- Workshop I.
- Implementation.
- Support groups meet.
- Further consultations.
- Design Workshop II based on current diagnosis of needs and key issues.
- Workshop II.
- Continuing implementation and support group meetings.
- Facilitator team reviews and plans emerging management development strategy, involving participants and key stakeholders including CEO and her/his team.

Figure 6.8 Overall structure of pilot program

- Building the climate; contracting and forming support groups.
- Creating a picture of the global environment.
- Rigorously reviewing our/my response to it.
- Developing a vision for the future.
- Deciding key strategic actions including influencing strategy.
- Identifying and working on key issues – the 'flexible program.'
- Planning action including support.
- Commitments and review.

Figure 6.9 Structure of workshops – Workshop I

- Recreating the climate.
- Rigorous review of progress since Workshop I; successes, difficulties, changes in the situation, learning, what now needs to be done, best use of workshop, ie, new issues.
- 'Flexible program' or 'open space' to work on key issues.
- Further planning including support.
- Final commitments and advice on next stage in RTMD.

Figure 6.10   Structure of workshops – Workshop II

- Agenda is your own work.
- *You* do it – it is what *you* make of it. We share responsibility.
- No contrived situations – working on reality.
- 'Core program' for key issues.
- 'Flexible program' for individual or shared issues.
- Climate: honesty, trust, being ourselves and being authentic.
- Balance: demanding, supportive, challenging, exciting, fun, serious, humorous, healthy, taking care of ourselves, knowing when to stop and when to review process, feeling and task, celebrating success and appreciating each other.
- Connection between workshop climate and what people want out there.
- Tutors model what they espouse.

Figure 6.11   Workshop approach

Having done this we (the facilitator team) now need some time to make any changes to the design and prepare and skill ourselves for the first workshop. We will have a good idea of both individual and group needs for which we may need to prepare ourselves. Some rehearsing, confidence building and giving each other support will be needed immediately beforehand. We will need to experience some of the processes if we have not already done so in our earlier meetings. Our aim will be to model an excellent partnership between women and men in providing empowering leadership. We need to be in good shape to do that and feel well

- Short inputs.
- Time to reflect and review.
- Work on own.
- Work in pairs.
- Work in small groups.
- Plenary to brief; build picture of global environment; share diagnosis and vision; review, work on key group or corporate issues and share insights and learning.
- Regular reviews of progress and learning.
- Giving and receiving feedback.
- Commitments to action.

Figure 6.12   Variety of workshop methods

supported by each other (there should be no competition, power struggles or big egos!) We need honesty and humility.

I have never found any problem in practice in getting managers and directors to release themselves for this work. They can readily see that the skills of facilitating individuals, teams and large groups are part of every leader's toolkit today and they are eager to learn them.

Workshop I

Space and time

The environment matters considerably. The venue needs to be away from the work site so that attendance is full-time in every sense. The availability of a swimming pool and other fitness or sports facilities, healthy food and places for walking are important. How meeting rooms are arranged sends out powerful messages. They need to be informal and flexible so they can be quickly rearranged. You will need a large room with comfortable chairs in a circle (not tables which make barriers) that can be moved about easily to form different groupings. Large wall spaces are needed that can be covered in flip charts or one huge flip chart when the whole group is building a picture of the global environment, how the system is now, and how it needs to be – their vision. Small rooms without tables are needed for support groups (unless the meeting room is exceptionally large) together with sufficient flip charts. Simple technology is best – all you need to provide are things like scissors, marker pens, masking tape.

The time allowed for the workshop is important too. This work really requires about three days to be done properly. People need enough time to 'get there,' leave behind their day-to-day concerns and overcome their doubts, fears and uncertainties about an important new experience. They need time to make major shifts in attitude or how they see things. Emotions are involved – the picture of global trends and the rigorous review can leave people feeling low in energy; vision building is exciting and moving. People need time to handle these rhythms. Opportunities to reflect and for the unconscious to work creatively overnight are important. At least two overnights are beneficial and attendance needs to be full-time.

Contracting and building a community

In a typical first workshop (see Figure 6.9) participants and facilitators begin by contracting, getting to know each other and building a community. It is best if this work can be done on the previous afternoon and early evening so that people are fully ready at the start of the first whole day. Each person needs to state clearly the outcomes they want from the workshop. We also need to contract clearly about process, roles and responsibilities and make agreements about the climate and behavior that will really support effective work and learning. This is important ground work in creating an effective partnership.

Self-introductions

Self-introductions can be profoundly important in a number of different ways: people get to know each other as human beings at a deeper level than ever before – *discover their common humanity*; start to break down divisions; are really open about themselves; build a climate of openness and trust; start to make decisions about who they would like to work with in support groups or otherwise; and, most important of all, get in touch with their own goodness and who they really are which is the foundation for so much of the work they will do in the workshop.

Usually we ask participants to pair up with someone they would like to get to know better, someone they trust. They listen to and support each other in turn talking about the points listed in Figure 6.13.

- My *full* name (often a revealing and humorous icebreaker).
- Where I am from – place and brief history.
- Two achievements I am most proud of.
- What matters most to me, what I am passionate about.
- Current issues for me as a leader – opportunities or difficulties I struggle with.
- Outcomes I want from this program.

Figure 6.13   Self-introductions

Then each person shares key points in the whole group – especially their issues and outcomes. It is best if a tutor starts and gently models the kind of honesty and feeling that others may wish to follow. I encourage the pairs to stand together up front, giving each other support for what can be a very moving and inspiring process. By this time participants are in a good position to decide who they would like to work with in support groups.

Using the Empowerment Model

Participants are now ready to do the core work of the workshop, ie, work round the Empowerment Model (see Figure 6.3). There are various ways they can do this work: starting with the whole group; then splitting into groups (facilitated or self-facilitated) of say six to eight people, or relatively intimate support groups of three to four people or pairs; then again as a whole group to share and review. These are design issues for the facilitators to decide, depending whether it is most appropriate for people to focus on the corporate organization or their own part of it or first the corporate whole and then their part of it.

I now favor getting the whole group to produce a huge wall chart of the *global environment* (stage 1), each individual contributing to the picture. This gets everyone on their feet and actively involved immediately. It shows how it is possible for a large group of people with different perspectives to build something together. It demonstrates how people can cope with a mass of complex data without distilling it into meaninglessness to which no one has any attachment. Each person's words are up there. It shows how we can respect everyone's truth which is an important lesson if we are to go beyond adversarialism. 'Everyone's truth is valid' is a ground rule.

A similar process can be used for the *rigorous review* of how the organization is responding (stage 2) – that may need to be boiled down to the *key issues the organization faces* – and the *shared vision* or *desired future* for the organization as a whole (stage 3). 'Common ground' and 'things not agreed by everyone' may need to be identified.

When people are working on their own part of the organization – rigorous review, vision and strategy – the work is best done either in well mixed, self-selected support groups with a facilitator, or in pairs, followed by some kind of sharing in the whole group. I favor, at least starting with, facilitated support groups unless there are large numbers. That may require working in pairs or self-facilitated small groups (given some ground rules or guidelines). People claim great benefits from learning from the experience of their colleagues.

Work on vision is very personal and involves the emotions as well as the head. It is rooted in values and beliefs. People need to get in touch with who they really are and sharing a poem, piece of writing or music can be helpful. Visions can encompass pictures and symbols as well as words. My experience is that people require support to do this work really well. It can be helpful to choose a 'friend' to walk with and talk about their vision for the whole organization, their part of it and themselves. The 'friend' listens and encourages. They do this in turn. They then write their vision on a flip chart before sharing it in their support group and perhaps later in the whole group, or by posting it on the wall as part of a 'picture gallery' of visions which everyone can view.

By the time people have worked round stages 2, 3 and 4 in their support groups they have learned a lot from each other, understand each other very well and are in a good position to give each other challenging and encouraging support.

Working on key issues

Then comes stage 5 of the model – *identifying and working on key issues* or obstacles that will get in the way of bringing about the desired future. There are three kinds of issues or obstacles – those out there in the environment or the larger organization; those in our team or group; and, finally and most important of all, those in you. These are the hardest to come to terms with and admit, but they are the ones over which we have most control. Usually I start by blaming things out there or others before I come round to me. This is where people have the opportunity to be really honest with themselves and with others and where important personal and organizational learning can take place. It is also the point at which participants empower themselves to take charge of their learning and the workshop gets out of control.

Issues and key issues

Something about *issues* and *key issues* may be useful at this point. The terms appear quite frequently in the text and in both the Empowerment and Internal Consultant's Models. I define an issue as something important that needs to be worked on or addressed. If it is not resolved it will impede or get in the way of progress. An issue can affect a whole organization. Defining it in this case is part of making an organization diagnosis. Or it can affect a team or group or it can be personal, ie, within a person or between that person and another (intra-personal or inter-personal). At another level it can be the issue 'in the room' when a group of people are meeting. In this case, it will not be possible to make progress unless that issue is addressed. A good process consultant will sense this and help the meeting identify and address the issue. It helps to express an issue as a question. In my experience this leads to more rigor. It is worth spending time carefully rephrasing the question.

Adding the adjective 'key' to the word 'issue' helps focus on what is most important. There are usually a number of issues in a situation. Time is limited and it helps to prioritize. Some issues may be described as *fundamental*. Some are *underlying*. Some issues *embrace* other issues. The idea of the *key* issue is that it is the one that is the key that opens the door that leads into a new room. It is well worth working hard to find the key issues in a situation. Sometimes it becomes apparent that there is one that is key. So the notion of defining the key issue is useful. I define this as 'the issue that if you identify it correctly and address it, will transform the situation.' It allows the maximum result for the least effort. Everything follows in its wake. It leads to a step change. Scales are lifted from people's eyes. It is energizing, awakening and perhaps leads to what is called a paradigm shift. Working on the issue is the best use of anyone's or everyone's time and energy. Getting to that issue may be an intuitive process and the question: 'What is the best use of your time right now?' may lead to it.

The 'flexible program' or 'open space'

I usually get people to pair up and 'give each other' a good listening to. Sometimes we first give a short input on 'helping skills.' I brief them to talk about 'What are the key issues I now need to work on out there, in my team, and in me?' Each person is asked to produce a flip chart headed: 'The best use of my time now.' It will list the three to four key issues they want to work on, how and with whom. Each person will briefly talk about his or her chart and put it on the wall. Then everyone will get into a 'mêlée' to arrange what they want. The less the facilitators get involved, the better it works. All they need to do is set the scene, state what room or spaces are available, suggest how the total time can be divided, describe some of the optional ways of working (for example in groups, pairs, on own, with tutors or not) and offer themselves as resources. Experience has taught me to keep out, not to attempt to organize it but let it emerge. It is exciting, frightening and it invariably works. Some people call this Open Space Technology (Owen, 1992). I call it a 'flexible program' where people pair up, call or lead meetings, make offers and make requests. Corporate issues get dealt with, relationships get sorted out; skills are exchanged, and people resolve difficulties, make momentous decisions, or even take a much needed break.

One managing director went off into the nearby hills for half a day and came back clear about what he had to do. Another top executive worked privately with a tutor on his relationship with his son, which was also a way of working on his relationship with his team of highly paid professionals. In another situation, the whole group wanted to work on gender issues and how they held back the top team. This took the form of a woman and a man sorting out their working relationship while the rest of the group simply gave their attention (facil-itated by a female colleague of mine). The silent attention of a large group is powerful; we all learned a lot. On another occasion it in-volved the male directors learning to listen to their female colleagues! Another whole group worked on resolving how the need for individ-ual accountability and corporacy could be reconciled. Often people take the opportunity to resolve or start resolving key interpersonal is-sues which nearly always boil down to changing their own attitudes or behavior. Sometimes people use the chance to pick brains and learn from the expertise that is in the group or simply to build bridges and forge alliances. An alliance between two people can achieve powerful results. Two men who had been rivals used the time to be-come partners.

Managers find it exciting and refreshing at last to be in charge of their own learning. It releases their enthusiasm. Why has it never happened before? It is also a model they can use in their own team events.

Developing key skills and learning

In these workshops managers will most likely need to learn and practice helping skills both as a key skill for developing their own people and so that they can facilitate each other in their support groups. Empowering leadership is also likely to be a key theme and they may need to work through the networking exercise refer-red to in Chapter 5 and described in Appendix 8. The support group is an intimate and important community in which learning can take place and it will often continue to meet for a long time after the formal program is over. Usually it starts with a facilitator – people need to learn how to work in a disciplined rigorous way – but gradually this role is handed over to the members who take it in turns to facilitate. In that group members practice giving each other feedback in an encouraging but challenging way. We brief them simply on how to do this. Also the group will learn to express their appreciation of each other. Some people find this embarrassing at first – others love it – and it plays an important part in helping change the culture of the organization to one where more appreciation is given more often. Learning is fostered by having reviews both in support groups and in the whole group in which people share what they are learning and the conclusions they have come to. Reflecting overnight and sharing insights at the start of the day is a valuable process. Reviews are important to make sure everyone is on track, to bring out important issues and to make adjustments and changes to the program, so is letting down at times and having fun and relaxation. Silly games can relieve tension, raise energy and spark creativity. Asking people how they are feeling can be an important intervention that breaks through blockages, opens up fundamental issues, leads to shifts in mind-set or indicates the need to change the design of the workshop.

Planning implementation and support

After the first workshop there needs to be a period of several months in which to implement strategies and plans for change and improvement. During this time participants are encouraged to network and meet in their support groups.

In the final session of the workshop, people make plans for decisive action and share commitments. We also encourage them to commit themselves to getting support and be specific about from whom they will seek it.

Finally, we review the workshop – ask what worked well and what needs to be altered for the benefit of future participants. We start discussing with them how the RTMD program should be extended to other people in the organization and how they want to be involved in this.

Workshop II (two days)

The nature of Workshop II is probably largely self-evident from Figure 6.10. Allowing two working days including two overnights seems about right. (This means starting at tea time on the day before the first full day and finishing at about the same time on day three.) Participants and facilitators need to spend time re-building the community they formed, recreating the climate, or 'getting there' after a gap of three to four months. The 'rigorous review of progress' takes place first in support groups or pairs – then in the whole group. We celebrate; tell stories about what has happened; draw conclusions and learning from that; identify the key issues now to be worked on and work on them using the *flexible program*. The key question for each participant is 'What is the best possible use of my time?' It is remarkable how both the most important individual and corporate issues which are getting in the way of the business, or may do so, can be addressed and, at least largely, can be resolved. Usually in the second workshop people are ready to work on far more fundamental issues and with greater honesty because, by then, sufficient safety has been created. Often they claim to get more value than from the first workshop.

We end the second workshop by planning further action and support; reviewing what worked and what we need to do differently; and again discussing with the participants how RTMD should be extended to other people in the organization, how the strategy for transformation should unfold and what part they want to play in it.

How does RTMD change attitudes and behavior?

RTMD methods and processes help people adopt new attitudes and behavior if they practice them during the workshops, in support groups, in networking and back on the job. Most often

- Continuing improvement and learning.
- Taking a view that is both global and strategic.
- Being visionary.
- Welcoming change and upheaval.
- Valuing difference and seeking common ground.
- Adopting behavior that empowers others.
- Creating a challenging and supportive climate.
- Using energy, emotion, intuition and both hemispheres of the brain – understanding the importance of the whole person.
- Being really authentic with others.
- Using process abilities and helping skills.
- Trusting, letting go of control and seeking balance.

Figure 6.14   Changes in mind-set and behavior

people change from being wary and competitive to becoming good friends and partners. *Above all, they experience what it is to be empowered and they understand how they can create conditions for other people in which they too can empower themselves.*

In the workshops and support groups participants develop and use many skills and practices that are vital for survival, among them those listed in Figure 6.14. Between the first and second workshops people apply these skills to real organizational issues, thereby making important changes which provide them with evidence that this new way of working is more productive. Once participants have experienced the effectiveness of a different approach and seen a practical pay-off in their businesses, they start to use it more widely, and it gradually becomes part of their everyday working life.

• Further programs at same level.
• Further programs at higher or lower levels.
• Work with the top management team.
• Work with several levels together.
• Large scale events involving representatives of the whole system at all levels – getting the whole system into the room.
• Continuing one-to-one networking and support groups.
• Training people at all levels to facilitate workshops and team events.
• Cascading through team programs in participants' own units.
• Using the Empowerment Model in self-managed work groups to plan improvement.
• Further work with specific corporate key issues that have emerged.
• Work on difference issues: gender, race, age, disabilities, etc.
• Work with individuals.
• Network events for past participants (alumni) to provide support for continuing change and create a thriving network.

Figure 6.15   Emerging strategies to embed change

Creating critical mass and embedding change

This first program is just the beginning of something that has the potential to transform the organization. A strategy needs to evolve in an emergent way to change how the organization does business and it needs to include ways of sustaining and developing the impetus for change. There are all kinds of possibilities. Some of these are listed in Figure 6.15.

I believe activities of this kind can transform an organization and its culture, but they need to develop organically. They cannot work miracles. Miracles require the leadership of committed, energetic, positive people who take responsibility and assume long-term persistent leadership.

Key factors that make for success

Over the past 20 years I have successfully introduced the RTMD approach in a wide range of industries including insurance, local government, avionics, higher education, information technology and retail. There are pitfalls, however, as it is not magic and it doesn't always work. Figure 6.16 lists the factors that seem to make for success.

Benefits to the business

Finally, here are some comments from participants – most of whom were or became directors – about how they benefited from one particular program and the effects it had.

> *'I now find myself once again firmly in touch with my personal philosophy and more importantly, confident and excited by what we can all achieve within (the company). Words somehow seem inadequate – a breath of fresh air, a common-sense revolution, of great significance to us all for the future – all these things and much more.'*

> *'As a result of this program, the integration of the two companies has been made easier and less painful. For this alone ... (the company) owes a considerable debt....'*

- Contracting well with the CEO who gives wholehearted support.
- A close partnership with an internal consultant who has credibility and assumes determined, long-term leadership of the program and shares ownership.
- Involving the CEO and executive as participants.
- Involving directors and managers as facilitators.
- A pilot program with carefully chosen 'champions.'
- Consulting and involving participants beforehand.
- Getting rid of competition in the training community.
- Building a highly supportive facilitator team. The blend of external and internal consultant and director or manager at the start.
- Modeling what we stand for.
- Sticking to non-didactic principles.
- Being bold, taking risks and speaking from the heart, with passion.
- The 'flexible program.'
- Being firm on principle but flexible and creative.
- Handing over ownership and involving the clients in creating an emerging strategy.
- Long-term support from an 'external' source.

Figure 6.16   Factors leading to success

'(The) management development function ... is already changing the culture within (the company).'

'I've enjoyed these three sessions a tremendous amount and am very different as a result. I'm more confident and am carrying through the changes very much into my working life. It's continuing as well. With some courses you forget everything in six months, but with these sessions, they're remembered and they impact on all aspects of managing a team. . . . This will change the attitudes of group management and really make (the company) No. 1.'

'This has been the best experience of my working life . . . I find it difficult to describe what I have got out of it but . . . I have

been inspired, encouraged and supported. This has given me the confidence to make it happen for me, my patch and my (company). I am positive the benefit will be lasting and ... when I recall events ... I will gain strength.'

Chapter 7 gives accounts of RTMD programs in four organizations.

References and suggested further reading

Gibran, K, (1991) *The Prophet*, Pan Books, London, UK.
Owen, H. (1997) *Open Space Technology – A Users Guide*, Berrett-Koehler, San Francisco, USA.
Revans, R. (1971) *Developing Effective Managers*, Praeger, New York, USA.

7

❖

Using Real Time Management Development
To change the culture of an organization

'There was a clear correlation between a factory's management culture and the degree of excellence that the factory exhibited – and virtually every winning factory had taken steps towards the establishment of an "open" management culture.

A collegiate style of management seems to correlate more closely with manufacturing excellence than a style based on fear, divide – and – conquer leadership, and autocracy. . . .

Smaller units tend to operate more efficiently, and are more effective at implementing improvement initiatives. Factories that are part of a large group ... would do well to adopt a "small business" mentality – a transformation in culture that needs to be directed from the top.' Independent *on Sunday* 3 November 1996, reporting on 1996 Management Today Factory of the Year annual award.

'We need to learn to do something by doing it. There is no other way.' John Holt, Educator.

'There is no such thing as a problem without a gift for you in its hands. You seek problems because you need their gifts.' Richard Bach.

Four case studies

This chapter tells the stories of trainers or internal consultants whose visionary leadership is helping to transform the cultures of their four very different organizations. They are people I profoundly admire for their courage and tenacity. Each participated in a long-term intervention ranging from two to ten years. In each case the approach was broadly similar and they had long-term support from outside sources. However there were interesting and significant differences and, in telling the stories, I shall bring these out. They will be honest, 'warts and all' accounts including an assessment of what they achieved, and what they did not, and the conclusions. I shall not name the organizations as I want to feel free to give my frank assessments without causing embarrassment. I shall call the case studies:

1. Bottom up.
2. Working near the top.
3. Top down.
4. Stuck at the top.

Basically there are two ways of managing a company. One – sometimes caricatured as the 'Genghis Khan approach' – is to manage by command and control, using punishment, manipulation, criticism, division and fear as the means of exercising power. (There are more benign forms of command and control such as

---

- Raise people's awareness of how they want things to be different by inviting them to express their views. Encourage them to speak from their hearts.

- Work with their energy to change things often expressed as complaints.

- Offer inspiring, visionary leadership which responds to their desire for things to be different.

- Provide different experiences of how work *can* be, that model a new culture and enable people to work successfully on their opportunities and the issues they present.

- Provide new, empowering tools and processes.

Figure 7.1 How to encourage cultural change

- The **subject matter is the exciting opportunities**, visions, strategies, issues, plans, struggles, reflections and learning of the participants.
- **Learning will be largely from visioning, planning, acting, reviewing, reflecting** and **learning from each other.**
- We **facilitators will try to be congruent** with our vision and walk our talk about empowerment.
- We will give only short talks or briefings to introduce the work that needs to be done. **Our role is to offer structures, processes and methods; to facilitate;** provide good conditions to work and learn in; avoid creating dependency or 'counter dependency,' be a presence and a resource to individuals and groups; speak out on major issues, say things that aren't being said and encourage others to do so.
- We will **use a wide variety of empowering processes** to maintain energy and excitement, respond to different needs and avoid monotony or boredom.
- There will be **no contrived exercises** such as simulations, role-plays, case studies, business games or other instruments.
- On the basis that there will be about 12 well-informed participants from a wide variety of backgrounds, we will not invite any expert speakers. Similarly, top managers will not be invited in, except as participants. People have access to both experts, benchmark companies and top management before or after the workshops. Such inputs would create a distraction from the work of the workshops. **All the resources we need for the workshop are 'in the room.'**
- The **unique needs of each participant will be provided for** by the broad core structure and the 'flexible program.'
- We will create a **new experience of working life** – challenge but not frighten off or alienate.
- **A long-term structure and long-term support** will be provided – ie, over many months because participants are making long-term strategic changes. Also they often need time to make fundamental shifts in mind-set and change the habits of a lifetime.
- We will **never allow ourselves to forget the business purpose** of what we are doing and the need for a practical pay-off for all stakeholders. Customers, jobs at all levels, suppliers, shareholders, the company and the community are at stake.

Figure 7.2   Key principles for RTMD

paternalism.) The other, not at all a soft option, is to manage by sharing power, providing open, inspirational leadership and to encourage, involve, empower, unite and bring out the best in people. The first can be summed up as *patriarchy* and the second *partnership*. All four case studies are about to attempts to encourage the latter.

All four, to varying degrees, illustrate the principles and ideas set out in Chapters 4 to 6. I learned a lot from these and other similar experiences and the principles have evolved from what I learned – both our successes and our difficulties (sometimes painful for me). That process of learning goes on. All four 'interventions' are based on the approach first outlined in Chapter 4 and repeated for your convenience here as Figure 7.1. They also reflect the following key principles summarized in Figure 7.2 (first shown in Chapter 6).

About having realistic expectations

Before starting on the four stories I want to say something about expectations and evaluation. I like quotes from artists – and remember, entrepreneurs and business people are *creative* artists:

> *'You are lost the instant you know what the result will be.'* Juan Gris.

> *'Only when he no longer knows what he is doing does the painter do good things.'* Edward Degas.

Of course we need to have clear goals and purpose and a vision of what we are trying to achieve, but it makes no sense to see the organization as a machine. There seem to be expectations that if you make an accurate diagnosis, and then design an appropriate intervention, the desired changes will occur and if they don't then you've got it wrong, you were incompetent and ought to be fired or hang your head in shame. Alongside this goes the idea that, after a suitable lapse of time, the intervention can be neatly evaluated in terms of whether goals and measurable benefits were achieved. All this can be encouraged by a desire to respond positively to management's natural anxiety about how the investment, often large, in both time and money can be justified. As a result of the above we may be tempted to make claims we cannot truly justify.

Perhaps we are beginning to understand that it is simply not possible, not within our power, to bring about cultural or large-scale system change in such a way. Organizational change is far too complex and there are too many unpredictable factors for it to be susceptible to a mechanistic approach. Unpredictable things happen – organizations get taken over or they merge, leaders change, key supporters leave or move. Also the idea of attempting to manipulate change as opposed to facilitating it is incompatible with empowerment. Organizations as systems and cultures evolve. Their evolution involves many people making choices. All we can hope to do is help things along – 'put our brick in the wall.' We can influence and facilitate people in working with the forces in the organization and its environment, helping them to adapt in a healthy way and make choices that enhance the chances of surviving and thriving. It is rather like the role of therapist – at the end of the day the choice is always made by the client. Perhaps the healthiest attitude we can have is one of great interest and high expectations whilst not knowing what the outcome will be.

If cultural change is to be more than cosmetic, widespread changes in attitudes and behavior are needed. Policies and practices may also need changing so that they are congruent with and support the desired culture. Despite the fact that there is an inexorable evolution in society of which cultural change in organizations is a part, not everyone walks at the same pace. Some just don't see it our way. Some don't want to change how they manage. In an organization there is usually a wide spectrum of belief and opinion. Cultural change involves letting go and giving up deeply ingrained habits and beliefs. Changes in what we say take place more quickly than changes in what we do, that is why the latter are more important to work on. We know from our experience of ourselves how hard it is to change habits. Changes in our attitudes and beliefs evolve over time as a result of influences and life experiences. It is all very unpredictable.

We have to be honest. Embarking on cultural change is an act of faith which requires belief and a strong commitment from the client if it is to succeed. A lack of commitment will be a self-fulfilling prophesy as we shall see in Case study 4. Similarly, evaluation of this kind of work can't be carried out in the same way as evaluating training. *Clients, the 'owners,' have to take* responsibility for finding out what has happened, what has changed, what the effects are, and for deciding how much further they have to go and what now needs to be done. They need to see evaluation as a way of keeping the action going – not as an ending or a way of distancing themselves from something they were not really committed to at the start, as in Case study 4.

Case study 1: Bottom up 'When trainers build partnership with their clients'

A large organization in the financial sector

This initiative was the work of a small group of internal trainers (of whom I was one) supported over a long period by external consultants. One helped me develop what I now call 'real time' methods; one of his colleagues then helped us become internal consultants, work strategically, overcome competition in the training community and work together as partners; then he became our 'shadow consultant'; finally, one of us who had become self-employed stayed with the project until it ended ten years later. The participants wanted an external presence and perspective.

We started where we could – almost at the bottom – with the section heads. That is where the energy was and we went with it. Here the need for development was most strongly acknowledged and the greatest potential pay-off was seen. There could be increases in revenue, reduced costs, higher service quality and improved efficiency. It would be fairly easy to measure results at this level. At this time (1978) there was very little acknowledgment of the need for development in the middle or at senior or top levels of management. Our practical approach produced positive results. As managers saw the results of our work with their people, our credibility grew. They started to want our help as consultants, or training consultants, in working with their teams. Managers at progressively higher levels wanted to come on our workshops. Increasingly our clients were telling us that something needed to be done to change the corporate culture. We should work with people higher up they said.

I therefore talked with some 40 top and senior managers; my colleagues did the same. Essentially we used the 'Useful Questions' Model and found a lot of agreement about what was getting in the way of better performance. They said the following was getting in the way:

- Lack of a sufficiently strategic approach.
- Inter-divisional rivalries and competitiveness between people.
- Lack of trust or openness about mistakes or development needs (seen as weakness).
- Over-control.
- Fear and feelings of inadequacy.
- 'Trashing,' blaming, complaining and criticizing instead of taking initiatives and speaking one's mind.

What they said was needed and wanted instead was:
- A more strategic approach.
- Values and beliefs articulated as a basis for mission and strategy.
- Greater skill in managing change.
- More inspirational leadership, particularly of large numbers of people.
- Commitment to common purpose and agreed strategy.
- Teamwork and trust.
- A climate that encourages people to take responsibility, develop and give all they are capable of.

These were the key issues. We set out to offer a Real Time Management Development program that would address them and enable the senior managers to bring about these changes. In retrospect it is clear that the empowerment model would have 'done the job.' In 1985 we approached six people at a senior level and asked them to work with us in developing a program for their colleagues. This first attempt did not start particularly well – one of the six had a severe trust problem and withdrew – but gradually, with the help of the remaining five, we got things right. We had discovered that the program could not work without trust. We also learned that we did not need outside experts (in this case I valued external input on strategic management), we could do the job ourselves. In 1986 we felt confident enough to offer a full scale program of three workshops spread over a year for 12 senior managers. We targeted managers at the two to three levels below corporate board level. Several of them later became directors of subsidiary companies. Again we worked where the energy was. This was the highest level we could reach. At this level there was a strong desire for cultural change but there was little recognition of this need at the corporate board level above them. We hoped that problem would be addressed by upward influencing and upward migration. We approached senior managers from across the divisions who we thought would be excellent participants and asked them to handle their politics and get approval, if needed, for their participation. We adopted this approach because of top level hostility towards personnel initiatives and the culture of warring barons at the top.

Luckily for us, the first full program was judged a huge success by a very influential group of senior managers – they asked for a fourth workshop a year later – and its continuation proved almost unstoppable. They claimed it made a huge difference to them as individuals, to their businesses and, as more programs were held, was changing the culture of the organization. Although managers were never involved as facilitators, who continued to be senior members of the training community, *ownership* was strong. The program evolved and took on a life of its own. It was almost as if the early group of senior managers had taken it over, protected it from hazards – top management were always ambivalent towards it and the relationship between the program and top management needed to be managed sensitively or they would see it as a threat and stop it – and ensured its continuation and supply of participants. Perhaps this was because they saw the facilitators as highly responsive to their needs.

The program continued for ten years. It evolved over time in response to the changing needs of participants. For example, participants sought 360 degree feedback before attending. They also wanted to know much more about best practice in other organizations. Input from a different industry was therefore brought in and a business school was involved. Some ex-participants got involved as presenters but not as facilitators. Altogether about 150 people participated. The number of participants dwindled as the most senior people had all been on the program and the program ended when nearly all suitable people had participated. It had done its job. It was always voluntary and people out of tune with its aims did not participate. It is noteworthy that very few women have been involved either as participants or as facilitators reflecting their small numbers at the senior level.

A significant minor variation in terms of the empowerment model, was that we did not use the rigorous review (stage 2). We went straight from stage 1, global trends, to stage 3 shared vision or desired state future. Our clients seemed to subsume stage 2 in building their visions. With some groups that would not have worked. They would have needed the rigorous review to get things off their chests before they could think about the desired future.

A year after the final program ended I tried to find out what was the effect of ten years of this intervention. It had *opened many doors to the facilitators* – team building and consulting work in the businesses and one-to-one consulting. It *raised the profile of corporate management development*. It *opened up a dialogue with the CEO* about culture, development for senior managers and the corporate management development role. Many of the *support groups (and networking) went on and on* and some still continue to meet after 9-10 years. It *built bridges, broke down personal and divisional barriers*, created a critical mass, moved the way people lead and manage change towards *a more inclusive approach*, a sharing leadership. One director wrote to me and said 'I look back on the … program as a major event in my managerial life in terms of self-realization and relationships.' There was a strong shift towards more *open, consultative, communicative* management. There was some filtering down of ideas and some influencing up. The CEO and some of his colleagues came along and contributed and it gave them food for thought.

It was evident that the program *only had a big effect on those who participated*, and *the corporate executive were never involved as participants*. I believed then, but even more firmly now, that top management do not participate, not through total desire to control but through their own fears and insecurities. They find openness threatening – indeed some of the participants found it very uncomfortable too! Thus, it was as if these able and dedicated top managers could not fully appreciate the importance of greater trust, openness and involvement if a culture of excellent team-work were to be created. I think for them the issue was not empowerment but *control*. They had a different mind-set. Top management don't always see what senior managers see so plainly (and vice versa) – each touches a different part of the elephant. They could see the program was doing something for senior managers so they allowed it to continue, but it was at times an uneasy relationship. They never really understood it and because of that it never had their wholehearted endorsement. For some it was a case of 'I work the way I work and I am not going to change.' No one ever really risked *really* explaining it to them. This is very understandable when people get punished for having a different view (especially in times of mergers, downsizing and among people keen to get to the top and be seen as 'one of us'). Fear plays its part. There was also the danger that if top people felt threatened, and feared loss of control, they would stop the program. A delicate judgment.

The conclusion is that what we were doing was partly for a future generation. What it tackled – the more senior strategic levels within divisions and operational management – it tackled very successfully. It helped those who recognized the need but not those who did not. Some were pulled along. However, the corporate level were largely unchanged, unmoved. When people moved up into it they did not change it, perhaps because they felt too isolated to challenge the top 'group think.' Also, role models have a powerful effect. Those who subsequently joined the top team did so by emulating the behavior of the current team *not* by practicing 'partnership' management. What else could be expected if those at the top were not involved as participants? As we have said, for them, I believe, the issue was not empowerment but control. If that level is to change they have to recognize the need and want to change. Corporate culture shifts when they shift. There has to be a belief at that level, and *they need to be involved as participants.* There has to be some push, perhaps some outside influence from someone trusted who is not completely 'one of us,' or perhaps a new generation, a new 'critical mass' at the top who think differently.

It looks as if we need to find ways of helping people at top, senior, middle and bottom level 'see' the whole elephant. This might offer the best chance of changing mind-sets – all of them *as participants*, in the same room, as equals, partners, speaking their minds without fear. But it takes a brave top management who actually want to do business differently and are willing to risk sharing some control in exchange for empowerment. How do you get them to want to is the big question. However, the story is not finished, all in good time.

Case study 2: Working near the top 'Real work with real people'

A large retail organization

Starting

My client and I had known each other for two or three years before he asked me to come and help him develop a new program. He had courage, vision and quiet passion about his work and was becoming more and more respected and trusted. His brief was to transform the existing rather traditional skills-based development program for senior managers. He wanted to create a program that would help senior managers actually bring about strategic changes, change the culture back in the business and improve results. A key feature of the program would be learning to lead in an empowering way. The current CEO was keen to develop an empowering culture in the organization. The new program would help him achieve this goal. Managers would learn to be strategic, visionary and empowering in handling change. They would use the new program to plan, implement and review changes with the long-term support of facilitators and colleagues.

Broadly speaking we followed the approach described in Chapter 6. We were not able to contract with the CEO. At that time my client did not have access to him but there was a clear link with the CEO's declared commitment to empowerment. The two of us held a planning meeting, made an organizational diagnosis and he talked about his vision for the program and who to target as participants. We also decided to invite a respected ex-store manager, seconded to management training, to join us as the third member of the all male facilitator team. This turned out to be an inspired choice. My client's boss approved our proposals and we started work in mid-1989. There was a clearly acknowledged need amongst senior managers and the proposal was likely to appeal to the carefully chosen target participants – a wide cross section at that level. They included large store managers, regional managers, senior members or heads of HQ departments and directors of small companies.

Issues

The three of us went out and listened to the participants. Their needs and issues sound fairly typical. They said they needed to:

- Look at the external environment, and review how well their businesses were responding.
- Manage change strategically.
- Learn how to cope with the change and the huge pressures involved.
- Lead in a way that inspires, empowers and develops people.
- Learn and get feedback from colleagues.
- Get encouragement to take risks and try new things.
- Learn how to bring more enjoyment into work and take better care of themselves.

As we talked with more and more managers, and worked with them over the months, we found that, like so many others, they felt relatively vulnerable; were relatively cautious; were often initially reluctant to talk openly about development needs; they often found that there were divisions between people who needed to co-operate; they had difficulty trusting colleagues and tended to blame upwards rather than take responsibility. The CEO, held in some considerable awe, was blamed for some of the difficulties (as is common). They were reluctant to work on gender issues perhaps because women at this level were in a minority and relatively junior.

How the work unfolded

We held the first program at a lakeside hotel and activity center. Each support group was based in a self-contained cabin where they not only held support group meetings but also slept. This helped to build really strong relationships. The sporting facilities, such as the pool and water sports, played an important part. There were wonderful places in which to walk like the nearby hills. Several people reported the influence these activities had on their energy, thinking and decisions – they used them as part of the 'flexible program.' Having an experienced store manager in our team made a big difference. He was highly credible to his senior manager colleagues. Often line managers become good facilitators more easily than trainers because they have less to unlearn and relate closely to the practical needs of their clients. We were very nervous as we were trying out completely different methods for the first time and he was able to reassure and encourage us to take even bolder risks. He told us our new approach was on the right lines. We invested time in building ourselves into a close team with a shared diagnosis and vision. We also practiced the skills we were going to use and impart to our clients – especially 'giving each other a good listening to' and learning how to support each other well. All this paid off. We were a really good team – we shared the work equally, not only leading large group sessions but also facilitating the three support groups, and defined each other's roles clearly. My client was the overall leader. My role was to focus on structure, methods, facilitate the team and be the external presence.

The first program exceeded our highest expectations. The CEO wanted these programs to continue as quickly as possible. I was asked to help facilitate a second program to bed in the approach and train another facilitator. Then we decided it was time for me to withdraw and hand over to my clients. My client, in turn, started handing over the program to colleagues. I suspect it became a little diluted, for instance, they moved away from the lakeside resort and the numbers were increased from 12 (three facilitators) to 16 (four facilitators). This made it harder to build safety. Nevertheless the program continued to flourish and was described as a 'flagship.' Sadly, in my view, managers were not at this stage invited to be facilitators and programs continued to be led by trainers, nor were managers trained to facilitate programs in their own businesses. I think this would have helped with 'ownership' – helped them see it as theirs rather than belonging to management training – and helped make management development and facilitating part of running a business.

Two years later I was asked to help initiate a program at a higher level – just below corporate board. This story shows how, unexpectedly, what looks like a 'sure thing' can go wrong. It also shows how much can be learned from an apparent disaster. My client's new boss and an experienced woman trainer joined us. We wanted a woman in the team to give support to women participants. We embarked on the initiative in our usual way and it all looked very promising indeed. My client's boss was an excellent ambassador and tireless recruiter. He also started building the needed relationship with the CEO.

But then things started going wrong. First my client was seconded overseas for three months. Both the newcomers were more at home with training than consulting, and were not used to working with underlying issues. For all his strengths, my client's boss was a dominant man with strong views who was used to being in charge and only just learning to be a consultant. He was often under pressure and was unable to come to meetings, or attended only part time. He wanted to delegate to the remaining two of us and use me as a hired hand rather than using me as a consultant and working with us as a partner. I had difficulty explaining that this would not work. The 'boss' was generally not open to my advice. He saw me as a temporary resource, to be managed, delegated to, not as a consultant. It became apparent that we were not all equally clear about or committed to a non-didactic, real time approach; nor clear about the importance of being congruent and modeling our beliefs rather than talking about them. Because of the pressures we felt, we did not give ourselves the time or space to discuss and learn about each other's values and beliefs and, importantly, understand the history and rationale for the work. A power struggle was developing – we were a competitive team, not a close partnership. We struggled on and I wrestled with whether I should continue. Fortunately my client returned just before the first workshop; that helped.

It was not an easy program. Some of the participants were particularly cautious and reluctant to do any practical work. There was not a lot of trust in the room because of certain personalities. This was not helped by the fact that our clients could sense we were not a united team, fully supportive towards each other. Some sessions over-ran considerably. Others did not get enough time to be fully effective. There were some lengthy didactic inputs, out of tune with an empowering approach. I did not perform at my best. There were rifts over the tutor team working late (analyzing the day's events and planning) instead of keeping ourselves in good shape for our clients and able to look at underlying issues. We were mirroring the culture out there in the organization rather than offering a better alternative. We later held a team day to try to sort out our differences but it did not work. At first it was proposed I attended unpaid! I was 'demoted' to participant status and my client tried to facilitate us. We really needed another external not involved in the 'stuff' to help us.

For the second workshop, my client's boss had decided to invite the CEO to come and answer questions. This had the advantage of building the connection with him and getting him involved. But it clashed with the real time approach. It was an example of 'mixed mode.' It proved to be a major distraction away from senior managers empowering themselves and a measure of the culture change needed. Certain grown men, normally ebullient, quaked at the knees and lost their 'bottle.' Preparation for this visit dominated everything for 24 hours. There was panic. No one talked about it of course. People competed to appear in a good light. We missed a golden opportunity to work the patriarchy or dependency issue. Because of the rifts within our team, we did not have the confidence as facilitators to bring this data out into the open and work with it as a key symptom of the organization's difficulty with empowerment – their fear and awe of the CEO.

I could see I was heading for the fall guy role. Criticism focused on me during and after the workshops. I think people unconsciously read the signs and attacked the weakest link – the person with least to lose, the one with least connection. I was not invited to help again and that hurt. Also I found it very disappointing to be dropped from work which had been so successful and to which I was so committed. I felt I had a lot more to give and they needed continuity. It seemed highly incongruent with our goals to punish the consultant for allegedly making mistakes or speaking his mind. They were acting out the 'distress' of their organization I thought. However, over time I learned a great deal as I reflected on the experience. My replacement for the next program was a woman for whom I have much respect. I hoped her strong presence would give better support to women leaders and bring out the gender issue, which until then had remained below the surface.

How the work continued after I left

My client tells me he learned a lot from this experience which seemed so bad at the time. The two programs – one at director level, the other at senior manager level – continued on and on. He made a number of key changes. Firstly, he further increased efforts to build the relationship with the CEO, the executive and the non-executive board members. He got them to sponsor the programs which meant that members of the executive participated in a session on every program; non-executive directors visited too. Secondly, my client decided to involve my successor in every program she could be available for. She gave him the continued long-term external support needed to tackle the really tough issues from then on. This enabled the two of them to openly address the issue of why it was so hard for top managers to talk to the CEO. They either addressed this at the time by encouraging dialogue or before or after the event. He also instituted a policy of involving a director or senior manager as a facilitator on every program. They might not always be so skilled as facilitators but they contributed passion, enthusiasm and knowledge of the business. Each facilitator team included a woman from now on. He was much more careful in choosing facilitators – people willing to be consultants, rather than didactic trainers, and people who would be good team workers. He also became more careful in choosing participants. Finally, he consistently invited women participants to the programs whether or not they met the 'rank' criteria, so that women were well represented.

Support group meetings and networking continued. 'Network events' for past participants from different programs and follow-up days between workshops were held. The program opened many doors for my client and his colleagues, including consulting work in the businesses. They influenced the way other programs were conducted. They raised the profile of HRD and equipped erstwhile trainers to move into internal consulting. But the most important result was to give him an opportunity to work at the most senior levels and do key strategic change work, and to see the CEO and other directors as normal people who needed help. A lot of home truths began to be heard. He encouraged the CEO to have a similar 'retreat' for the executive (participants were asking why they held themselves aloof from this useful process) but there was resistance to this idea and it did not happen. My experience is that a leader may have to insist if this kind of work is to happen.

Before it ended in 1995, some 200 directors and senior managers had participated in these programs. Work at the most senior level ended when the new CEO was appointed. By then all top managers and directors had been through the program. Lower level work ended when the new CEO, wisely I think, decided to disperse management development into the businesses and only retain a tiny corporate presence. My client had not built the relationships with the new corporate HR director for the work to continue. Perhaps by then this six-year initiative had largely completed its mission. Now there is a new piece of work to be done. My ex-client is now an independent consultant bringing this approach to other organizations.

Effects on the business

The effects of this kind of intervention are inevitably intangible. Dozens of managers and directors have reported on the changes they have made. They have recommended the program to their colleagues. Busy directors and managers are unlikely to do this unless they have benefited significantly. These are typical reactions, reported after the first program:

> 'It has focused my attention and energies in searching for and expressing a real vision and convinced me I could do it!'

> 'It has re-emphasized the importance and value of people and how to motivate them more fully.'

> 'A major effect on my life – business and elsewhere – raised my self-esteem, helped me give up smoking.'

> 'Spiraling upwards. The package is great, it has given me a new way of life in terms of fitness – really has changed my life that way.'

> 'Huge opportunity – the space for me. It gave me a certain sort of strength.'

> 'I got really positive help. I have learned to focus my attention and energy on where I need to go'

> 'Tremendous – I enjoyed the chance to come back to Part II. The second workshop was almost more valuable.'

> 'Clarified things that were abstract. Feel I have had an overhaul.'

> 'I had much confusion, many issues to deal with. It got my feet back on the ground and gave me the ability to see things through. Quite radical for me.'

My client tells me he constantly meets people who say how much the program affected them. Essentially it was personal development that had a powerful effect on how they managed and led their organizations. He does not know how far this cascaded down to the front line but it gave the participants tools for strategy planning, ways of working with people and ways of conducting their meetings. He is in no doubt that the model will work for organization development and work for teams.

Another powerful effect of the programs was in opening up channels of communication with the CEO and corporate board, including non-executive directors. It helped get messages upward; it brought issues up to the most senior levels and helped accelerate change that was needed. People learned to speak frankly.

Learning

I asked my client what he learned from the experience. This is what he said:

- 'It is possible to do development for individuals which has a powerful effect on the organization.

- You have to get the executive involved and they need to be open and listen.

- It is about partnership with directors and managers, not didactic teaching.

- People who come need to be prepared to do the work – no good pretending. So selection is vital – participation must not be compulsory.

- Those who got most from it have done best in the company. Those who got least have not done well. You have to be prepared to learn.

- You need a team of facilitators who really understand and support the approach and each other.

- You have to resolve the issue: are you in organization development or management development?

- It is a great way to do real work with real people. The model works – there is no doubt in my mind.'

My learning after a considerable period of time is that, yes, I could have done better, been less sanguine when my client was seconded overseas, done a better job of recontracting with his boss, explained better that he needed to be a full time partner, been more authentic *and* relaxed in challenging and bringing out the difficult issues. But, at the end of the day, it probably would not have made much difference. Sometimes the combination of people and circumstances (facilitators and clients) will lead to difficulties and sometimes the external consultants will be the scapegoats and not get the credit they may feel they deserve. The negative or unhealthy patterns of the organization's culture can play themselves out in microcosm, you, the external consultant, are in the thick of it and it is all happening so fast. I have to remind myself:

> *'Do not fear mistakes – there are none.'* Miles Davis.

The main thing is that I, my client and the organization learned, but it did hurt!

Case study 3: Top down 'When everything works well'

A small borough council – 1,000 people

This intervention had everything going for it: a supportive, open CEO who decided to be a participant and to whom empowering behavior came easily; a respected and skillful internal consultant (the development and training manager) with a boss who backed her; directors who wanted to participate, most as facilitators; a good balance between women and men at all levels; good contracting with the CEO and his team and thoughtful handling of the ownership issue. Also, top and senior management had been closely involved in developing the emerging strategy. Finally, it is a relatively small organization and that helps. Not surprisingly many benefits have resulted, even so, there were some difficulties as time went on and these are interesting to anyone trying to bring about change of this kind.

Issues

The organization was facing huge pressures in trying to become leaner and at the same time deliver higher quality services. It was in the midst of changes resulting from compulsory competitive tendering and the formation of business units. There was a lot of insecurity. Many people felt the odds were against them and were discouraged by an unappreciative public. Some were fighting for the survival of their units. There was conflict between the need for a corporate approach and pressure on business units to be cost effective. Old attitudes needed to change. In particular people needed to take individual responsibility for solving problems, improving services and reducing cost, instead of blaming upwards or thinking they could not do anything. Quality improvement and cost reduction depended on both individual empowerment *and* collaboration. The connection between the way employees were treated and the service they delivered to customers was well understood by the CEO and most of his colleagues. They had published a mission statement setting out their goals, values, objectives and strategies. This document made a strong link between the paramount importance given to customers, quality and cost-effectiveness *and* having high quality staff who felt well supported and encouraged to contribute their full potential. It emphasized the need to encourage initiative and creativity within defined corporate objectives and that teamwork and co-operation were essential. Our intervention was seen as a means of bringing about the changes in attitudes and behavior needed to make this vision a reality. Whilst the CEO was widely respected, some thought he could give stronger direction and perhaps the initiative would provide him an opportunity to do so.

How the work started

In 1991 my client decided to invite me in to work with her after attending my open program on organization transformation. By then she had known me for two years (the development of trust between client and consultant seems to be a repetitive theme!) She wanted support for a long-term intervention to change the culture of the organization. We first spent a day together making an organization diagnosis, developing her vision for the organization and planning the early stages of an intervention. Her vision for her organization included the following:

- Everyone in the organization should feel part of it and responsible for themselves, their destiny and responsible for the organization.
- An organization that is learning all the time and adapting, ie, is healthy.
- Support for everyone in the organization to cope with change.
- The talent, energy and potential in the organization to be released.
- A leadership style and culture that enables this to happen.

She knew her organization well and this was a vision to which many people could relate strongly. It would inspire not only her but also many others who were to support her.

Soon afterwards we contracted with the CEO about his objectives, how the proposed intervention would help him achieve them and the support he would give the work. He was very clear about his expectations – he wanted to bring about the changes in behavior needed to make the mission statement a reality. He wanted an empowered workforce that would respond flexibly to change and take responsibility at all levels for providing high quality, cost-effective services. He wanted extraordinary performance from ordinary people. He wanted people to look forward to coming to work. This was his vision and it required a change in how people were led and managed. He wanted the intervention to help bring about that change. He agreed to our initial proposals including the involvement of the director of technical services to act as a third member of the facilitator team.

Next we met to build ourselves into a team, plan a pilot program and develop proposals for top management. A key decision was the choice of director of technical services. He had all the qualities we needed for a good partner: astuteness, vision, credibility with colleagues, openness to new ideas and the natural skills to be a good facilitator and supportive team member. The choice of 12 participants at director level and their reports was also crucial – a good mix (women and men), some cynics but mainly leaders who would make good use of the opportunity and help us make it a success. We decided not to include the CEO in the first workshop – it would only add to the nervousness. Between us we went to see all the participants, consulted with them and came back to design the first workshop of the two-part pilot program. We shared the data we had collected, diagnosed it, set objectives and designed a workshop intended to meet these goals. The workshops would facilitate participants in bringing about changes in the business and tackling key corporate, unit and individual issues. The program would encourage empowering leadership and develop helping or facilitating skills.

In order to save costs, the workshops would be non-residential (except for the tutors who would need to do reviewing work and preparation). Participants would start with coffee and stay for dinner and not try to fit in visits to the office. The venue was a local manor house set in beautiful countryside and gardens. We presented our proposals and the diagnosis on which they were based to the top management team and then to the participants, making whatever changes were needed. (In all the case studies I keep stressing the rigorous way the facilitator team worked: contracting and team building with each other, and then with our clients, collecting data, building relationships, first individually and then [harder] as a group, diagnosing the data, goal setting and finally contracting structure and processes. I do this because it is fundamental to a successful outcome.) We then spent a day together developing the skills needed to facilitate the workshop, partly by facilitating each other, rehearsing and fine tuning.

My client tells me that the first three-day workshop was an exciting and nerve-racking experience for herself and her colleague – it was for me too – different from anything they had experienced before. The workshop would start at tea time and we met several hours beforehand to do more skilling up, preparation and give each other whatever support we needed. The participants were nervous too. We all sensed it was a critically important event – make or break. At that stage we were holding the anxiety of the whole organization. The first day was exciting but not easy. At the end of if we wondered if it was all going to work and we approached the second day with trepidation. By the end of the morning of the second day we knew 'we had done it.' The process had worked and one of the 'cynics' was brimming with enthusiasm. Their first experience of the 'flexible program' was daunting, my two colleagues say, but it worked brilliantly, the participants really taking charge of it. One key issue for everyone in the flexible program was 'Following the setting up of business units, what do we now mean by corporacy?' The whole group met for two hours to work on that issue. Many other issues, both individual and of interest to varying numbers of people, were worked on. Every participant came out of the first workshop with plans to make important changes in the organization and some planned to make changes in their behavior. Support groups had been the principal working groups. They all made dates to continue meeting.

How the work unfolded

It had been a successful breakthrough and the way was now open for four more two-part workshop programs to include all members of the top two levels of management and some members of the third level. Each program would have three facilitators of whom one would always be a director and at least one a woman. From now on all facilitators would have been participants. The plan was that I would help facilitate the next workshop in which the CEO would participate (he had no difficulty working as an equal partner with other participants nor they with him) and then I would withdraw from training facilitators and act as 'shadow consultant.' Similarly, a key part of my client's strategy had been to transfer ownership. Therefore she progressively withdrew and handed over her role as facilitator and workshop leader to others. Of course some have performed this task better than others. However this policy has enabled her to concentrate on managing the intervention and helping the CEO, directors and senior managers to develop the emerging strategy and provide the necessary support for facilitators.

As all the directors have participated in the program and most have been trained to facilitate workshops, the effects on their attitudes and behavior are considerable. This led to my client and I being asked to facilitate their annual top management retreat and help them improve the way they function together as a team and in their formal meetings. Workshops were held to train more directors and managers as facilitators. A second series of five workshop programs has been held for middle managers. Work was harder at this level as powerless attitudes were more prevalent. The programs have continued to be facilitated by a team consisting of a director, a senior manager and someone from HR, including at least one woman. 'Network events' have been held for participants of the first ten programs. Support groups have continued and one still meets after four and a half years. At the time of writing, nearly all managers of people, some 120, have been involved in the programs. There was interest in involving council members in the program but this has not yet been pursued. There is now an annual program for newly appointed managers. Finally, a third phase for non-managerial staff has been initiated. My client concluded that these employees needed a different kind of program to develop their self-confidence and other skills if empowerment was to work. One of these programs is offered annually for voluntary participants. However, as there are over 800 people in this category, progress will be very slow. I had hoped there would be a demand for real time programs in business units to consolidate the change in how people do business together but that idea was not supported (with one important exception mentioned later). The directors preferred a corporate approach. My client feels she has not sufficiently succeeded in transferring ownership and responsibility to her clients. I think that has contributed to her getting exhausted – a common phenomenon in this kind of work. (She tells me, however, that certain factors in her life, such as her mother's death have contributed more to this.) For a time I acted as 'shadow consultant' but then she felt able to manage the intervention without outside help. I think this kind of work requires outside support, partly to avoid exhaustion but partly because there are some issues which an insider alone will find it hard, if not impossible, to tackle.

Effects and Benefits

This is what my client said about the program some three years after the start:

'It is always hard to ascribe changes in culture to one specific event or intervention. However I believe that this has achieved the following:

- People are adapting more willingly and effectively to change.
- Responsibility is being pushed down the organization.
- People are supporting and helping each other more.
- To quote the CEO: 'Changing attitudes, change in the culture. People giving real commitment at all levels – not just senior people.'

There have been many tangible benefits in all parts of the organization as participants have implemented their strategies and plans. For some people it has opened their eyes to the benefits of development and they have made great changes themselves, and in their part of the organization. Here are some comments from participants:

- "A new approach to people management which attempts to put empowerment into practice and leads to more delegation of responsibility."
- "I am more positive, communicative and committed and feel more part of a team."
- "Clear understanding of the experience has enabled me to approach/react/respond differently both with others who had attended as well as others in the organization."
- "What I will, will be."
- "I've learned how to handle difficult situations and stand back."
- "My impression is that it is having continuing impact, for the good, on attitudes and morale."
- "Very positive – lots of corporate thinking and suggestions coming out of groups." '

A year later, I met with my client and one of the directors. He said the following:

'It has had a profound and lasting effect on me. In essence it has made me welcome change. I was dyed in the wool. It has made me embark on new endeavors. It has lightened up the whole organization. I was very cynical previously. I am lastingly changed.

Where it has had an effect it has been lasting, particularly with boosters every now and then. My support group has flourished and continued for four and a half years. Maybe others too.

It has given me skills I did not possess in leading small and big groups and a huge amount of confidence and insight into other people and their needs; it has made me like people more.

I have run my own departmental program ... Through me it has opened doors for others – they've learned skills from me.'

Of another director he said: 'He has completely changed how he operates in a team and how he runs his meetings. It has confirmed the style he was developing.' Others have been influenced: 'I can be myself and have ideas about what I want to do.'

There has been a wide range of effects on fellow directors (seven) including one on whom the effects were 'temporary' and another assessed as having 'none.' Their team meetings have become more supportive (with certain exceptions recently) and they always conduct a review. Further down, the effects have varied too, with facilitators being most affected. Generally there is a greater desire to work well together, give and get support. People are aware when behavior departs from the way it was in the workshops. It has freed up a lot of people to say *'I'm not going to complain and blame. I'm going to do something.'* It has introduced a vocabulary, tools and an awareness of blaming and complaining. It has liberated people. Networking has had beneficial effects, particularly in support services units where people have got together, shared common issues and given each other support. For others it has done nothing and some are blatantly cynical and dismissive.

A number of valuable corporate projects have grown out of the programs and have benefited from the management team delegating more to them, making their work become easier because of greater co-operation. Some managers have changed their style and that has benefited their teams and their customers. But this has not happened where managers have been frightened to let go of control. Many people have reported obstacles above them in implementing a new approach. Lower down in the organization the program has had less effect. People feel they have less autonomy than senior managers. Here it is harder to get over the message: *'You are in charge of you; the only person you can change is you.'*

They summed up the picture as: *'Significant effect on 40% participants; some effect on 75%.'* (The first figure is included in the second.) It looks to me as if the effects are fading somewhat and a boost is needed. Also the 850-plus core workers and team leaders have not really been engaged – this is where the most tangible benefits are to be achieved – and could not be, given what has been done so far.

As to the benefits for my client, she says she has got to know the CEO and his directors well (she has high credibility with them). It has raised her profile and increased her confidence (and stature) such that she applied for and nearly got her director's job when he retired. However, she experiences strains and role conflict because her organization development function is located in Personnel rather than the CEO's office – a significant and not unusual difficulty for internal consultants who are attached to the personnel department.

The way forward

My client and her director colleague believe that the following points need to be addressed:

- The CEO and his team need to review where they are in terms of changing the management style and culture and achieving their objectives for the intervention; they need to review where they want to be and what they need to do now.
- Cracks are emerging in the top management team and they need support and challenge from outside to help them address relationship issues.
- The top team needs to provide a new 'way forward' – the whole organization needs to know where it is going, particularly now there is a new (political) administration.
- The work needs to cascade within units.

I back all this but I think they need not only to engage the core workers but also to involve council members. Somehow they need to take the brave and risky step of *'getting the whole system into the room'* to decide together the way forward and plan its implementation. I think the CEO needs to be given support to take a further bold step.

Learning

My client believes the key success factors that helped the intervention work are as follows:

- 'Contracting clearly with the CEO and involving him early on as a participant.
- The partnership between myself, as leader of the work, Bruce, as external consultant, and successive directors as facilitators, and particularly involving a director in the first pilot program.

- Using directors and senior managers as the principal source of facilitators.
- Ownership of the strategy being clearly within the organization – myself and my clients.
- Working on real issues within the programs.
- Facilitators modeling the values and behavior we wanted to encourage.'

In retrospect she would do the following differently:

- 'I would start the intervention with a "whole system" approach.
- I would share the leadership of the intervention with at least two other people within the organization.
- I would concentrate on a smaller team of facilitators, thus ensuring more of the limited resources could be put into dedicated facilitator training.
- I would be clear from the outset with the external consultant about when her/his involvement would finish. (Is this possible?)
- I would put more energy into encouraging programs within business units.'

She has struggled with the following issues:

- 'How to stop the "secret club" syndrome that seems to have developed amongst those who haven't been on the program.
- How to build on the success of the programs, without doing more of the same.
- How to sustain my energy and enthusiasm over the long period it takes to achieve a change in culture.
- When is the right time to manage the intervention with no help from the outside consultant?'

She and her director colleague's reflections are as follows:

- 'People have a lot more to offer than you first credit them with.

- Changing the culture of an organization takes a long time and requires enormous patience and energy.

- You must not get discouraged if you don't get 100% success, but aim for it and give it your best shot.

- You need support – other champions who encourage you.

- You need very conducive surroundings for workshops. [I would add, not luxury and the same venue for everyone.]

- Hit all 1,000 participants at the same time (the message can get subtly altered).

- You need confidence and a basic way of operating.'

Case study 4: Stuck at the top 'The severe, absent father'

A large organization in the education sector

Starting

I contracted with the training and development manager. We had known each other for many years and she had read many of my articles. One day, at a conference, she told me her organization was ready to take a major initiative to help change the culture and she wanted my help. The proposed intervention would start at the top. It had a strong emphasis on quality and equality. Transforming quality and coping with rapid change, in part, depended on women and men working well together, bringing out people's potential and valuing difference. The idea was that the top team would set an example. It was an imaginative and exciting proposal and I felt privileged to be invited to help. I admired her boldness and courage and felt the project was extremely worthwhile.

The CEO was intellectually committed to management training and equal opportunities and he approved her proposal. In retrospect, he did not really understand what he was letting himself in for. He gave me the 'once over' for an hour and agreed to her using me. A former academic with a good mind, extremely well informed about his world and a good strategist, he was in the midst of bringing about many bold and needed changes. He cracked along at a punishing pace and not everyone could keep up. I heard that working for him could be hard and not particularly rewarding for some. He was absent a great deal in the external environment of education and not particularly interested in managing internally, apart from the strategic and structural aspects of change as opposed to the so-called 'soft' or human side. He had a reputation for setting up a lot of initiatives then walking away, later holding meetings that began 'why haven't you?' It was said that he did not give sufficiently clear guidelines or monitor rigorously or give support. So when things went wrong he apportioned blame. Later he did the same with us! In short, he was a stern, critical 'absent father' of whom many people were afraid. (A few knew how to stand up to him but they tended to be of a like mind.) This was how he controlled. Was this like his own childhood I wondered?

I made several unsuccessful attempts to meet and contract with him about purpose, objectives, how this initiative could help him achieve his goals, what support he would need to give it and what it would really be like. Nor was I able to contract with him and his executive later on. This began to worry me. He was committing large sums and a lot of time without being clear about his objectives or really understanding what he was embarking on or how he needed to make it succeed. If the top people were not committed, it would not work. The outcome was almost predictable. I wondered whether I should continue with this, yet people felt it was worth going on and he might be won over. It was a dilemma.

As soon as I was 'approved,' I invited a trusted woman colleague, interested in and skilled with gender issues, to join us. Also two of us would have a better chance with something so difficult. Work started in 1992. We were to work with the CEO, his executive and their direct reports – some 36 people. The goal was to help them change the way they worked together, especially the two genders, and help them lead their people more effectively through rapid change. Broadly speaking we followed the approach described in Chapter 6 and for the most part it worked well, winning them over, gaining the enthusiastic support of most of the participants, and later, their ownership. Our client (the training and development manager), my woman associate and I formed a facilitator team and we went out and talked with the dozen carefully chosen people who would attend the first of three, mixed level, two-part workshop programs. The CEO would be a participant on the last program. The strategy (risky but perhaps the best we could do in the situation) was to win him over if the first two went well.

Issues

What we learned was this. The urgency and pace of change were exceptional. There was a high degree of over-working, some people failing, getting ill or having accidents, and being side-lined and replaced, sometimes by fresh people from outside. People supported the changes – their difficulty was with the style. I gather the culture was fairly typical of the academic world. On the whole it is good academics who rise to the top. They do not necessarily make good managers, especially of rapid change. They do not usually have experience of other worlds of work. There is some arrogance and egotism around. The place can be intensely political. They can misuse their intellects to avoid taking responsibility for changing, talking about it instead. They can be 'in their heads' and highly critical, rather than supportive. We found many exceptions to these stereotypes. Many were enlightened, creative, aware and open to new ways of working. Basically they seemed little different from their counterparts in other organizations.

A strong interest emerged in improving the way the top and senior management worked together. Also, perhaps because of a relatively high proportion of senior women, many wanted to work on the gender issue. Some of the men were relatively unaware of their impact on women colleagues and reluctant to work on the issue. There were varying degrees of optimism, pessimism, openness and resistance. But in general they were keen to work on the issues that emerged including how they led people and managed themselves in a period of rapid change. However, they were afraid of the CEO and frequently expressed concerns about how he would react when he got involved.

How the work unfolded

Having collected this data from the first group we contracted with them at an introductory meeting, agreed objectives and how we would work together. It was very different for me to work with a close colleague. That mutual support meant we were stronger, perhaps bolder and more creative with our client's issues and I learned more. We did most of the facilitating and our client played a major part in diagnosing and interpreting the situation. We encouraged her to stay close to participants between workshops. With gender issues so important it was good to have two females and one male facilitator. The first program worked well, as did the second. Both programs comprised the two levels below CEO. Indeed, many things went well right up to the end. However, there was a lot of part-time attendance but perhaps this was inevitable in an educational institution with teaching obligations but I wondered if it demonstrated ambivalence amongst those close to the CEO. We learned to live with that and also to work flexibly in one very large room in which we could break into three support groups. They learned to work in a circle, use the empowerment model, work on real, and here and now issues, to co-counsel, watch silently whilst a senior woman and a man were facilitated, and do other things that must have seemed strange to some. They grew increasingly enthusiastic and, at the follow up workshops, many reported changes in how they managed and all kinds of improvements. However, I think we all knew at some level that a time bomb was ticking away. There was always a lot of attention given to the 'absent father' who was due to attend the third program.

We involved participants in developing the emerging strategy at the end of each workshop. The key features were two network events to bring together all participants after the second program; another after the first workshop of the third program; similar events for participants' organizations or teams co-led by participants or co-led with one of us; a facilitation skills workshop to help participants lead or co-lead workshops in their organizations or simply facilitate their people; lunch meetings for participants; articles in the organization's newspaper to communicate what they were doing; a charter representing their values and intentions; and support group meetings. Although participants did not become involved in facilitating the main program, some helped at introductory meetings and co-facilitated the second network event. Ownership was high by now.

The main focus and energy in the workshops was on how the senior and top management worked together and their relationship with the CEO. They made considerable progress with the first issue but not the second. That would have required the CEO's full-time presence and willing involvement. When he did get involved – in the third program – his membership was very part-time and in the second workshop he began expressing grave doubts as to whether the investment was value for money. He called for an evaluation to be conducted before any more money would be spent. Perhaps we were getting too close for comfort. The evaluation was used to turn the intervention into a phenomenon – something that could be studied, rather than a joint endeavor, the results of which everyone, including the CEO, was responsible for, as partners.

The evaluation, carried out, not by the participants but by two experienced post-graduate students (did they unconsciously read the politics?), was sufficiently ambivalent to achieve the goal of stopping it all just when it was getting close to the fundamental issue, ie, the relationship between the stern, critical absent father and his team. My interpretation is that he didn't want to look at this because it might have meant changing. He did what he often did – poured cold water on it. He thus wasted a big investment in energy, time and money and further discouraged his team. But no doubt he did this with the sincerest conviction that he was acting in his organization's best interests.

The effects

Looking back, should we have gone ahead? Was it professional to continue without properly contracting with the CEO and his executive? Was it possible to insist? Would it have worked better if we had or would it have been stopped at the start? We will never know. I believe you do what you can do. You take the opportunity and make the best of it that you can at the time. 'Chaos theory' supports the notion that lots of little changes have big effects in the totality. Had we not gone ahead, many people would have been deprived of the considerable support and learning they got from the program, and the many people working for them would have lost out too. There was also a great deal of learning for the three facilitators which they were able to take elsewhere. So what were the benefits? It touched many participants personally and has affected how they manage their people, and perhaps changed the culture of their organizations. In the senior team it opened up dialogues between people who previously had not talked. It improved relationships between academics and services. It broke down barriers and built relationships. The methods we used are still being applied in their meetings. One senior manager left and is applying what he learned in another important industry. Another has profoundly changed how he manages several hundred people and he says that, as a result of the program, he grew in confidence and it gave him the courage to go for his beliefs. He has done amazing things which are benefiting large numbers of people and increasing the flexibility and quality of the service they provide. This is described as a big success story and it has reached right down to manual workers. He credits it to the program. This alone would make it worthwhile for me.

Conclusions

It didn't change the corporate culture. How could it if it did not really *involve* the CEO and his closest colleagues who were insufficiently present? You cannot expect people in a prevailing climate of fear to significantly influence upward. *For people to be influenced they need to have the experience of being fully engaged, full-time participants.* For that to happen they need to believe that it is essential and want it. How do you bring that about? Not, I think, by insistence. People have to come to it in their own way, at their own pace. You may perhaps help if you can build a relationship of trust (it is very hard to do that with some people) but it may result from individual experiences, reflection, reading, listening and this sort of real time development program. A big influence sometimes is a person's experience of their parents. I suspect this applied in this case. *Being a good enabling CEO is very much the same as being a good parent – not being too stern, critical or controlling, certainly not punishing. Being more encouraging and enabling and letting go – yet being firm about those few crucial things. It is the kind of balance a good parent has to learn with teenagers. A good parent learns from their children. A good CEO needs to learn from her or his whole team and the whole system. A learning organization needs a humble, learning CEO.* She or he has to be strong enough to be open to it and they have to be strong enough to speak their minds. They won't do that if the parent is punishing. Today's CEO has to move away from patriarchy to something more like partnership with strong adults, one of whom is leader. Like all the others, this story is not finished. This CEO gave his gifts and set good foundations. Another with different gifts, who is better at the more difficult softer arts of leadership, which are even more needed in times of retrenchment, may follow.

While reflecting on these four case studies many interesting issues emerge and many tentative conclusions can be drawn. To select just a few I would include:

- *The role of the CEO* is absolutely crucial.

- *Long-term support* from a trusted external consultant seems to be very important, otherwise the most difficult issues may not be tackled and energy and imagination may wilt. Like anything else, this cannot be predetermined at the start and needs to be managed wisely and with awareness to avoid dependence or counter dependence. It needs to be a dynamic partnership in some ways like a good marriage (but not 'till death us do part').

- *Partnership* is another essential: between client and external consultant; and all her/his clients; CEO, the executive and employees at all levels.

- *'Ownership'* runs parallel with partnership. Handing over ownership without abdicating is crucial.

- Being constantly aware of the importance of everyone be-having in a way which is *congruent* with goals is crucial. There were so many departures from this in Case study 2. We need to ask each other frequently 'are we being congru-ent here?'

- I doubt that you can successfully mix modes, ie, facilitate or empower *and* be didactic and patriarchal in the same pro-gram. This is likely to bring out powerlessness, dependency or counter dependency and set back your work a long way, for example, as in Case study 2.

- *Only those who participate* (especially as facilitators) *really get the benefit*. Given the prevailing culture of fear of the top and powerlessness at the bottom, it is hard for individual participants to influence people above or below them. Ways have to be found of involving *everyone* and without class distinctions, and involve everyone as facilitators too. There are all kinds of ways of doing this – in small groups; in pairs and later in their own or other units.

- Ultimately we have to *get the whole system into the room* – all stakeholders, too, perhaps. We are all co-creators of the organization. However, this may not be possible at the beginning, the need may have to emerge. You start where you can!

- *Support* for the leaders of such an intervention is vital because giving and supporting others cannot be sustained indefinitely without it. And, if the external consultant gets 'stuck,' as I did in Case study 2, it is wise for her/him to get *supervision* from someone not involved.

- *Evaluation* needs to be seen as a positive way of supporting change and helping it to continue; not as a detached study of whether it worked or not.

Some of these conclusions point the way for the next chapter. I keep asking myself 'Should I and my client presume to help change the culture of an organization?' Who are we to do this? Of course we should. That is what the internal consultant is there for and she/he is perhaps one of the few people best able to think in terms of the whole system and best able to see her or his client as the whole system.

References and suggested further reading

Bach, R. (1995) *Illusions – The Adventures of a Reluctant Messiah*, Mandarin Paperbacks, Random House, London, UK.
Holt, J. (educator) quoted in Cameron, J. (1995) *The Artist's Way – A Spiritual Path to Higher Creativity*, Pan Books, London, UK.

8

Getting the Whole System into the Room
Gaining the commitment of the whole workforce to change

'We are going to win and the industrial West is going to lose out; there's not much you can do about it because the reasons for your failure are within yourselves. Your firms are built on the Taylor model. Even worse, so are your heads. With your bosses doing the thinking while the workers wield the screwdrivers, you're convinced deep down that this is the right way to run a business. For you the essence of management is getting the ideas out of the heads of the bosses and into the hands of labor.

We are beyond your mindset. Business, we know, is now so complex and difficult, the survival of firms so hazardous in an environment increasingly unpredictable, competitive and fraught with danger, that their continued existence depends on the day-to-day mobilization of every ounce of intelligence.'

Konosuke Matsushita, founder of Matsushita Electric Ltd, quoted in *Managing on the Edge,* Richard Pascale, Penguin Books, 1991.

My journey

I experienced a growing unease as I reflected on the work described in Chapter 7. I felt sure that the Empowerment Model was thoroughly sound and the approach based on it could work very well indeed, given sufficiently favorable conditions such as the support of the top. However, I had a number of concerns.

It is all very well working with managers but what about the mass of people in the organization 'doing the actual work' of making things, providing services and dealing with customers? How much effect was our work together actually having on the way things are on the shop floor or on the quality of product or service received by the customer? We were not sure. Also these programs were taking a long time to roll out. Where there was an attempt to involve 'ordinary workers,' it was in a diluted form in less affluent surroundings. What message did that convey? It was another reflection of our class attitudes perhaps.

I had other concerns, some more fundamental. Systems thinking tells us that in deciding the way forward or resolving fundamental issues you need data about the *whole* system. People at the top or in the middle, inevitably, only have data about *part* of the system. If good strategic decisions are to be made, data is required from people at every level, including the bottom, and from people outside the system, such as customers and suppliers. Of course that data can be obtained, and often is, before decisions are made. But for maximum organizational learning to take place, different stakeholders or people from different parts of the system need to be in the room together. They all need to be listening to each other and the process needs to be interactive. There needs to be a common or shared data base built *together* by everyone in the room. People at the bottom need to see people at the top taking on board what they have said, responding to it in a way that demonstrates a change in attitude and actually behaving differently; showing that they really mean what they say about involving people, valuing their contribution and wanting an empowered workforce. Also people at the bottom need to be given the opportunity to act powerfully, speak their minds honestly without fear of adverse consequences and take responsibility. Top management need to experience this and see it works. People need the experience of hearing diverse views expressed, sometimes with passion, and perhaps being moved by this. They need to discover how constructive and valuable difference can be and have their fears and stereotypes dispelled by a constructive experience that worked. In other words a huge amount of organizational learning can take place only when you get the whole system into the room. Real sustainable change occurs when people experience the paradigm shift that enables them to see beyond their small part of the system. For the organization to learn a different dance, the partners all need to be present. As we concluded at the end of Chapter 7, 'only those who participate, especially as facilitators, really get the benefit.'

It is not only about making sound decisions and learning from each other. It is also about successful implementation. For people to be committed to changes, they need to be involved in and informed by the process of making those decisions and take responsibility for their part in implementing them.

I had another concern. Sometimes, we had encountered dependency, counter-dependency, resistance to really doing serious work or taking responsibility for the outcomes. Was this because we facilitated too much? Would this be less likely to happen if we stood back more and gave *everyone* a share in facilitating the small groups at least? That also fitted well with our conclusions that people who become facilitators benefit most.

With these thoughts in my mind I started reading Marvin Weisbord's *Productive Workplaces* (Weisbord, 1987) and I organized a development program for myself to learn about 'large group interventions', in other words ways of working with much larger groups that make it possible to get representatives of the whole system working together in the same room. I attended workshops which not only described the methods but also gave me experience of how they work either by my being a participant or through simulations. I looked in depth at the following four approaches:

- Future search
- Open space technology (OST)
- Real time strategic change (RTSC)
- Search conferences

In this chapter I shall do no more than introduce you to these four approaches (there are many others) and tell you how you can find out more about them. As yet I have limited experience of using them (though I have been a participant) and I have no big stories to tell. I hope that will come later! The principles and methods have influenced all my work.

The case for getting the whole system into the room

First I will summarize why I think these approaches need to be considered. The concerns I have expressed above do not invalidate real time management development. RTMD can have a powerful effect on individual managers who may then lead their organizations very differently. It gives managers a new vision of how teams and groups can work together. It gives them some of the tools. It is also a good way of going with the energy, acknowledging where the organization is and starting where you can. Like every good methodology it has its strengths and its limitations. It may offer you the best way forward given where your organization is and it may open your managers up to the possibility of 'getting the whole system into the room' – something for which the organization was not ready when you started out. This chapter may help you to prepare yourself for when your clients are ready. To be ready to help your clients you need a new mindset.

I see essentially four possibilities for initiating transformation, as shown in Figure 8.1. The first two are 'starting where you can' strategies. The last two are possible when your client is the CEO of the relevant system or sub-system. The last is appropriate when the CEO is really ready to share control.

- Starting at the bottom and working up.
- Starting somewhere in the middle and working upwards, outwards and downwards.
- Starting at the top and cascading down.
- Getting the whole system into the room.

Figure 8.1 Four possibilities

Top-down approaches to bringing about change have limitations. Strategic decisions made by top management may prove flawed because they were not informed by data possessed by people elsewhere in the system. Often top management has difficulty gaining 'buy-in' or the full commitment of the workforce because the latter do not have a full appreciation of the situation and they were not involved in the decision making. Key mes-

- Decisions are informed by the whole system.
- A high degree of involvement and engagement and hence commitment is created.
- Collaborative behavior is encouraged.
- There is a high degree of organizational learning and the organization increases its capacity to adapt.
- People learn to value diversity and work with conflict.
- A sense of common vision and purpose is created.
- A huge groundswell of energy is generated to bring about change.
- Top management learn to let go of control and respond to feedback; people at the bottom (or in the middle) learn to act powerfully and contribute more confidently.
- New organizational norms about how to behave are created.
- People learn how to cope with uncertainty, complexity, confusion and fluctuating emotions.
- Top management can signal that things are really changing.
- A large number of people can be involved.
- A high degree of personal responsibility is encouraged – dependency and counter-dependency are minimized.
- People learn self-management and facilitation skills.

Figure 8.2   Major benefits of large group methods

sages may be diluted as they pass down the organization. Similarly there are obstacles to information passing upwards. Traditional processes of communication are relatively lifeless as they are not sufficiently involving or interactive. The top-down approach to change does not provide adequately for organizational learning. Increasingly often today, traditional linear methods of making decisions are simply not up to the job because the data involved is so complex and the situation is in a constant state of flux. Finally, the process of cascading strategy downward can take a very long time. That can be too long in today's world.

Some of the major benefits of using large group methods, or getting the whole system into the room are listed in Figure 8.2.

However, large group methods should not be contemplated where top management wants to tell or sell, and has no intention of sharing power or implementing whatever has been decided in the event. They are only appropriate when top management is genuinely interested in involving its workforce or co-creating with it. If top management does not respond honestly to feedback or demonstrate that it is 'changing the way it does business,' more harm than good will be done.

Background history

Large group methods can be traced back to the collaboration of Fred Emery, an Australian, and Eric Trist at the Tavistock Institute of Human Relations, London, in the 1950s. Together they developed the first search conference in 1960. Two British aero-engine companies had recently merged to form Bristol Siddeley. The purpose of this conference, to be known as the Barford Conference, was to help the newly formed company create unified strategy, mission, leadership and values. After the Barford Conference, Fred Emery, Merrelyn Emery, Eric Trist and others facilitated hundreds of search conferences in North America, Australia and elsewhere over the years. The search conference also inspired the later development of future search (Weisbord, 1987 and Weisbord & Janoff, 1995); the work of Dannemiller Tyson Associates in developing interactive strategic planning and real time work design; and real time strategic change (Jacobs, 1994).

Recent examples of well known US companies using large group methods are Marriott Hotels who have used them to embed quality methods into the company worldwide; the Ford Motor Company using large group interventions as part of their successful strategy to turn around their business; and Boeing using the methodology to plan and build the 777 in record time. In the UK the approach has been used very successfully in the Employment Service.

Each of the four approaches I shall describe offers a generic model. None of these approaches is merely an event. The event is only a stage in a much longer process for bringing about change preceding and following the event.

Future search

The future search conference is a method co-developed by Marvin Weisbord and Sandra Janoff in the late 1980s for involving a wide range of interdependent 'stakeholders' in an organization or community in working together to build a picture of the desired future they want and to plan to bring it about. A typical future search conference gets 30 to 70 (ideally 64) people into one large room for 16 hours work spread over three days (ie, 2 overnights). Participants from all levels are selected from eight carefully chosen stakeholder groups. The approach departs from top-down meetings or consultation. Its purpose is to enable the stakeholders to take responsibility for co-creating their desired future and planning to bring it about.

At its very simplest the future search design is:

- Past – where we've been.
- Present – where we are.
- Future – what we want.
- Action – how we get there.

Certain basics underly the design of a future search conference. These are listed in Figure 8.3. Fundamental to the approach are bringing together all those who have a stake in the outcome, have key data to contribute and who will play a crucial part in implementation; creating together the big picture and an understanding of it before deciding and planning action; focusing on the desired state and what is agreed, rather than on problems and conflicts which are relatively unproductive and sap energy; and, finally, people managing themselves and taking

---

- 'Whole system' in the room.
- Global exploration before local action.
- Future focus and common ground.
- Self-management and responsibility.

Figure 8.3   Future search basics

1. **Review the past** – milestones in global society, self and our organization or community. Everyone writes on huge wall charts building a picture of the past. Mixed groups identify trends and patterns.

2. **Explore the present** – stakeholder groups identify trends affecting our future; what we are doing about them and not doing that we want to do; what we are doing that we are proud of and what we are sorry about.

3. **Create ideal future scenarios** – mixed groups prepare an ideal future for the organization or community and dramatize it to the whole conference, presenting the future as if they were there.

4. **Identify common ground** – mixed groups and then the whole conference identify the common future, ways to work towards it (projects) and unresolved differences (not agreed).

5. **Make action plans – co-operating and taking individual responsibility** – stakeholder and volunteer groups make plans to bring about the common ground future, steps they will actually take and report back to the conference.

Figure 8.4   Five main stages

responsibility for action. All these enhance the chances of successful outcomes.

The generic design has five main stages (see Figure 8.4). The basic methodology is as follows:

Before the conference

- The event is carefully planned by a steering committee of eight to ten people representing the stakeholders.

- Great care goes into ensuring that participants represent a broad spectrum of viewpoints.

- The purpose of the event is clearly defined.

- Top leaders' backing is secured, as is their agreement to be there only as full time participants and support whatever outcomes emerge.

- Three to six months' lead time.

During the conference

- People work in eight groups of eight (hence the ideal number of 64 participants), either stakeholder groups or mixed groups as appropriate.

- There is a mixture of work done individually, work done in groups or work done in the whole group (not always in that order).

- Large wall spaces are covered in white paper, or groups cover the walls with cut up charts. Self-adhesive colored dots enable people to vote on priorities.

- There is a high degree of self-managed learning and planning; groups facilitate themselves, everyone taking turns as discussion leader, time-keeper, recorder and reporter.

- Two facilitators run the event as a whole, managing task and time boundaries, handling large group process issues, avoiding creating dependency and counter-dependency, and not getting involved with small groups or with content issues.

- Administrators provide the small groups with briefing papers, worksheets and take care of logistics.

- There are no top management or expert lecturers – top managers or experts are included as participants; no training sessions.

- The focus is on common ground and shared desired future; differences are acknowledged but not worked on.

- The focus is also on discovery, learning and co-operating rather than hierarchy, power, conflict, passivity, adversarial behavior and dependency.

- Everyone takes individual responsibility for planning action to bring about the desired future.

Certain ground rules need to be accepted by the conference. These are listed in Figure 8.5. Amongst essential conditions for success are the full time attendance of all participants, healthy meeting conditions and public responsibility for follow-up.

My experience of the methodology is that it is excellent in helping people learn that they can cope with a mass of complex and confusing data and make sense of it by trusting the right-hand, in-

- Everyone should acknowledge that all ideas are valid – respecting everyone's truth.
- Everything should appear on flip charts.
- Participants should listen to each other.
- Everyone should observe time frames.
- Everyone should seek common ground and action – not problems and conflicts.

Figure 8.5   Ground rules of future search

tuitive part of their brain. Particularly through dramatizing the future (in stage 3 of the conference design) they learn to bring to bear all their creative, and not just rational, faculties. People experience and learn how to cope with the 'roller-coaster' of their feelings at various stages of the process of getting on board, facing the complex mess that seems outside their control, owning up to what they are doing and want to do, becoming energized and excited by their vision and, finally, realistically planning what they will do. People also learn a great deal about diversity and difference. Working productively with people who are different breaks down stereotypes and encourages respect. They find that constructive outcomes and much learning are the result of *listening* to each other, accepting that everyone's opinion is valid and focusing on common ground rather than problems and conflicts. I think people are usually surprised that, whilst conflicts and differences are expressed and not avoided, there is a huge amount of common ground. That is enough to enable people to move forward in constructive action planning. The methodology also maximizes the chance that people will take responsibility and not engage in dependency and counter-dependency perhaps because everyone is encouraged to actively contribute from the very start and take a turn in facilitating their group.

Future search is best limited to about 70 people. That is the maximum number that, in the experience of the co-creators (Marvin Weisbord and Sandra Janoff), works well. So what about the people who were not involved? Catering to their needs has to be a major issue for the action planning stage; alternatively, additional or parallel future search conferences can be held.

Future search seems to be an excellent approach to use in a

community or an organization where leaders are prepared to co-create with other stakeholders. It is particularly suited to creating sustainable development plans for Local Agenda 21. (At the Earth Summit in Rio de Janeiro in June 1992, world leaders signed a global environment and development action plan called Agenda 21. Over two-thirds of this plan required the commitment and co-operation of local authorities to implement it. Each local authority was encouraged to create its own sustainable development strategy, through local participation, known as its Local Agenda 21.) It has been widely used in USA, Canada, Australia and Scandinavia (Weisbord, 1987).

Open space technology

As I have only experienced this approach at professional and personal development conferences, not yet for a business purpose, I asked my friend, Martin Leith, to write this section for me. Here is his account.

Open space technology (OST) was developed in 1984 by Harrison Owen, an American organizational consultant. It is a method for organizing a self-managed meeting or conference, the program of which is created by the participants themselves. The method enables people to create and manage an agenda of workshops, discussion groups and other sessions in which they discuss the things that really matter to them, explore issues and opportunities and find new ways forward. An open space conference has no invited speakers, just one facilitator who explains the procedure and facilitates the plenary sessions. Although OST tends to be regarded as a meeting management method, its principles can be applied to create a whole new way for people to work together in organizations.

Most open space conferences take place over one, two or three days. A typical one-day conference would have four open space timeslots, for example 1000 to 1130 hours, 1130 to 1300, 1400 to 1530 and 1530 to 1700, each with a number of different sessions taking place in parallel.

The approach is suitable for any size of group, 12 is probably the minimum number of people, and the capacity of the venue is the only factor that limits the maximum group size. An open space conference with 500 participants would not be unusual.

When to use open space technology

OST is a highly effective method for surfacing people's heartfelt concerns, exploring strategic issues and opportunities, promoting discussion and decision making, developing action plans with a high degree of ownership, and transforming a group of disparate people into a vibrant community. The method should be considered whenever a project involves high levels of complexity, diversity and conflict and decisions need to be made quickly.

Principles

- Provide the absolute minimum of structure and control.
- Participants are encouraged to display passion and responsibility.
- Participants self-manage everything except the plenary sessions, including the development of the agenda, the open space sessions and the production of the session reports.
- 'Whoever comes are the right people' – even if only one person shows up at a session, this will be exactly the right person to do the work that needs to be done.
- 'Whenever it starts is the right time' – if a session starts earlier or later than the advertised time, that is OK. No one need get impatient or feel anxious.
- 'Whatever happens is the only thing that could happen' – in other words, let go of expectations.
- 'When it's over, it's over' – if everything has been said, move on.
- If a participant is in a session and is not giving or receiving anything useful, he or she should use 'The law of two feet' to move to wherever a worthwhile contribution can be made.

Methodology

- Potential participants receive an invitation that shows the title of the conference. This should be neither too general nor too specific, for example: *What are the issues and opportunities facing the XYZ Corporation?*

Time	Place ⇨	Plenary room	Seminar room 1	Seminar room 2	Seminar room 3	Seminar room 4	Lounge	Bar	Terrace	Garden
0900	Opening plenary									
1000	Open space sessions (1)									
1130	Open space sessions (20									
1300	Lunch (restaurant)									
1400	Open space sessions (3)									
1530	Open space sessions (4)		Post-it note ☛	1530 Room 2						
1700	Closing plenary									

Figure 8.6 Open space matrix

- People arrive at the venue and take their seats in the plenary room. The chairs are arranged in a circle to indicate that everyone is a leader.

- The facilitator welcomes people and explains the open space principles and procedure.

- Participants offer as many sessions as they wish. Those offering sessions prepare a handwritten poster, make a brief announcement to the whole group and tape the poster to one of the walls. This wall becomes the conference agenda. A meeting space is booked by taking, from a matrix, a post-it note which shows times and places, and attaching it to the poster (see Figure 8.6).

- The 'market place' commences. Everyone signs up for the sessions they wish to attend.

- The open space sessions take place. One participant in each session takes notes and produces a written report using the computers and printers located in the 'news room.' One copy of each report is taped to the wall under the banner 'Breaking News' to create a conference newspaper.

- The conference closes with a plenary session during which participants return to the circle, reflect on their experiences and share them with the others. Sometimes participants get together before this final session to prioritize actions arising from the different sessions and to form self-managing project teams.

- As people leave the conference they are handed a copy of all the session reports.

- In the weeks and months following the conference, individuals, project teams and informal groups carry out the agreed actions and keep everyone informed about progress.

Results delivered

- People's *genuine concerns* are identified.
- *Creative and relevant ideas* are developed.
- *Concrete action plans* are specified and committed to.
- On-going *self-managed teams* are established.

- *Productive working relationships* are created.
- *New behaviors* are practiced and become the norm.

Open space technology has been used successfully in most parts of the world. European organizations which employ the method include Dutch Railways, Guinness, ICI, Prudential Assurance and Shell. Despite a long and growing list of success stories, open space technology should never be regarded as an easy option. It should not even be considered if anyone wants to exercise control, when the answer is already known or when the achievement of a specific outcome is essential. But for those who are willing to step into the unknown and allow the unexpected to happen, open space has the potential to produce breakthrough results.

Real time strategic change (RTSC)

Real time strategic change (RTSC) was developed by Kathie Dannemiller and Robert Jacobs in the 1980s and is 'a *principle based* approach to fundamental, organization wide, rapid, sustainable change.' (Jacobs, 1994).

The underlying principles are:

- *Treat current reality as a key driver* – a continuous focus on the simultaneous and sometimes conflicting realities which exist in the internal and external environments.

- *Work in real time* – simultaneous planning and implementation of individual, group and organization or community wide changes. '"Real time" means working through real issues, with real people affected by them and getting real results.' (Jacobs, 1994).

- *Create a common data base* – a common understanding of strategic issues informs the discretion of people at all levels so that they can make wise decisions individually and collectively.

- *Create a preferred future* – a collective 'image of potential' for the future forms the basis for action today. A compelling representation of what will look better and how it will feel is created by participants.

- *Create community* – foster an environment where individuals come together as part of something larger than themselves that they created and believe in.

- *Foster empowerment and inclusion* – engage the entire organization in ways that lead to ownership of and commitment to a shared purpose and future direction and the actions needed to get there. This includes fostering *ownership* of the process, content and outcomes.

As well as these six principles, the RTSC approach is based on open systems theory which translates into a whole system focus. A second all encompassing notion is to continually pursue and clarify purpose and desired outcomes. The whole system focus means involving the whole system (or a critical mass). Thus a microcosm of the system designs the overall change effort and microcosms of participants design key initiatives. Everyone who needs to make changes happen is involved.

Amongst the key characteristics of RTSC are the following:

- There is no limit to the numbers of participants – 2,200 people took part in an event held at Ford and 500 to 5,000 people took part in events at Boeing.

- There is great emphasis on events being only part of a chain of initiatives to bring about change in how the organization does business. RTSC is not just big events. The work with top management and other levels of formal and informal leadership, design work and planning are as important a part of the change process as the events themselves. Apart from events, change efforts are made up of initiatives such as benchmarking, work design, local implementation of action plans and leadership development to support and sustain the changes.

- Whereas future search is clearly for the purpose of 'co-creation,' RTSC can include both 'consulting' and 'co-creating' (see Figure 8.9 on page 155). Often there are some issues which are not 'up for grabs' or fall outside the parameters of the effort. When this is the case a critical piece of the work to be done by the leadership and design teams is exploring and defining exactly where the system boundaries lie and what issues are under discussion. The RTSC approach encourages leaders to undertake a change effort focusing on and working in the preferred future mode as much as possible. This means that norms and processes around authority, decision-making and accountability are developed during a change effort, so becoming the preferred way of doing business in the future. Leaders carefully choose how much or how little to include others in decisions of various sorts, understanding the longer term ramifications of precedents set via those choices and via the processes used for making such choices. Senior management may be more willing to take the risk with a system-wide RTSC effort because of the flexibility and customization possible in how power is shared in the organization. An example of this can be found in the design shown in Figure 8.7 illustrating how strategy can be developed.

- There is no generic design as the processes of each change effort are designed to fit each organization situation. Each event is different and tailored to the unique purpose and circumstances.

- Events are designed by design teams usually consisting of 10–30 diverse people who are a microcosm of the system as defined. One of the first tasks of the design team is to define the purpose of any initiative within the change effort. Design teams partner with the organization's leadership team to make good decisions for a change effort which have broad based ownership and support. A logistics team handle all the administration before and during events.

- During an event designed to align the organization, a critical mass of the organization will be in the room as full-time participants. People outside the organization such as customers, industry experts, or representatives of other companies who have been trying to transform themselves, may be invited to come in to contribute. The emphasis is on involving key stakeholders in a change effort. The people who are needed to contribute to 'building a common data base,' deciding strategy *and* the need to plan and implement system-wide action are the ones who become involved.

- Much of the work is done in small groups of eight ('max mix,' ie, tables representing the widest mix of participants). The

Getting started

Welcome and purpose, logistics, roles, guidelines, self-introductions, climate building.

Building a common data base

- View from leadership team: challenges and opportunities; strengths and weaknesses; vision for the future; key strategies.
- Organization diagnosis: what you are glad, sad and mad about.
- Expert input.
- View from customer perspective.
- Presentations from other organizations who have trod a similar road.
- 'Valentines' (ie, feedback) from group to group: receiving and responding to feedback positively.
- Reviewing organization norms – how we have done things until now – and identifying priorities for change.

Reviewing organization strategy

- Revisiting leadership team's strategy.
- Giving feedback on the strategy.
- Leadership review strategy overnight.
- Leadership present revised strategy and get further feedback before finalizing.

Planning action

- Planning system-wide action.
- Back home planning.

Figure 8.7   Real time strategic change generic design: broad outline

usual process is that people first work individually; then as a group and then one of the group reports back to the whole conference. The 'max mix' tables are self-managed.

- There is an effort to build and embed the capability for transformation within the organization during a change effort. This is an important hallmark of success for an RTSC initiative.

- The consciousness for the change effort has to be how the organization wants to live in the future. An underlying theme of RTSC is to design and use processes that the organization wants to be an everyday part of its future.

There are myriad possibilities for events to focus on issues such as process redesign; organization culture; company mergers; diversity; re-engineering and strategy. Figure 8.7 shows a generic design for an imaginary event which focuses on developing the organization strategy and planning to implement it. When many people come together, it is an exciting experience. A huge amount of energy is generated. Much time and energy needs to be spent working with the leadership during the whole change effort to educate and support them (a two-way process for clients and consultants). This will enable them, in turn, to lead the creation and support of a preferred future for the organization. They have to show they really mean to change the way they do business. This requires their really hearing what they are being told, really showing they have heard it and making changes that convince other participants. If they fail to do this, they will sabotage the whole endeavor. Also their behavior as members of 'max mix' tables will matter enormously, for example, senior people not dominating. The scale of the event also requires very detailed planning, well structured and designed processes and impeccable organization. It also requires flexibility. Daily reviews are carried out and these may require a complete overnight change in the design. In addition to formal daily reviews, corrections in 'real time' are a regular part of an RTSC effort. As well as two facilitators, a logistics manager is needed and a team of logistics staff who keep the participants' tables supplied with briefings, worksheets, review forms, etc. A variety of methods are used including individual work, group work and whole group work. Participants at tables of eight each get a turn at discussion leading, time keeping, recording on flip charts and presenting.

The RTSC approach helps clarify the power, authority and decision-making infrastructure of an organization so that the most appropriate people make decisions for all the right reasons. RTSC will best suit the organization which has a preferred future that is a good fit with the six principles of RTSC. It will suit an organization that wants to involve very large numbers of people; wishes a very much tailor-made design and prefers perhaps to include elements of 'involve and consult' as well as 'co-create.' The latter seems to represent the ultimate in letting go of and sharing control. For example, it can give top management the key role in formulating strategy and reformulating it in response to the common data base that is co-created by all participants.

Search conferences

The search conference, the original method developed in the 1950s, offers an alternative. Fred Emery and his partner, Merrelyn Emery, still practice from Australia and Bob Rehm and Nancy Cebula, working out of the USA, are amongst many exponents.

Two key principles underpin the search conference. The first is the *democratic design principle.* An organization, designed according to the democratic design principle, locates responsibility for control and co-ordination with the people doing the work, to the greatest extent possible. The bureaucratic principle locates responsibility for control and coordination of work one level above where the work occurs. The second principle is *open systems theory.* In a search conference people experience a learning community in which they systematically explore their entire environment. The purpose is to actively plan so that they are both responding to and changing their environment as they go. It means being actively adaptive – developing the system's capacity to be a community that continuously learns from and changes its environment. A system can *reduce* turbulence by changing the conditions that surround it and by influencing their direction. To become adaptive, a system needs to make sure there is alignment between its own desirable future and the desirable future it has for the world (see Figure 8.8).

The key features of this approach are as follows:

- The system is clearly defined and only system members are in the room – not members of its environment. Only those people who are responsible for changing the system are included. Data from outside the system can be sought beforehand. It is not considered necessary to get the whole system into the room.
- Optimally there are only 20 to 40 participants, ie, the number of people who can engage together in face-to-face dialogue.

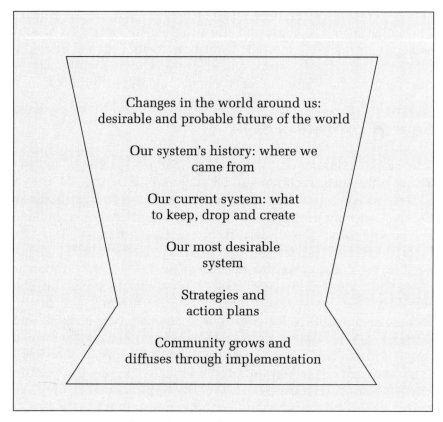

Changes in the world around us: desirable and probable future of the world

Our system's history: where we came from

Our current system: what to keep, drop and create

Our most desirable system

Strategies and action plans

Community grows and diffuses through implementation

Figure 8.8   Search conference design: the open system's 'funnel'

- Search conference is a large group method and the basic building block is the whole group. Sometimes, for the sake of expediency, small mixed groups of eight are used to analyze data or brainstorm ideas on behalf of the large group. However, the search conference is basically a large-group self-managing process from beginning to end.

- All work is done in the whole group or in the small groups – none individually. There is great emphasis on all work being done openly and displayed publicly on flip charts.

- Because numbers are smaller, the conference is not timed to the minute and the program is 'chunked out' broadly into thirds spread over three days: one-third covers changes in the world (environment); one-third our system; and one-third strategy and action planning. The reasoning behind these thirds is Emery's open systems thinking theory which suggests that, for a plan to succeed, the system and environment need to be directly correlated with one another. Thus the search conference starts by exploring the turbulent field to agree on desirable and probable future worlds; then work can proceed on developing the most desirable system and action planning in such a way as to be adaptive (directly correlated) with the environment.

- Because of the smaller size, working in whole group and more flexible time frames the conference feels more relaxed, free flowing and less structured.

- The approach need not involve the whole system and could be used for several levels of management or a team. Search conference is not a whole system event, as defined by other methods. It is an open system method – system in environment.

The biggest difference apart from the relatively small numbers who participate is the model used. Within the boundaries of this *environment, system and action planning* funnel, each search conference needs to be carefully designed for the client and managed 'on the run.'

The search conference is the middle part of an overall three-part process consisting of preplanning, the search conference event itself and implementation. It is in the implementation phase that large numbers of people can be involved. How this is done will make or break the intervention – whether it is done in a participative, democratic way or a bureaucratic way, using the standard committee format that tends to frustrate people (Emery & Purser, 1996).

The following four conditions are fundamental to the method:

1. **Openness**   A climate of openness and absence of manipulation is created partly by displaying all work on chart paper. It is assumed that differences in opinion are healthy and mutual learning follows from sharing different experiences and perceptions.

2. **We are all humans with the same human concerns**   When people see that the behaviors and motives of others are similar to their own, they can admit that they can learn from each other. If anyone acts as expert or talks down to others,

mutual learning is reduced. People discover their similarities through sharing ideals about their desirable future world and system. These ideals transcend gender, race, status and age.

3. **We all live in the same world**   The rule is that all perceptions are valid. Building together a shared picture of the changing world helps establish the validity of the notion that we all live in the same world and forms a shared context for planning and action.

4. **Trust**   Trust develops when people experience an open learning environment, appreciate we are all humans with similar concerns, and live in the same real world. This trust strengthens and deepens interpersonal relations, and increases the probability of mutual learning and networking.

Though expressed differently these conditions and their consequences echo the experience of real time management development, future search and real time strategic change.

The search conference may better suit a situation where the organization's leaders prefer what feels like a lower risk entry into large group interventions; where they would be more comfortable with smaller numbers; do not consider it essential to involve the whole system; and would prefer the less structured, more fluid process that is possible with a smaller scale event. This might better suit the style of some facilitators.

Comparing the four approaches

It may help in comparing the four methods I have described to look at the five modes for creating a shared vision described by Peter Senge's colleague, Bryan Smith, in *The Fifth Discipline Fieldbook* (Senge, 1994) shown in Figure 8.9. As Martin Leith points out in his *Guide to Large Group Interventions* these five modes can be applied differently to policy, vision, strategy and planning. My understanding is that real time strategic change involves people through a mixture of 'consult' and 'co-create' used as appropriate. Its effectiveness depends upon contributions to strategy being evidently taken on board there and then.

Modes for creating a shared vision	**Tell**	**Sell**	**Text**	**Consult**	**Co-create**
	Requires compliance	Seeks buy-in	Invites reactions	Requests contributions	Create together

Figure 8.9   Bryan Smith's continuum

There are significant elements of co-creation especially in creating a common data base and in planning implementation. Open space, future search and search conference are firmly in co-create mode.

Conclusions

My conclusion is that for large group methods to be effective you need a robust model – the Empowerment Model could be one of these; carefully thought out underlying principles; appropriate processes that *reduce* dependency, conflict and task avoidance and *encourage* partnership, learning and taking individual responsibility; and simple techniques (for example, lots of wall space, huge sheets of white paper to cover it, scissors, tape and colored self-adhesive dots) that fit large-scale working.

What characterizes these approaches, in common with RTMD, is that people learn a new way of working. Without even talking about it they learn about:

- Involving the whole system.
- The learning, self-adaptive organization.
- Self-managed groups.
- Distributed work groups.
- How to handle complexity and chaos.
- The fluctuating emotions involved in changing and learning.
- Valuing and respecting difference.

Afterwards the organization will never be the same again. It is not just an event. It is a whole new way of doing business.

You, the facilitator, need to be true to yourself. You have to be really clear about who you are and who you can be. Therefore, in addition to matching the methodology to your client's needs, you need to decide what approach fits your values, beliefs, needs and style. Perhaps you first need to apprentice yourself to experienced practitioners or get one to work with you. With experience you may develop your own methodology, drawing what you need from different methods, or you may decide to adhere to one of the proven methods. Whatever you do, as with real time management development, it is the principles that matter. It is important that you think these out and articulate them clearly. You also have to learn to let go of outcomes completely. We talk about leaving the ego at the door – tricky but being client centered is demanding enough without other competing needs getting in the way.

If you acquaint yourself with these approaches, I promise you that all your work will be affected. You will be influenced by the principles, by whole system thinking and open systems thinking, by the ground rules and by the techniques. I doubt your work will ever be the same again. And you will be open to the opportunity to offer the approach to your organization. You will be able to encourage it to take a brave new step. Also you will be getting involved in the quest for communities to find a more human way of working together.

I am convinced that the time has come for these methods to be widely used in bringing about system wide strategic change. They need to be part of the toolkit of tomorrow's company – and yours!

References and suggested further reading

Bunker, B. and Alban, B. (1992) 'Large Group Interventions' special issue of the *Journal of Applied Behavioural Science*, Vol. 28, No. 4, December.

Bunker, B. and Alban, B. (1997) *Large Group Interventions: Energising the Whole System for Rapid Change*, Jossey-Bass, San Francisco, USA.

Emery, M. and Purser, R. (1996) *The Search Conference: Theory and Practice*, Jossey-Bass, San Francisco, USA.

Jacobs, R. (1994), *Real Time Strategic Change*, Berrett-Koehler, San Francisco, USA.

Owen, H. (1997) *Open Space Technology – A User's Guide*, Berrett-Koehler, San Francisco, USA.

Senge, P. (1994) *The Fifth Discipline Fieldbook*, Nicolas Brealey, London, UK.

Weisbord, M. (1987), *Productive Workplaces – Organizing and Managing for Dignity, Meaning and Community*, Jossey-Bass, San Francisco, USA.

Weisbord, M and Janoff, S. (1995), *Future Search*, Berrett-Koehler, San Francisco, USA.

Sources of further information

Future search:
- Searchnet, Philadelphia, PA, USA.
  1-800-951-6333
  1-215-951-0328
  www.SeachNet. org
- New Economics Foundation, London, UK.
  44(0)181-878-8062
- Maurice Dubras,
  Jersey, Channel Islands.
  44(0)1534 237 39

Real time strategic change:
- Dannemiller Tyson Associates,
  Ann Arbor, MI, USA.
  1-313 662-1330
- Robert Jacobs and Frank McKeown,
  5 oceans,
  6027 Tory Lane, Chelsea,
  MI 48118, USA.
  1-313-475-4215
  e-mail: 5 oceans@tmn.com
- RTSC Global Learning Community
  on the World Wide Web,
  http:\\www.rtsc net.com
- Paul Cox
  Vista Consulting, Birmingham, UK.
  44(0)1527-837930
  e-mail: anne@vistabrook.win-uk.net

Search conference:
- Nancy Cebula & Robert Rehm,
  Boulder, CO, USA.
  1-303-499-1607

Open space technology:
- H. H. Owen & Co
  Potomac, MD, USA.
  1-301-469-9259
  e-mail: owen@tmn.com.
- Romy Shovelton,
  Wikima Consulting, London, UK.
  44(0)171-229-7320
  e-mail: romys@compuserve.com.

All methods:
- Martin Leith,
  Martin Leith Limited,
  PO Box 4YY,
  London W1A 4YY, UK.
  31(0)20-681-2518
  e-mail: mleith@mleith.com

I am indebted to Martin Leith whose *Guide to Large Group Interventions* I have found invaluable in writing this chapter. I am also grateful for his valued comments in general and the section on open space technology in particular, which he wrote for me. Harrison Owen kindly approved our account of open space technology.

I am grateful to the following for their valuable comments and help: Marvin Weisbord on future search; Paul Cox of Vista Consulting and Frank McKeown of 5 oceans on real time strategic change; Robert Rehm on search conferences.

9

Giving and Getting a Good Listening To

Releasing individual potential

'Everyone is the expert on their own life.' Romy Shovelton.

'Often, to discover what I think, I first need to talk. This way I find out.' Anon.

'People have a lot more to offer than you first credit them with.' A director.

'All problems contain the seeds of opportunity.' Deepak Chopra.

'Trust in yourself. Your perceptions are often far more accurate than you are willing to believe.' Claudia Black.

'Listening to others talking about their lives and deepest concerns we learn more about ourselves because we are all part of one another.' Anon.

Listening is an important part of your strategy

Just imagine the positive effect on an organization if hundreds of people in it get a *'good listening to'* (I am indebted to my friend Ken Harrison for this phrase. His thinking is that most often what people get is a 'good talking to' when what they need is a 'good listening to') and decide to trust their own thinking, take personal responsibility and initiative, solve problems and get the customer what she/he wants, on time and to the required price and quality. It could transform the business!

If we want our organizations to thrive, there are two things we can offer: one is *to help every individual give their full abilities and talents*; the other is *to help people work collaboratively* despite our competitive genes. The two are inter-linked because most people will not offer their full potential in a hostile, intimidating or adversarial climate (some thrive on it of course – nothing is ever that simple – but in my experience most do not). Bringing out individual potential and fostering collaboration are two of the most important skills needed by leaders. They are the two core skills most needed by consultants too. We also need to do a lot of asking and listening if we want to understand the 'whole system.' From giving people a good listening to I have learned more about businesses, people in them and the issues they face than from any other source. In this way I have learned more about myself, too. I have learned that in everyone else there is another part of me.

This chapter will concentrate on the one-to-one relationship in releasing individual potential. The next chapter will focus on leading or facilitating teams in ways that bring out collective excellence and foster creative and responsible collaboration.

Skill in one-to-one facilitation or helping (use whatever term you prefer or will be most acceptable in your organization) is the bedrock underlying many of your potential strategies as a leader or internal consultant (refer back to Chapter 5). It is a core skill – see Figure 9.1. A 'good listening to' can vary from a half or one day consultation to a few minutes. It does not have to take up a lot of time – especially if both of you are good clients and know how to use support well. It depends what you want to use it for too. Developing a strategy may need half a day or one day. Dealing with some feelings or getting ready for a crucial meeting may take only a few minutes laced with a touch of humour.

For directors and managers, teaching their people to give each other a good listening to can be an extremely important part of their strategy. On the one hand this can *save huge amounts of their time* because, instead of coming to them for day-to-day support, people can more often go to each other. On the other hand, this also helps build *one team*. It breaks down barriers, helps people build trust, understand how interconnected they are and how

- Encouraging individuals to unblock organizational treacle by deciding to take the initiative and 'do it.'
- Giving your support to leaders who continually face massive change and uncertainty.
- Getting out into the business and developing widespread friendships.
- Understanding the whole system.
- Building readiness for change and collecting data before real time development programs or team events.
- Facilitating people in small groups or consulting to individuals on RTMD programs.
- Training managers, consultants and other leaders in facilitating.
- Teaching mentoring and coaching skills.
- Encouraging support groups and networking and skilling people for this.
- Breaking down barriers and internal competition; fostering partnership and collaboration instead.
- 'Giving and getting a good listening to' is another key way of discovering our common humanity.
- Getting support for yourself and giving it to key partners and allies.

Figure 9.1   One-to-one facilitating: a core skill for your strategies

much they need to inform and involve each other. It helps people see the whole system. It also frees up the manager to hold less frequent, more strategically focused support meetings with her or his people. A half-day off-site meeting every quarter to review progress (using the 'Useful Questions' Model) can be invaluable as compared with a string of short meetings or 'Why haven't you?' meetings, and in my experience it is far more effective than formal appraisal meetings. You can go a step further in creating partnership and make it a 'co-counseling' or mutual listening to in which the time is split between the two of you, each giving the other a good listening to in turn.

For top managers, a notoriously lonely role, the concept of 'getting and giving a good listening to' with a few trusted friends or colleagues in the business world could be another attractive way of getting support.

Why one-to-one facilitating is so important

Facilitating one-to-one is fundamental to transformation. It is *individuals* who take initiatives, whether on their own or in partnership with others. Everyone is capable of offering leadership in their own workplace, community or society at large and in an excellent organization or thriving society they will do so. People like this change the world. By leadership I mean taking responsibility, showing the way and encouraging others to do so in whatever role, be it ever so 'humble.' People are more likely to do this if given support that is both encouraging and *challenging*. We will come back to this point at the end of the chapter.

There are two things going on for us: all those changes out there – the world and how other people are reacting to it; then there is how you and I are reacting to all this (see Figure 9.2.) How we react inside and therefore outside has an effect on what goes on

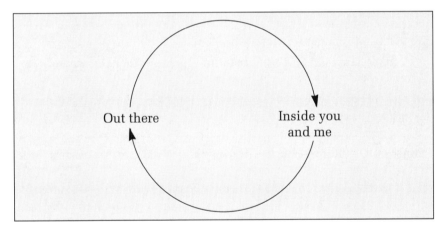

Figure 9.2

out there in the world – how other people react to you and me but also how the whole universe reacts to what we think and do. If we want to change what is happening out there we need to change what happens inside us: our fundamental attitudes and beliefs; how we see things; our expectations; what we project as well as our actions (Chopra, 1994).

> *'When your inner situation is not made conscious, it appears outside as fate.'* C. G. Jung.

'Undoubtedly, we become what we envisage.' Claude M. Bristol.

'Life shrinks or expands in proportion to one's courage.' Anais Nin.

'Every time you don't follow your inner guidance, you feel a loss of energy, loss of power, a sense of spiritual deadness.' Shakti Gawain.

How we react to what is going on out there

Many people face more uncertainty, more unpredictable and rapid change, more stress than ever before. We can be victims of it. Or we can thrive on it. It is our choice. Much of that choice is about how we react inside, but some of it is about how we choose to react outside despite what is going on inside. Or, maybe, at some point we can choose a less stressful lifestyle but we can never escape it all. Uncertainty, unpredictability and change are the very essence of life. We can never avoid that and we all need a way to thrive on it. The key thing is that we have choice.

I have found that it is essential that I trust my intuition and my heart and that I learn to distinguish between intuition and other kinds of feelings. To do this I have to look into myself and recognize and follow my 'inner guidance.' Often I also need to ask what it is in my heart to do. I need intuition, heart and head working together. Sometimes I have a very strong urge to do something and I cannot explain or justify it rationally. Afterwards it becomes abundantly clear why it was so important. Furthermore, following your intuition is often the only way through a complex, changing and unpredictable situation. Good listening needs to encourage people to learn this life skill. You cannot do that unless you have started to learn it yourself.

Figure 9.3 outlines some of the most common reactions that people have. They may not reveal this at first but when they feel safe enough, this is what they tell me. Clearly a lot of the time we 'contain' these feelings and get on with whatever we have to do, maybe putting on a brave or smiling face to the world. This is appropriate. Inside it may be different. Also, especially if we exercise choice, we can have a great many 'positive' feelings in this interesting and exciting world of ours which is full of creativity

- Insecurity, anxiety, fear or panic.
- Frustration and disappointment.
- Anger about things that don't make sense.
- Resentment and bitterness.
- Confusion in the complexity of everything.
- Feelings of self-doubt, inadequacy, powerlessness, cynicism, even hopelessness.
- Guilt about what we have to do or mistakes we made.
- Grief about what is passing and we have to let go of.
- Exhaustion from the pressures.
- Fatigue from listening to the difficulties of others.
- Fatigue from just 'getting on with it.'

Figure 9.3 Ways we react inside to what is going on out there

and potential: anticipation, enthusiasm, high expectations, hope, joy, satisfaction, calm and good feelings towards others. These are not the problem. The problem occurs when we have difficulty coping with the so-called 'negative' feelings. These can, particularly if we hold on to them, sap our energy, diminish our creativity, damage our immune system, affect our sleep, distort our judgement, and affect what we see, what we think and how we act. We can take it out on others, act out our feelings, dump them on others, make poor decisions, act when we need to reflect and not act when we need to act. If a lot of people are doing this, it creates a deadening climate. Instead what we need is a vibrant, exciting one which people want to be a part of and which is attractive to customers and suppliers as well.

Our task at work, especially in times of change, is to think and act flexibly, make wise decisions and learn from our experiences. Also it is to provide excellent leadership to others who are facing similar difficulties, to be hopeful, inspiring and empowering. For this we need all our energy, goodwill and intelligence. It is hard to do this if we are weighed down by feelings that are not dealt with. We can contain feelings for a while, 'fake it to make it,' but not for too long.

Really feelings are not the problem, they are just part of being human. The problem is thinking they are a problem. It is more about reconciling our needs with what is culturally acceptable in our environment. Latins typically express their feelings; Brits hold on to them and confuse thoughts and feelings. Ultimately feelings can be the source creativity and energy; sometimes they are telling you something very important such as 'I don't want to do this.' There are all sorts of ways of working with them – walking, running, swimming, riding, music, dancing, beating with a baseball bat, kicking a ball, dramatizing them, being funny or silly about them, singing, yoga, meditation, prayer, reading or writing 'morning pages' (Cameron, 1995) or *getting a good listening to.*

> I remember when I was starting to write. A friend, Richard Allen, and I decided to write an article together. We booked a meeting room to sketch out the article. I started saying 'Who am I to write this article? I don't have an MBA. I'm not a professor or business leader. What right have I to write an article like this?' Richard listened to me with a knowing smile whilst I expressed all my feelings of inadequacy. Then he said 'Get on your feet; walk round the room and talk. I'll write what you say on flip charts.' We did this for 20 minutes or so. Then we exchanged roles. After a couple of hours we both had notes for what proved to be a very popular article that got us on to several conference platforms, made many friends, helped in recruiting people to our teams and later brought us clients. I went on to publish another 30 or more articles. That all sprang out of Richard giving me a good listening to whilst I walked and spoke with passion.

I am indebted to Richard Allen for the diagram in Figure 9.4. It makes a lot of sense to most groups to whom I present it. (When Richard uses the term 'fizz out' he is thinking of people who, without saying anything, exude anger, resentment, cynicism or pessimism. You know they have feelings they are not expressing directly. You just don't want to be around them if it is a chronic state that goes on and on.) I find that if I get my feelings out, express them, what seemed like a problem then seems like an exciting opportunity. 'Negative' feelings are soon transformed into 'positive' energy and excitement.

Useful assumptions about people

In my work, in my relationships and especially when I am facilitating someone I find it useful to make assumptions about peo-

As with physical hurts, so with emotional hurts there is a natural healing process. Basically it is to get a good listening to so that you can talk about or express how you feel and get it off your chest. Small children do this brilliantly if we let them.

Unhelpful process

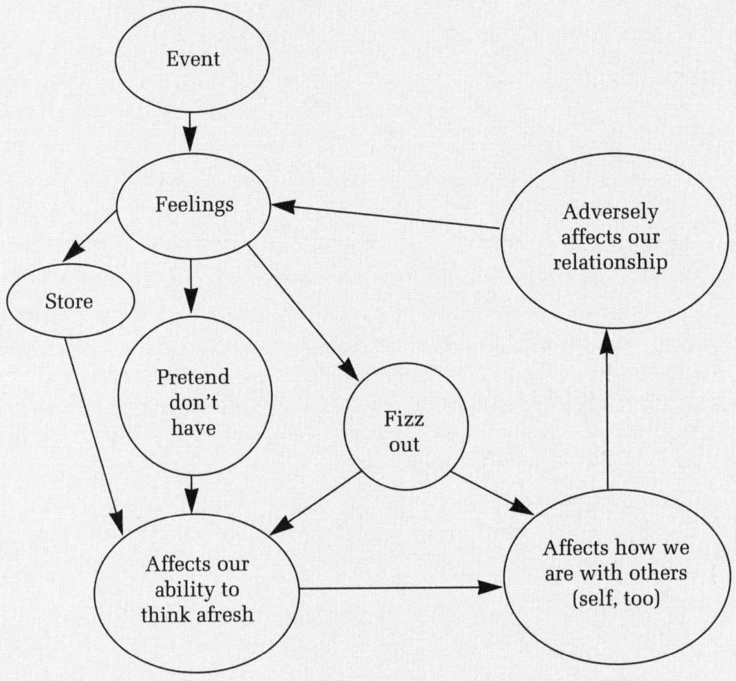

Helpful process

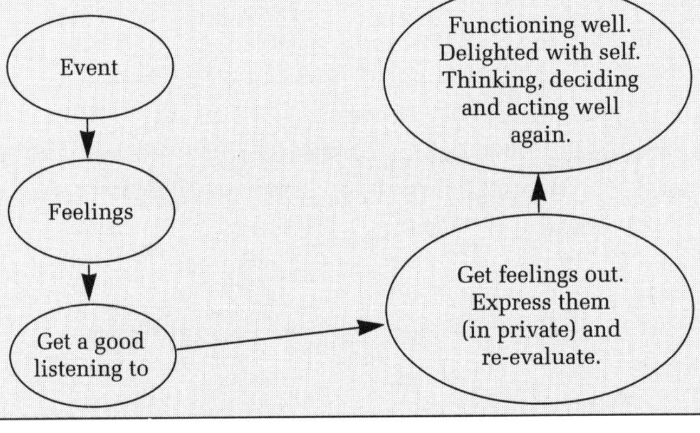

Figure 9.4 The good news – 'getting a good listening to'

We are inherently ... or have the potential to be...

- Highly intelligent,* flexible and creative.
- Welcoming towards change.
- Co-operative and loving.
- Attractive and likeable.
- Keen to do our best and improve.
- Enthusiastic, energetic and fun-loving.
- Inquisitive and eager to learn.
- Relaxed and confident.
- Powerful.

*By intelligent I mean, primarily, able to make fresh, appropriate responses to each new situation. However, as Charles Handy says (Handy, 1994), there are many different kinds of intelligence not just academic, (eg, factual, analytical, linguistic, spatial, musical, practical, physical, intuitive and interpersonal).

Figure 9.5   Useful assumptions about people

ple – see Figure 9.5. Does this set of assumptions stand up to scrutiny? Certainly intelligence varies but there are all kinds of intelligence. We need them all. It is silly to rank some higher than others as we do in our class-driven national culture. As a result, many people greatly underestimate themselves or are significantly blocked about their intelligence. I also observe that almost everyone I know, including me, is capable of behaving in these positive ways. I think most parents see this inherent nature or potential in their small children – on good days at least! Of course we do not always behave intelligently or in the other positive ways described. Indeed human beings are *all* capable of doing the opposite – being destructive and dysfunctional. But I do believe we always have a choice. I also think that these are *useful assumptions* to have in our minds about the people who work for and with us, about our customers and suppliers, about our partners and our children – about anyone if we want to bring out the best in them and *particularly in a facilitating relationship*. In a facilitating relationship it is our job to hold up a mirror and reflect with unshakable certainty the other person's inherent nature or potential. Julia Cameron calls this being a 'believing mirror' (Cameron, 1995).

When I was a child of seven or eight I was constantly told by my teacher that I was stupid and bad. That is exactly what I became. It got to the point where I was too ill to go to school. My parents took me away and moved me to another school where the 73-year-old headmaster (it was wartime!) believed in Christian love. In all kinds of ways he told me I was intelligent and good. I flourished and became academically successful – always near the top of the class for the rest of my school career. From that experience I learned a lot about how to release potential.

How our potential gets blocked

So what is it apart from some feelings, that gets in the way of people behaving in the way described in Figure 9.5? My friend John Thatcher has a useful way of describing this – see Figure 9.6.

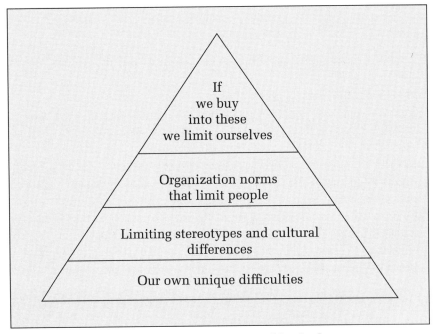

Figure 9.6   How we get blocked

Our own unique difficulties

Starting at the bottom of the pyramid, in those formative years of childhood, if we are lucky, we are loved by our parents and family. We have good role models and get a good start at school from wise teachers and good friends. But, despite everyone's best efforts, mistakes will be made and we may pick up unhelpful messages like: 'be careful', 'don't take risks', 'you cant trust people', 'you are not very clever' and 'don't have high expectations or you'll be disappointed.' This is really the *distress* of our parents or other role models being offered or interpreted as guidelines for living. Also there may be ways in which our parents are poor models, for example, they are poor at handling conflict or forgiving or getting what they want in life, so we do not learn how or we over-compensate. Dad may have trouble expressing feelings or be an absent workaholic. Mum may accommodate others, put herself second and avoid conflict, or an only child may not learn about give and take. Fate can deal cruel blows like losing a parent or sibling. You may have no parents. Most people triumph over these difficulties but they can leave scars. One very able and successful entrepreneur I know was constantly told by his father 'You'll never make a success of anything.' That did not help and it shows up in how he leads people and leads his life. He puts too much effort into being a success and making money at his own expense and the expense of others. The quality of his life suffers and so did his team's. I told you about the teacher who told me that I was stupid and bad. Also at night I was always listening for aeroplanes, bombs dropping nearby and my parents' fights. We overcome these hindrances but they can leave us with *patterns*, habitual, unhealthy ways of reacting or seeing the world which may emerge particularly in times of stress. I am sure you will recognize this in yourself and others who are close to you at work or at home. It helps explain why able and successful people sometimes act inappropriately in particular ways that limit them. It is a difficulty they seem to have. The same applies to me and you, we are all in the same boat – awareness helps.

Limiting stereotypes and cultural differences

Human beings have a fundamental difficulty about difference and it seems to start around middle school years. Little children seem to play together quite happily whatever their color, race or religion. Then something happens.

My 13-year-old daughter has lovely wavy hair. Most of her friends have straight hair. They criticize her for having wavy hair and she gets upset about this. There are many other examples. In the end they all fear being different in *any* way. I tell her to be delighted about herself exactly as she is. Never mind being 'cool'; proudly be herself.

A few months ago I heard a storyteller or children's entertainer describing his experiences. Four- to six-year-olds squat in a circle and just enjoy themselves and laugh heartily. At ten to twelve years they start looking round to see if their colleagues are laughing. Fear of being different has replaced spontaneity.

Right from the time we are having stories read to us at bed time, in all our experiences as young people, we are getting messages about people in 'our group' and people who are different from us. These may instill stereotypes about male and female, black and white, our race and others, our religion and others, people with disabilities, people who speak like us and people who do not, people from our social class and people in other social classes, people from our region and people from other regions. We may not realize this is going on so we end up with ideas and prejudices about how young people should behave, how men and women respectively should behave and their roles in society, prejudices about working class or middle class or upper class, prejudices about black people or white people, people from the North, people from the South, young people, older people, and people with disabilities. Instead of seeing them as who they uniquely are, we see them in terms of stereotypes and even as less than completely human – how else could we justify treating them the way we do (for example, the way the Nazis treated Jews, the way Israel treats Palestinians, how the West see Arab countries, how America sees Cuba, the way imperial powers treated the people they colonized and recent massacres in the Balkans and parts of Africa)? We demonize foes.

These stereotypes can affect us in two ways: firstly, the thoughts we have about those not in our group, different to us, and the way we behave towards them, and, secondly, we can *internalize* the stereotypes in society about our group and that limits us. This restricts the way we behave, limits our expectations, and gets in the way of expressing our unique individuality and potential. This adds up to a huge waste of human potential (our own and others). It can lead both to massive underachievement and oppressive behavior and the injustices that people have been fighting for generations and war.

We rightly believe we are decent, fair-minded people. The chances are that we are not fully aware of the extent to which we are influenced by these stereotypes and the subtle and hurtful ways in which we react to them. If this is pointed out to us, we are likely to be defensive and resistant. We do not like to feel judged or guilty.

'Despite its bad reputation, awareness is everything (or almost everything).' B. Oshry.

How can we become more aware? Partly by reflecting about:

- What our prejudices are.
- How we acquired them.
- What we have done to overcome them and fight for justice.
- What more we will do to put things right in our relationships, our workplace and the wide world.

You can address those questions on your own with a notepad or in a support group of people like you with whom it is easier to be honest and where you will not cause offense. Another option is to listen (non defensively and without guilt) to people in other groups from yours telling you what it is like for them (if they will tell you), for example, black people, people of different religion, women, young people, older people, breadwinners, single parents, fathers, mothers, working class people, and people with disabilities. You may be deeply moved by what they tell you about the obstacles they have had to overcome and the abuse and discrimination they have suffered. If so, your viewpoint will almost certainly change profoundly. There is nothing to beat listening to people who are different from you. If you feel prejudice, catch yourself. The odds are that you lack information – seek it. Remember, feeling guilty or being defensive has no place in this. You did your best at the time.

As the world shrinks, we travel more and more of us work in transnational organizations and cross-cultural teams. We are learning more about our cultural differences. In some respects, as we learn from each other, we are becoming more alike; yet in others we are becoming more differentiated, more aware of our unique cultural differences and more anxious to protect and enjoy them.

In business these differences can be bewildering and a source of difficulty, conflict and frustration. At first we think people in other cultures are extraordinary and wrong. This can be ruinous to business performance. Perhaps, because business survival is at stake, we are gradually learning to understand cultural differences, to respect them and, a stage further, to learn from them (Berger, 1996 and see Chapter 10).

Organization norms that limit people

As soon as you start working in an organization, you pick up its cultural norms. Some are useful; some are not. For example: you do not challenge your boss; you work long hours and don't take all your holidays; leaders must lead on their own, know all the answers and not admit mistakes or show any weakness; don't get close to people you lead; don't admit to putting your family first; don't say what you think; don't show feelings whether they be excitement or dismay; and we are the best.

> One boss said to me when I went to him privately after being side-lined in a reorganization: 'Bruce, you'll never get on if you show your feelings like this.' His advice was probably sound and well-meaning but I thought 'poor man' and 'poor family.'

Some norms are unique to the particular organization; some common to many others and some, such as the roles of women and black people, are taken from society; some are essentially national. The effect is to encourage dysfunctional behavior of various kinds, such as not speaking up, competing and over-working to our own, the organization's and our family's detriment. This limits the contribution that all sorts of people make. Of course, if we want to be effective, we have to be sensitive to an organization's norms, but we do need to sort out in our minds which ones work well and which do not and wisely challenge the latter.

Practical implications

What are the practical implications of all this? Firstly, if we want to help people bring out their potential, perhaps by giving them a 'good listening to,' being a coach or mentor, being a 'believing mirror' or simply to help in our day-to-day contacts with them, we need to be aware of the following four things that may be getting in their way (and ours as a helper):

- Straightforward *feelings* about the situation they face that may need to be acknowledged and expressed.

- Difficulties or *patterns* established when they were growing up that they need to *contradict* in their lives today.

- *Stereotypes* affecting *how* they view themselves or others.

- *Organizational norms* that limit people and need to be wisely challenged and changed.

These four factors not only affect our own lives, they can also creep into our helping of others.

These ideas may also explain why we have difficulty in our relationships with some people. Our own unique difficulties or patterns may clash with theirs. That's why X is '*like a red rag to a bull*' when she meets Y. Our stereotypes may prevent us seeing the real human being under the patterns. Likewise they may have difficulty seeing the real you (or me). But remember, any change in a relationship has to start with you (or me). You, only, have control of your own behavior.

Giving people a good listening to

As with any form of facilitation – in management development programs, support groups, team events, whole system events – you need suitable:

- Conditions.
- Processes.
- Models.

Whilst having a good model you also need to be fully responsive to your client (be client centered). This means your being (this is the paradox) completely flexible and able to cast aside your model and trust your intuition – those little messages that are

- Giving complete attention – listening and observing.
- Thinking about what the other person is saying and what you notice.
- Remembering what they said earlier and linking things together.
- Listening to yourself, hearing your intuition – those messages that are coming up – and evaluating them.
- Noticing your feelings which are so important and indicative. What are they telling you? Perhaps what is not being expressed.
- Resisting the temptation to get involved in the content – not ever asking more questions about it than is absolutely necessary to help your client.
- Planning and controlling the session – thinking about what the other person wants, the structure to get them there and how much time is left.
- Deciding how to respond.
- Responding by silence, expression, posture and words.

Figure 9.7   The inner task of listening

coming up all the time. Giving a good listening to is complex. You are trying to do a lot of things at once – not easy – and to manage this you have to trust your intuition. The inner task of listening is outlined in Figure 9.7. When you read through it you will see that there is no wonder that listening is harder work than talking!

The conditions

There are some essential conditions for one-to-one facilitating and these are listed in Figure 9.8. Let me comment briefly on them: You cannot impose helping. To work well it has to be wanted. Also it is no good if you give it reluctantly and only with half a mind; it is better to postpone listening until you are really ready. Secondly, trust and safety are absolute prerequisites for the 'client.' This means explicit confidentiality, freedom from being judged or punished and security from intrusions. The person being listened to needs to be totally in charge – *they* decide what they will talk about, how much they will reveal, what suggestions they will follow and what action they will take. This is an essential

- Voluntary and by mutual agreement.
- Confidential and safe.
- Person being listened to is totally in charge.
- Reciprocal facilitating, preferably equal time for each person.

Figure 9.8   Essential conditions

part of safety. I believe facilitating is best done on a mutual basis, ie, we co-counsel or listen to each other in turn – first you, then me – and we split the time equally. This avoids dependency or counter-dependency; reaffirms that we are equal partners; dispels the false notion that one of us is superior to the other, wiser or less in need; re-inforces our common humanity; and we learn more, far more, by listening to each other and teaching each other to facilitate.

> When I managed a team we all co-counseled each other and I got as much benefit from the least senior members as I did from the most. It helped break down all kinds of barriers, fostered partnership between us and helped people develop faster. My 18-year-old secretary was superb at giving a good listening. Some years later she had acquired a masters degree and had become a senior consultant. Now she has her own business. I like to think that the listening to she got from me and others helped her overcome many obstacles including prejudices about her gender, age, education, race and class. As a manager I found that half a day, of quality time, 'listening to' every quarter was far more constructive than formal performance appraisal meetings.

The process

Figure 9.9 gives my summary of the process. *The big issue with most people is to unlearn giving advice and solving problems for people and instead to learn to support the client in 'doing it for her/himself.'* This means letting go of control (very difficult at first for most managers) and letting go of content. It means focusing all one's effort on facilitating – two minds attending to one life. 'How can I best empower my "client"?' is the big question. Respect means trusting your client to come up with their own unique solutions, confident that they will. Disrespect means offering solutions instead of saying 'Trust your thinking.'

- Give respectful and complete attention.

  Respect her/his brilliance.
  Show delight, smile.
  High expectations.
  Relaxed confidence.
  Complete interest – not concern.
  Listen, listen, listen, look and think.

- Holding a mirror to her/his true nature.

- Follow your 'client' doing it for her/himself – do not lead.

- See where she/he is functioning brilliantly and where she/he is having difficulty, ie, where 'distress' or a 'pattern' is operating.

- Similarly notice where you are thinking brilliantly (and where not) about how to give a hand. Trust yourself and act on your best thinking.

- Achieve a good balance between challenge and support.

  I am indebted to my American friend, Charlie Kreiner for these simple powerful ideas.

Figure 9.9   The process

Models

Model A: Just listen

The simplest model of all and maybe the most useful is *just listen* and *be fully present*. This is a brilliant exercise for people who normally offer advice. Sometimes 15 minutes of being listened to can make all the difference and is *all* that is needed – no comment, no response except a loving face, a 'believing mirror' but maybe the occasional 'go on'; 'tell me more' and 'keep going.' I should know better, but my wife and children keep telling me 'All I want you to do is *listen*; I don't want any advice; don't tell me what to do; I know; and most of all don't give me any "lectures".' But sometimes I forget and get sucked into inappropriately concerning myself with the content, usually because I get worried about them.

Model B: The facilitating model

The next one is highly acceptable in businesses. I have used it to train hundreds of managers, internal consultants and people working with small and large consultancies. The model has worked with a huge range of people including allegedly hard-headed engineers and accountants who are not supposed to be good at such things but most often are.

> One large consultancy who used this model to train its people found it gained a key competitive advantage. Because its consultants were more client centered as a result, it got much more repeat business. That is the cheapest way of getting good business. So it had a big business pay-off.

With the help of John Seddon, now an independent consultant and author, we developed a five-stage model when I worked in a large financial institution. We used it to train ourselves, other internal consultants and an army of managers. They loved it. It is based on Gerard Egan's three-stage helping model (Egan, 1997). I used to call it the helping model but I now call it the '*facilitating*

1. **Contracting**	Initial definition of purpose or desired outcome of meeting. Agree ground rules, role of 'helper' and physical setting.
2. **Building a relationship**	Get to know each other; share key information; build the relationship through trust, integrity, mutual understanding and self-disclosure. Understand the person and their difficulties.
3. **Exploring the issue**	Get to know the issue presented. Explore the data, feelings and issues underlying it.
4. **Understanding the issue/ opportunity and setting goals**	Help the client see underlying causes and patterns, make sense of it all, gain fresh insights and learning. Challenge and confront your client to help them see things differently. See the opportunity under the issue. Set goals for change. Clarify what success would look like. What will the pay-off be? What have you done before that has worked/not worked?
5. **Planning action and support**	Turn the need for change into practical strategies for action. What will you actually do to improve/transform the situation? What might get in the way and how will you tackle it? Identify support needed for success. Commit to action.

Figure 9.10 The facilitating model

model,' a name that has no connotations of 'therapy' or 'weakness' that can initially put people off (see Figure 9.10).

As Gerard Egan originally pointed out, this is a developmental model and the two parties may need to return to earlier stages. You may need to go back and recontract. You may find you need to go back and build greater trust before you can work with what now appears to be the issue. You may need to build a stronger relationship before you can confront your client on a key issue, or you may find that by confronting them you are deepening the relationship. You may need to go back and explore the data further, or, only now that safety has grown, can you work on the feelings. As one of my manager clients said:

'It's a bit like peeling an onion. There are layers and layers.'

Another feature is that the model is not entirely sequential – for example, you are building trust all the way through, not just at the beginning. Every step you take demonstrates your humanity and integrity.

Model C: The empowering model

Another model I use is based on the Empowerment Model. Before I start with this model, or indeed any other model, I use what I call *beginning questions*. I invite the other person first to talk about two to three things they are pleased about and then maybe to share anything that is getting in the way, for example, an awful journey, a row with a partner, or a bad night. Then I ask goal-setting questions like 'What outcome do you want from this 20 minutes?' 'What do you want to talk about?' 'What is the best possible use of this time?' 'What would make the biggest difference if you could resolve it?' and maybe 'How do you want to get there?' and 'What support do you want from me?' The answers to these questions will enable you to plan a structure together. Often, however, the headings of the empowering model (Figure 9.11) can be a useful structure to propose.

To keep things on track, your intuition may prompt you to ask 'Are we working on what you want to work on?' 'Are we working on the most important issue?' 'We have 10 minutes left – what would be the very best use of that time?'

With this, or any of the other models, you have the option of using flip charts to record the goals of the meeting, the structure

- **Airing the current situation** Talking about it. What is good/difficult; what would you like to change? Sharing facts, thinking, feelings. Symptoms.

- **Diagnosing the situation** Making sense of it all; drawing it all together; what it boils down to; defining the key issue or key issues.

- **The desired state** Your vision of the future – how would you like things to be? If everything were going really well, how would it be? If you settled for nothing less than everything, how would things be?

- **Strategy or action** What will you do to bring this about? What do you need to do? What are those few crucial steps you need to take?

- **What might get in the way?** What are the potential obstacles? How might you sabotage yourself? What will you do to ensure complete success? What support do you need/will you get for yourself to maximize your chances of succeeding, from whom and when?

- **Commitment and support** Finally then, what will you commit yourself to do (including support)?

Figure 9.11 The empowering model

you agree and, the key points or decisions. You can present the flip chart to your 'client' as a gift. (You can do the same work on a clipboard.)

Model D: The contradicting model

In the section on 'Our own unique difficulties' (starting on page 168) I talked about *distress* and *patterns* and *contradicting* patterns. I got these ideas from co-counselling or re-evaluation co-counseling (Jackins, 1973).They give rise to another simple model which I call the 'contradicting model' (see Figure 9.12). As with all these models, you can share the model with the other person, write it on a flip chart, put it on the wall and ask them if they would like to use it. I believe in being completely transparent with my clients, always sharing my models with them, what I am doing and why. We can then collaborate better together as partners. It is another way of building safety and trust. It gives them a say in how we work too. It also helps develop their skills as facilitators.

Stage 1 –   What is the underlying difficulty or *distress pattern* here? And how did it start?

Stage 2 –   How can I best help the other person *contradict* it?

Stage 3 –   Suggest or offer a *contradiction*.

Stage 4 –   Ask the 'client' what the *pay-off* or *benefits* will be if, from now on, they contradicts the pattern.

Stage 5 –   Ask what *specific steps* she/he will take to make these happen and what support she/he will get.

Figure 9.12   The contradicting model

Let us take an example. The other person keeps showing lack of confidence in their intellectual ability and saying in various ways 'I am not that bright.' You know how this started – her elder brother excelled at school and university and got all their parents' praise and encouragement. In fact you know she is very intelligent. One thing you can do is simply say 'You are very intelligent' or 'Trust your thinking – you are very astute' or ask 'What would you do if you trusted your thinking absolutely?', or you can offer an affirmation. Suggest to her that she says 'The truth is I am very bright indeed.' This will almost certainly make her laugh (with relief?) or encourage her to write down an affirmation like 'From now on I am going to recognize just how bright I am' and keep looking at it daily. Another approach is to suggest she completes this statement: 'I now accept that I am a very bright person and the benefits (or pay-off) will be.............' She then tells you all the benefits of living her life on the basis that she is highly intelligent. You list all her answers on a flip chart and keep asking for more. Finally, you list all the changes she will commit herself to making. This kind of exercise usually produces a lot of laughter and it is best done with humor. It is fun but has the serious intent of committing the person to making important changes. It can be used for a wide variety of 'patterns,' for example, over-working, lack of confidence, criticizing, worrying, accommodating others, having low expectations, neglecting our needs, constantly hurrying, putting ourselves under unnecessary pressure, etc.

It is easy to think up appropriate contradictions. They are usually simply the opposite of the distress, for example, for someone constantly hurrying, 'I have all the time in the world,' or 'I will take the time I need' or 'I will do this effortlessly.'

'Contradicting' can also be used to challenge present thinking, help people reframe, get themselves into a different mind-set and see things in an entirely different light, for example, to see some-thing that appears threatening or a set-back, if not a disaster, as an exciting opportunity full of promise. Therefore, the 'client' may be encouraged to say about the apparent disaster 'What a gift!' or 'I welcome this golden opportunity,' or, about a mistake, 'Whoops, here I go again.' The more humorously and light-heart-edly this is done, the better! It helps to make light work of our distress patterns. *We can laugh our way into a completely differ-ent mode of thinking!*

Human beings are capable of holding many models in their heads at the same time and drawing upon them as appropriate. I know that, when I am facilitating others, I draw on these and probably many other models. I start by finding out what my 'client' wants. Then I use my intuition to guide me to use one model or to pick and mix or maybe not to use any model at all and just trust my intuition to guide me, or I trust my client to know what she needs to do and ask her the best way.

Model E: The reviewing progress model
Before you finish giving a good listening to someone, it is a good idea to ask whether you can give them any further support, for example a follow-up meeting to review and sustain progress. For this purpose a useful model is given in Figure 9.13.

There is a good reason for starting with triumphs. Most people will have difficulty appreciating just how much they have achieved, sometimes against the odds. It 'contradicts' the harsh self-critic that is in us all and instead puts us in a more balanced, self-valuing, hopeful state of mind. When we feel good about

---

- What is going well? Celebrate my triumphs.
- What has been difficult? What are the set-backs or disappointments?
- What have I learned from these experiences?
- What changes have taken place out there?
- Set new goals.
- What do I need to tackle now that will otherwise get in the way?
- Commitments: action and support.

Figure 9.13   Reviewing progress model

ourselves, as we deserve to, we think better, we are more creative and we are more likely to aim high and have high expectations of ourselves and others. We won't do this weighed down by self-criticism or guilt.

Continuous learning and improvement

I have advocated 'co-counseling,' ie, two people facilitating each other in turn, both giving and getting a good listening to. One of reasons for this is that we learn a lot more by taking turns in both 'helper' and 'helped' roles. Also, it is as important to be a good 'client' as it is to be a good 'facilitator.' There is something incredible, and incongruous about helping others and yet not being skilled in being helped. That can seem arrogant too. (Indeed, I would go so far as to say that if you are in any major facilitating role it is *dangerous* not to have a 'supervisor' or 'shadow consultant').

> It is important to develop an authentic relationship with clients and partners. For me, it was a huge step forward in my development when I discovered that one of my consultants, whom I greatly admired, had as many difficulties as I did – just different ones! Roger Harrison's book had the same effect on me (Harrison, 1995). It is one of the most honest books I have read.

We need to develop both sets of skills – helping and being helped. So, at the end of each listening to, both parties need to take part in a brief review to develop their skills as 'helpers' and 'clients.' This is about being humble and rigorous. *First* do a review of the helping:

- What the facilitator did that helped or seemed to help (two to three specifics).
- What the facilitator might do differently next time (one specific).

The facilitator reviews first and then receives feedback from the 'client.' *Next*, review what the 'client' did that helped, then what the client might do differently. First the client reviews; then the helper.

Notice the way the questions are phrased in a non-judgmental way. That is important as it is easier to receive feedback like that. Also notice that the favorable feedback comes first. Most of us are quite sensitive to what we interpret as criticism. We can hear suggestions for improvement more easily when there is more praise than criticism, when it is phrased in a non-evaluative way and when we have commented on our own performance first. It is important to be concise and to the point with feedback. Rambling long pieces of feedback take up a lot of time and can be quite boring, so think first. Conducting a review like this at the end of a helping session, is a simple and effective way of teaching people how to give each other feedback.

Giving feedback

Giving, seeking and receiving feedback are extremely important skills for people in organizations. Yet a lot of people flinch from giving honest feedback. Equally, people are reluctant to ask for it and have difficulty receiving it non-defensively. Most of us are sensitive to criticism and neither wish to hurt nor be hurt. Many of us have had bad experiences of being hurt by insensitive feedback or being punished for giving honest feedback. Yet ultimately we can be more hurt by not being given honest feedback. This is one way businesses fail – 'No one ever told me I was falling down in the job until it was too late' and 'How can I trust people if they only tell me the good news?' People often talk about the problem with everyone except the person who most needs to know. How can we trust people if they are not authentic with us? Authenticity is the foundation of trust and partnership.

Although it is not easy, there are principles for giving feedback (see Figure 9.14) and these are more likely to prove constructive.

Phrasing feedback in the following way is most likely to work:

First, 'These are the things I most appreciate/value about you...' or 'What you do that really helps/contributes is...' or 'Your most valuable contributions are...'

Then, 'As a good friend, my single piece of advice to you is...' or 'My single "do differently" is...'

It is important to be concise, truthful, not to wrap it up and yet

Feedback is more likely to be acted on when:

- It is asked for by the recipient or offered and only given if the other assents.
- The timing is right. As immediate as possible but when the other feels receptive.
- There is a strong relationship of trust and goodwill.
- The balance is right, ie, much more appreciation is given than criticism.
- It is phrased in a non-evaluative way – concise, accurate and descriptive.
- It is given as from one loving friend to another – someone who cares a lot about you and the organization in which you work.

Figure 9.14   Giving feedback

to be sensitive in how you phrase it. As the recipient it is important not to qualify praise nor to defend yourself against advice or
suggestions. You may clarify it if you *really* need to, but otherwise say, with genuine appreciation for what is a gift and often
requires both courage and much careful thought: 'Thank you.'
You may decide simply to reflect or sometimes say what you will
do about it if you are ready to. Resist the temptation to explain,
justify or defend. This quality of feedback is not an attack. In this
sort of climate it is recognized that everyone is trying to do their
best and does not deserve to be blamed. Feedback like this is
given in a spirit of loving concern for you and the organization.
The least we can do is be grateful and aware that almost everyone's initial reaction is likely to be resistance.

Giving and receiving feedback is not a major part of 'giving and
getting a good listening to.' Generally, the role of the facilitator is
not to express opinions or get involved in the content, but sometimes the 'client' will ask for feedback and you may decide to give
it. Also challenging your client by offering feedback is appropriate. Sometimes your integrity demands that you give it. I have
included it in this chapter because it is an important part of building really trustworthy and loving work relationships. It is such an
important part of learning and yet we seem to have so much difficulty doing it. So often it leads to argument and punitive and
damaging conflict. We have to agree not to go down that route.

If we do not want to be members of what my friend Mary Thompson calls the 'cozy club' we need to learn how to give lovingly and receive gratefully what she calls the 'loving boot.' I know I struggle with the pain of it unless I am given a lot of reassurance that I am 'OK,' particularly in the eyes of the person who is giving me the feedback.

References and suggested further reading

Berger, M. (1996) *Cross-Cultural Team Building – Guidelines for More Effective Communication and Negotiation*, McGraw-Hill, Maidenhead, UK.

Cameron, J. (1995) *The Artist's Way – A Spiritual Path to Higher Creativity*, Pan Books, London, UK.

Chopra, D. (1994) *The Seven Spiritual Laws of Success*, Amber-Allen/New World Library, San Rafael, USA.

Egan, G. (1997) *The Skilled Helper: A Problem Management Approach to Helping*, 6th edition, Brooks/Cole Publishing, Pacific Grove, USA.

Handy, C. (1994) *The Empty Raincoat – Making Sense of the Future*, Hutchinson, London, UK.

Harrison, R. (1995) *Consultant's Journey – A Professional and Personal Odyssey*, McGraw-Hill, Maidenhead, UK.

Jackins, H. (1973) *The Human Situation*, Rational Island Publishers, Seattle, USA.

Oshry, B. (1995) *Seeing Systems – Unlocking the Mysteries of Organizational Life*, Berrett-Koehler, San Francisco, USA.

10

Transforming Teamwork
Valuing diversity *and*
fostering collaboration

'Real learning comes about when the competitive spirit has ceased.' J. Krishnamurti.

'When we don't see systems, we are at their mercy.' Barry Oshry.

'Power is the ability to act as if you can make happen whatever it is you want to make happen, knowing that you cannot and being willing to work with whatever does happen.' Barry Oshry.

'God loves diversity.' M. Scott Peck.

'Responsibility is believing that I am in charge of my own behavior.' Sir Colin Marshall, Chairman, British Airways.

This is a straightforward and practical chapter which will be useful to anyone who wishes to help a team or group work better together – whether you are a member or someone outside invited in to help.

The name of the game for organizations is to survive in an unpredictable and potentially hostile, potentially benign environment. This requires the diverse contributions of everyone in the team, all their data and more, all their different kinds of intelligence, energy and initiative *and* their commitment to a common purpose. We human beings do not find this easy.

I started the chapter with some quotes from Barry Oshry whose insights into the patterns of relationships in organizational life are fascinating (Oshry, 1995). I am particularly indebted to him for his analysis of the behavior of 'tops', 'middles' and 'bottoms' and their ill effects on the customer – more about this later. Now I want to put aside his book and draw on my own experiences and what hundreds of people have told me about what goes on in their teams.

The big issue in teams is how can they rejoice in the diversity and difference of individuals (see this as a blessing rather than a problem) *and* yet combine to achieve common purpose. Often this seems impossible, for example when a team is doing the 'dance of the blind reflex,' as Barry Oshry calls it, unaware of the patterns that affect it. There are two common solutions: one is to *dominate*, marginalize people who are different and force them to submit; the other is to *expel* people who are different and re-cruit clones or people who submit. Both are dangerous strategies. They often lead to blindness, deafness and complacency. Is there a third way? In this chapter we shall try to find it.

> *The family meeting* – recently my wife, Suzanne, and I were shouting at each other over some conflict. The children heard us. First George, the youngest, said 'Why don't you sit down quietly and talk about how you feel?' Hannah offered us a hug and then said she had read in a book about a family who held 'Indian meetings.' They regularly got together, sat in a circle, each spoke in turn, while everyone else listened. Why didn't we come to her room and do that? She spun a 'talking stick' and the person it pointed to was to start first. No one was to interrupt, she explained. Suzanne, my wife, suggested we first speak about how we felt. The children facilitated us – kept us to the ground rules we had agreed, ie, to listen and not interrupt, justify, defend or criticize. We did the same for them. First we talked about how we felt, then the issues that concerned us. At the end we all felt better; there was a kind of calm. We had all been heard. Suzanne and I had resolved our conflict, given each other some essential information and decided on an action. Also we had made some agreements with the children that would remedy some of their frustrations. We all agreed to make this a regular meeting on Sunday mornings (I am sorry to say we have lapsed on this *regular* part).

Teams, big or small, are not unlike families. I think this illus-trates simply what often goes wrong in teams, how anyone, no matter how junior, can intervene to break the 'dance' and what can be done to make things work well. Perhaps the simplest and most important thing people can do is *agree to listen to each other.*

What goes on in teams – the patterns

Here are some of the things that happen in teams when they are not functioning well. The *tops* (often white, middle-aged males) feel burdened, isolated and responsible; dominate the talking; control too much; bully or talk loudly and for a long time to get their way; think they are right; do not welcome divergent views; and do not admit mistakes or that they do not know. They behave like warring barons and fight over territory. The *bottoms* hold the tops responsible; blame the tops; complain about lack of direction; stay quiet; criticize them behind their backs; and are oppressed and feel powerless. The *middles* tend to feel like piggy in the middle, and are in an impossible position, trying to meet everyone's demands, and seeing all points of view. Sometimes they adopt tops' behavior; sometimes bottoms' behavior. Often they compete and blame each other too. Customers (internal or external) wonder why all these people cannot get their act together and they often suffer poor service, poor quality, poor value and huge frustration when they try to get complaints put right. Bottoms also wonder why tops and middles are in such chaos – particularly as they are often closest to the product, customer or supplier and see the consequences.

Other things happen, not necessarily connected with tops, middles or bottoms. All the factors described in the previous chapter can come into play – stereotypes, the cultural limitations of the organization and individual blockages. Some people do a lot of talking and not much listening; their views prevail while others stay quiet, get drowned out or are not heard. There may be undercurrents, feuds and battles for power and control. These issues are not addressed. Indeed many issues are not. Often the atmosphere is hostile: there is a high degree of competition, criticism, 'trashing' done openly or outside meetings. Issues are not brought out into the open because of fear or feelings of inadequacy. Similarly, people do not admit to mistakes, not knowing, or not understanding. There is a lack of openness to new ideas. 'Group think' prevails. Because they are not sufficiently involved or do not risk expressing themselves and their views are not heard or appreciated, many team members feel 'turned-off', disengaged, cynical, angry or frustrated. Not that they show it, of course. They try to look happy and accommodating. Sometimes they suspect the meeting has been rigged and the issues 'sewn up' beforehand. They may have little interest in the agenda if they have not helped create it and the meeting feels boring and ritualistic. People are waiting for the meeting to end so they can get out and get back to some 'real work.' And meanwhile the issues that matter most to them have not been resolved and they still have no sense of common purpose or clear direction.

This is a dangerous and wasteful way for an organization or team to behave. A team needs to understand the whole situation and the whole system needs to contribute their data. It needs a shared vision and a sense of direction and common purpose. The whole system needs to contribute to agreeing key strategies and individuals need to enthusiastically decide the actions they will take within the bigger framework. This cannot happen in the climate described above.

In a team there is always the possibility of either *destructive, dysfunctional behavior* on the one hand or creative, responsible behavior on the other. It helps if we can first see clearly what we are doing (*awareness*), see that it is partly patterns that are systemic rather than personal failures (ie, they tend to happen in any organization) and then exercise *choice*. Anyone can help the team do this. However they need to *expect resistance* – 'the sound of the old dance shaking' (Oshry, 1995) – and *not take no for an answer*.

Breaking the patterns and creating a new vision of teamwork

Here I should like to offer practical suggestions – things you can do. I shall include a number of models which you can bring into play, adapt, pick and mix. Some have their roots in the 'empowerment model' or 'useful questions model.'

Beforehand work – building readiness

Assuming that there is an intention to hold an event such as a meeting, it may help to talk to each member of the team beforehand to start their thinking, bring out their energy to change things

- What do you enjoy about being a member of this team? What does it do that works?
- What is difficult about being a member of the team? What does not work?
- How would you like things to be different in the team? What is your vision?
- What would be the pay-off if it were like that?
- What are you prepared to do differently to bring this about?
- How could the meeting we plan help? What would be the outcomes if it were a complete success?

Figure 10.1 Quality of life in the team

for the better, help them become clear about what outcomes they want, collect data about their thinking, and start involving them in planning the event. Usually it is much easier for people to express their views in private to an individual they trust than to do so in a group. It is usually easier to build trust, and develop readiness with individuals than with a group. If it is a very big team, you can talk with a cross section. Some suggested questions are given in Figures 10.1 and 10.2. The first set is appropriate if the key issue is how the team works together. The second set may apply if the issue is how well it functions as a system in its environment.

- What are the key changes taking place in the environment affecting this organization or team?
- How is the team responding: well/not well; succeeding/failing; system working/not working?
- What is your vision of how things should be (the desired state or system if everything were working well)?
- What needs to be done to bring that about?
- What key issues or obstacles will get in the way unless the team tackles them?
- How could this event help?
- What would be the outcomes if it were a complete success?

Figure 10.2 How the team performs

Questions like these will provide the team with the data they need to set provisional objectives for their event. Depending on the numbers involved, two facilitators, perhaps one who is a member and one who is not, could collect this data, summarize the key issues very concisely and propose objectives and a simple structure to enable the objectives to be achieved. It is likely that the team will be surprised by the degree of common ground.

Symbols

If we want to transform teamwork, symbols are important. Where the event or meeting is held, the way the room is arranged, whether everyone is included, who speaks first, how long people speak, how late people work, the attention paid to physical needs (food, exercise facilities, whether there are alternatives to alcohol or stimulants like coffee), whether top people are full-time participants or visitors, how they behave – all these things and more convey messages about the values of the organization. Careful thought needs to be given to ensure that, whatever choices are made, they are congruent with the kind of teamwork the leadership wants to create.

Other things to consider are seating arrangements. If people are seated and work in a circle this suggests *no hierarchy here.* If tables are removed this suggests openness, flexibility and no barriers. If people are invited to take a turn to speak, in turn round the circle, that may make it easier for diffident people to express their views and it implies *no pecking order.* You may suggest *contradicting* some of the *stereotypes* (mentioned in Chapter 9) by inviting younger people, women or those who have not yet spoken, etc., to speak first. But this could seem patronizing. Explain why you are suggesting it and see how people react. Always be transparent about your process suggestions and explain your thinking. Encourage people to try new things before deciding whether to reject them.

Beginning work

I call these beginning questions *opening circles* because people speak in turn, going round the circle. It is similar to the *talking stick* which is another option. I find, particularly if I have not been able to talk to people individually beforehand or if we

---

- Some things I am pleased about. One or two successes to celebrate.
- How I am feeling. What it has been like for me.
- Outcomes I want from this meeting – my highest expectations.

Figure 10.3   Feelings and expectations

have not had a pre-meeting, a few simple questions will enable a team to clarify their goals for a meeting or event (see Figure 10.3).

The purpose of the first prompt is to contradict the feeling that 'I haven't really achieved anything. It's all been pretty bad really.' It is to get in touch with the reality that we *have* made progress despite difficulties. The second question enables people to get things off their chests, express their feelings, learn from each other what it has been like in different parts of the system and understand their common humanity. They will build trust by risking being open with one another. Through this process they will also *diagnose* the fundamental issues they need to tackle. Time and again I find that how people feel is how many other people feel in the organization. They are a microcosm, a barometer. This diagnosis will enable them to set objectives or outcomes for their meeting. The process will enable them to recover their energy too.

I successfully used feelings to diagnose, release energy and set goals when I was asked to facilitate a group of leaders who were trying to transform quality in their organizations. Their energy was low and they looked depressed. I got them to talk about how they were feeling and I wrote what they said on flip charts. Basically they felt dejected, manipulated by top management and powerless. After an hour we had a fairly comprehensive diagnosis of what was getting in the way of quality improvement. By now they were feeling much more energized. We soon set objectives for the meeting. They developed a shared vision, fresh strategies and plans for transforming quality in their organization.

Figure 10.4 gives questions which will produce not only a shared vision for the team but also the ground rules necessary to create that vision and against which periodic process reviews can be held. It is likely that the ground rules will be added to and

- How I want things to be in this team – my vision for it if we are to perform and learn to our highest potential.
- The ground rules this requires – the behavior that I want from others and that I will contribute.

Figure 10.4 Developing a vision of the team we want to be

modified with experience. It is often a good idea to get people to work first in pairs, listening in turn, while the other says what it is like now; how they would like it to be; and what behavior that requires. People can then work together to build a team vision and team ground rules. First, the team talks about its vision; then the behavior that is needed. Each person offers one idea not already mentioned; then there may be another round. Then the team identifies what all agree to, ie, 'common ground' and what is 'not agreed.' Figure 10.5 lists some of the most important ground rules for transforming the climate in a team.

- Show respect for everyone's opinion.
- Listen, really listen, and don't interrupt.
- Be as concise as you can.*
- Propose a review or time-out or some light-hearted, silly games if the group seems to be getting stuck.
- No blaming, 'trashing' or jokes at another's expense.
- Appreciate others.
- Be honest – risk speaking your truth.
- Respect confidences.
- Everyone takes responsibility for the outcome.
- Have fun.
- Have good working conditions. Take care of your physical, energetic, emotional and spiritual needs. We are complex beings.

*The importance of being concise is that, if you are not, people may feel bored and lectured at and find it difficult not to interrupt you.

Figure 10.5 Ground rules for a team

Core work

The core work of a team is to constantly scan its environment, rigorously appraise how well it is responding and take the necessary steps to improve and survive. The Empowerment Model provides a useful basis for this – so do the other models in Chapter 8. Let us assume the team is holding an event to do this work. It has already agreed goals and ground rules. Figure 10.6 gives a useful structure it can use.

The trick here is to *create a big picture together* working in the whole group and use the freedom of *open space* or *flexible program* and individual work to *enable everyone to take individual initiatives*. Work in the whole group requires lots of wall space. A basic ground rule is *respect everyone's truth and value everyone's contribution to understanding the whole system*.

Whole group

- *Our environment* – what is happening out there?
- *Our current system* – how well are we responding?
- *Our vision* – the desired state – how would things be if everything were going well?
- *Our strategy* – what are the key steps or decisions we need to take or changes we need to make to survive and thrive?

Open space – flexible program

- *Key Issues* – what are the key issues we/I need to tackle that will otherwise get in the way? Work on them.

  Groups work together on shared issues or interests.

  Individuals work in small groups or pairs on individual issues.

- *Actions and support*
  The actions I will take and the support I will seek.

Whole group

- *Public commitments* to actions and support.
- *Review and decisions about follow up or involving others.*

Figure 10.6   Creating shared vision and strategy

When creating a shared vision and agreed strategy it may help to distinguish between 'agreed by everyone' and 'not agreed.' Include the former and set aside the latter. The 'flexible program' enables individuals to propose issues that need to be tackled, enlist the support of others and decide on the individual steps they will take to bring about the shared vision. This approach releases individual energies and gives everyone a sense of contributing in the best way they can. It avoids creative people feeling constrained or tyrannized by a majority.

After work

It really is essential to have a follow-up session. Some clients do not. The reasons are understandable – daily pressures and cost – but not having a follow-up greatly diminishes the chances of succeeding. I would go as far as to say it is not rigorous or fully responsible to invest time in planning and *not* review progress together. It sends out a message of not really intending to succeed. It squanders the investment of time and money; encourages disappointment and cynicism; implies a lack of commitment to changing and is quite simply unprofessional. A useful framework for a follow-up is given in Figure 10.7. Typically a day or two are needed. Half a day might be sufficient.

- Rebuilding the climate.
- Rigorous review – celebrate successes, share difficulties, where I did not succeed, how the environment changed, what I learned, key issues I now want to work on.
- Open space or flexible program to work on key issues, new goals and strategies.
- New commitments including support.
- Review and plan further follow-ups and how to involve others.

Figure 10.7   Follow-up

During work

Letting go of control and going into the mess
Often a team needs to get into a mess, sink into what feels like the depths, step into confusion, express its resistance, feel anger,

fear, cynicism, resentment, grief or whatever it needs to feel. Most of us do not like this. It is extremely uncomfortable for many people: members of the team, its leader or a facilitator. We may feel responsible, incompetent and afraid we won't come out of this into a clear blue sky. As facilitators we may feel tempted to help the team out, make proposals, solve problems, soothe the team and take charge of the situation. Usually this is quite the wrong thing to do. Instead we need to stay with the discomfort of the team and our own; encourage or allow to happen whatever it is that needs to happen; show relaxed interest and confidence in the team (sometimes this is not easy; I can panic inside). Resisting it will most likely bring trouble falling down on your head. We have to *trust* that this is the work the team needs to do and when it is done, the team will recover its energy and creativity.

> One team I was working with were facing reorganization. Some would do well in the new set-up; some would not. There was a lot of grief and some anger towards the leader for the way the review had been carried out – not involving all of them sufficiently they thought. They needed to get into the mess of expressing their diverse feelings. The leader was wise enough to listen to them without defending himself. When they had done this, they were able to get on with the constructive, creative work of planning implementation with goodwill and responsibility.

Working in pairs

In the previous chapter I described the process of giving and getting a good listening to, ie, pair up and listen to each other in turn. In my experience this is an extremely good process to use during team meetings or events – to help people access and deal with their feelings, process or reflect on what they have heard, access and work on their own resistance and discover what they really think and want to do. Often it is useful for people to pair up and listen to each other in turn before they share their thinking with the whole group. It can be extremely valuable if the group seems stuck. People first work in pairs saying what they think is happening before they share their insights with the whole group. It is a way of avoiding 'group think': if you first discover what *you* think, you will be less influenced by what others think.

It has other advantages: teaching people how to listen and demonstrating the benefits of listening; breaking down barriers; developing trust; helping people respect and value diversity; and helping people discover their common humanity. And when you listen to another human being expressing their intimate thoughts, you learn about facets of yourself. The golden rule is *listen; be a believing mirror; do not interrupt.* When people are working in pairs, listening to each other in turn, the room is noisy with the buzz; it's full of energy. It is quite different from what often happens in groups – deadness, dullness and silence.

Giving feedback

When a sufficiently close and trusting climate has been created, it may be appropriate for people to give each other feedback, perhaps one-to-one and privately, perhaps in small groups, perhaps in a whole group. The event may be a good opportunity to do this work well. Figure 10.8 gives a useful format for this. The recipi-

---

- What I most value about you as a member of this team (maybe two sentences).

- One suggestion I make to you as a good colleague or loving friend - something you should do differently.

Figure 10.8   Giving feedback

ent may thank the other person, clarify if really necessary but it is wise not to discuss, defend or justify. It must not be used as an opportunity to 'dump,' attack or settle old scores. Feedback needs to be given in a spirit of generosity.

The 'rugby ball'

There are three things that require attention in an event: task; process and feelings (see Figure 10.9). There is a tendency in most teams to concentrate single mindedly on the task. You sug-

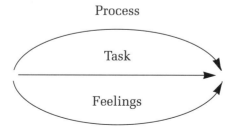

Figure 10.9   The 'rugby ball'

gest the team decides purpose, objectives and a framework for getting there but before you know what is happening, they immediately plunge into the *task*. They do not hear what you are saying to them about *objectives* and *process*. It helps the team to contract with someone from outside the group who will facilitate them and focus single mindedly on the process and noticing feelings. Or the team can decide to rotate this task round the members of the team so that everyone learns how to do it and thus the team develops its awareness of process and learns to share responsibility for it. The task entails contracting with the group about what they want the facilitator to do; what they the team will be responsible for; what the objectives of the meeting are; what framework will enable them to achieve those objectives; reviewing how the team is working together and agreeing whatever changes in the process are needed; reviewing progress with the task and with learning; noticing feelings and deciding what those feelings mean; drawing attention to time boundaries and, if agreed, giving feedback about what the facilitator observes.

Feelings are important. The feelings of the facilitator are often a reflection of the feelings of the group. The facilitator may be a 'barometer.' Sometimes feelings may simply be part of the normal 'roller-coaster' that human beings experience as they work on different stages of the task. Sometimes the feelings may indicate an issue that needs to be brought out into the open – a key issue that is not being dealt with – or that the process needs to be changed. A review to bring these feelings out into the open and facilitate a discussion may be most constructive.

Reviewing work

Reviews are an important part of effective teamwork – checking how well the event is working and deciding whether any changes are needed. Useful review questions are given in Figure 10.10.

- What I have gained (thus far).
- What I have learned.
- What has helped our progress.
- What I suggest needs to be changed or 'done differently.'

Figure 10.10 Review of benefits and process

This work can first be done in 'listening pairs' and then shared. Notice that the focus is on the positive – not on criticism but positive suggestions. This approach enables people to appreciate how much they are gaining and learning and what works, rather than encouraging the destructive patterns of complaining, fault finding and blaming which human beings are just as capable of. An end-of-day review could include the question 'What I will do to help myself and the team work even better tomorrow?' This encourages people to take responsibility for the success of the event rather than blame others.

Another set of questions can be useful if the group seems stuck – see Figure 10.11. First people 'listen in pairs'; then they share

- What I have noticed.
- My diagnosis of this.
- What I suggest we do differently to sort this out.
- What I will do differently to help.

Figure 10.11 Diagnosing the process

their thinking and agree the way forward. It really is essential that everyone accepts responsibility for the success of an event; they do not blame or hold the facilitator responsible; and they choose to intervene constructively when they see a need and risk making a 'mistake.'

Ending work

I call these 'closing circles.' The work of ending includes making commitments, expressing gratitude, appreciating people (including self, other members and leaders or facilitators), celebrating the success of the event, reviewing and learning from what worked and what may need to be done differently, planning follow-up, preparing for the outside world and sending people away feeling good about themselves. You will be able to think of all sorts of ways of doing these tasks. Some have been described already. They need to be brief as people are usually tired and keen to get away by now. Perhaps it is most important to make sure everyone gets some appreciation. It can be public – each person receives appreciation, for example two or three sentences from the person on their left, or it can be private – each person is given a sheet of paper, the person next to them writes their name on the top, writes a sentence of appreciation underneath, folds the paper over the words and passes it to the next person. Thus it goes round the circle and the recipient has a nice gift of appreciations to keep and read as often as they wish. Usually this means a great deal to people and they can refer to it when life is difficult. I have an old briefcase full of such pieces of paper to cheer me up when I am giving myself a hard time.

Cross-cultural team building

I am indebted to my friend, Mel Berger, for this contribution on cross-cultural team building. For more information and case study examples, see Berger, 1966.

When dealing with people of different countries and cultures, 'rejoicing in diversity' takes on an added dimension. People who have grown up and lived in another country or regional culture are going to have different basic approaches to work and personal relationships and about what is the 'natural,' 'commonsense' way to do things. This is likely to be deeply inbred, stemming from different child-rearing practices, educational differences and work methods. We are all raised with a set of values which influence our attitudes and behavior. These values are reinforced by parents, teachers and managerial bosses. To not conform is to risk non-acceptance by our community.

Because values are so basic to each person, and often not conscious, you are unlikely to get others to change their behavior towards yours. The best you can hope for is to understand the other, at least partially, and to respect differences. Based on understanding, it becomes possible to recognize the cultural strengths and skills that each has to offer, and blend them to achieve 'cross-cultural synergy.' For example, some cultures tend to focus more on the long-term while others focus on short-term results, and yet others on building a consensus.

When consulting to a culturally diverse group, the starting point is to collect data about people's views and preferences. Cultural values which are relevant to business practices are well spelled out by Hofstede (1980) and Trompenaars (1993). They have identified values which differentiate countries, some of which are set out below:

Openness

While most Western countries value openness, in many parts of the world it is seen as upsetting the harmony of the group. People will not speak negatively towards others in the team and they will not be impolite to you, the question asker. They may not even tell you that they don't understand you for fear of insulting you.

Authority

While we value participation, delegation and empowerment, this is contrary to many cultures in which the most senior manager is expected to know all and make the decisions. If you start questioning a junior manager in front of a senior manager, both people will be upset and embarrassed.

Structure

When organizing work, some cultures like all the rules and procedures to be spelled out, while others like to have the freedom to act as they wish, as long as it is directed towards agreed objectives.

To tease out the cultural biases, you need to ask people how things are done in a descriptive manner, and later ask them how they would ideally like things to be. For example, they may feel the boss is an autocrat but that is what they prefer. You also need to be careful to phrase your questions neutrally without revealing your views. Otherwise, people from a polite culture, for example many Asian cultures, will tell you what they think you want to hear. You are likely to get closer to an open answer in a one-to-one, more private setting. The group setting may be too public for people to really say what they think. You may also get some good answers from a syndicate group discussion but recognize that the most senior manager is likely to be the one to tell you what the group thinks. If you value everyone being open, you will probably be frustrated. If you push for full and open sharing of views, you will probably alienate yourself from the team. Remember, also, that it will take longer to get information and have a dialogue with people from different cultures than from your own. Trust may be harder to build and critical to achieve. This will be most strongly felt where there are differences in language fluency and in one's native language.

In summary, when working with multi-cultural groups, you need much patience to fully understand everyone's views and preferences. It will take much more time to reach a consensus amongst different parties than you expect. If you can remain curious and inquiring, you will succeed and learn a lot about the culture of others and yourself.

Conclusion

I have used all these models and approaches. They can work with teams large or small, a few levels or many. The processes just need adapting. They do work. People may find new ways embarrassing and express resistance, but that is just 'the sound of the old dance shaking.' You will help them if you are relaxed, confident and flexible. Pushing hard against resistance will only make it stronger. Don't give up, don't take no for an answer, and keep on and on but in a relaxed and confident way.

I think you will find that, by using some of these methods in teams, you will give people a glimpse of what is possible and what most of them have, in their hearts, always yearned for. You will give them a taste of the team they have always wanted to belong to and a vision of the team they will create.

References and suggested further reading

Berger, M. (1996), *Cross-Cultural Team Building*, McGraw-Hill, Maidenhead, UK.

Hofstede, G. (1980), *Culture's Consequences*, Sage Publications, London, UK.

Oshry, B. (1995), *Seeing Systems – Unlocking the Mysteries of Organizational Life*, Berrett-Koehler, San Francisco, USA.

Trompenaars, F. (1993), *Riding the Waves of Culture*, The Economist Books, London, UK.

11
❖
Using Support Groups
and Networking
for Change

'Surround yourself with people who respect and treat you well.' Claudia Black.

'Choose companions who encourage me to do the work, not just talk about doing the work or why I am not doing the work.' *(An affirmation.)* Julia Cameron.

Why you need support

Transforming your company can be hard work. It has its joys but it can be exhausting and at times discouraging. You encounter all the feelings, stereotypes and 'patterns' described in Chapter 9 – your own and those of others. In particular you encounter resistance and because that usually requires patience, it can be frustrating. It is not easy to keep up energy, optimism, enthusiasm and goodwill. It is hard to maintain respect for difference when you believe someone is profoundly mistaken. Maybe it will be easier if you decide to give up judging. Nevertheless it is hard work. It can be extremely lonely for top people who may feel there are many things that they cannot confide in their colleagues.

It is not surprising that people look to others for support. It makes good sense to do so. Throughout history people have been gathering round them people they trust. This chapter is about doing this more effectively and making deliberate what people do naturally.

When it works and when it does not

There is a tendency to seek out colleagues and build a team around you who are like-minded. History provides numerous examples of people doing this. At an extreme they may be yes-men and flatterers. This is a dangerous thing to do. And yet we need an oasis, a haven from the normal day-to-day, often hostile world where not everything is sweet reason and light; where people behave less well than they would like; lose their tempers; attack each other and compete; and sometimes betray confidences or stab you in the back.

At times you need a place where you will be nurtured; your wounds well dressed; where there is a 'believing mirror'; where you can reflect on what happened and how you acted without being judged or attacked; where you can express your feelings without guilt, no matter how extreme or outrageous they may be; where you don't need to hide anything; you can trust people; you can talk about the most difficult and confidential issues. This place may be amongst your friends inside the company or outside amongst people who have no connection with it and who have an equal need for complete confidentiality.

Getting robust support

My friend Mary Thompson has a neat model, the support group model (see Figure 11.1). Good support means a good balance of gentle *nurturing* on the one hand and *challenge* on the other (what Mary calls the 'loving boot'). That's real love. It takes a lot of trouble, care and judgment to know when and how to deliver the 'loving boot' – and to judge when there is enough trust for it to be accepted as a gift from a friend who really cares. I have learned not to trust people who do not tell me what they really think and only give me the good news. Equally I have learned to avoid people who are addicted to cruel criticism (I have known some consultants like that); discourage me; don't nurture my tender ideas; can't really give anyone else attention for more than a few seconds without 'turning the tables,' reverse the process and talking about their own problems instead; like to offer me solutions; can't stand it when people express feelings; try to protect me when I need to feel my feelings fully – in

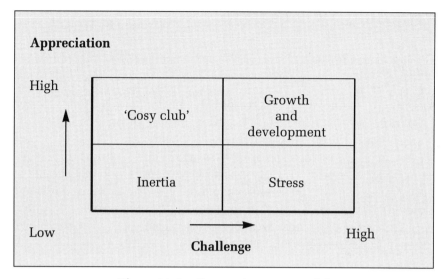

Figue 11.1   Support group model

other words do not really *respect* me. 'Respect' says it all for me: it implies they know I am strong enough to face the truth; handle my feelings and that I am creative enough to find my own solutions. Also I do not want someone as a supporter who will take sides or *collude* with me in any way – for example, with my tendencies to block myself; react inflexibly; resist change; forget my vision; look on the black side; underestimate myself or blame others instead of taking responsibility. I want supporters who will encourage me; believe in me; remind me of my vision; and challenge me gently but relentlessly; not protect me from the truth nor allow me to delude myself. That is the kind of person I can trust – someone with awareness and integrity.

A support group is a place where people are giving their very best to each other. We can't keep this up all the time in the heat of the kitchen – but we can and must do it in a support group.

Call it whatever you like

If you do not like the term 'support group' call it whatever you like. Call it a 'golden circle.' Julia Cameron describes 'Sacred Circles' in her superb book (Cameron, 1995).

Choosing membership

Whenever I get the chance – on a real time management develop-ment program, at a teamwork event, working one-to-one with people or when training them in facilitating skills – I encourage people to form support groups. A support group can consist of people from inside or outside their organization – ideally both. I simply ask them whose support they want or need and, if they name only two or three people, I ask again and again, if necessary. It is unwise to rely on only one or two people because it places too great a burden on them – especially if one is your partner. I also encourage the formation of support groups as one of the main workplaces during any workshop I facilitate. I invite people to choose their own membership. I offer the criteria listed in 11.2.

- Intuition – take first thoughts seriously.
- People you trust and admire.
- People different from you.
- People who will not collude with you.
- People who challenge you in some way. You may not find them 'comfortable.'
- A good mixture.
- People who can *listen*.

Figure 11.2   Criteria for selecting members

Avoiding the 'cosy club'

If a support group becomes a 'cosy club' it probably will not last long. Often people say: 'Let's meet for lunch or dinner' or 'have a drink together.' This is an enjoyable, nice thing to do. But this is leisure time, relaxation. It is not a support group meeting. In these conditions there are too many distractions to work rigor-ously. Nor is a support group a discussion group or a debating so-ciety. *The purpose of a support group is to help people transform their organizations, or society or their lives.*

Nor will it work unless there is sufficient time for each person (say four to six people) to get enough time for the work they want to do. Probably half a day or at least two hours is needed. Also someone needs to facilitate. The role of facilitator is to think about the group and its needs beforehand; find and arrange a venue (or delegate this task); plan and propose a simple structure or program; actively facilitate the group when needed; make sure everyone gets an equal amount of time to do their work; keep time; or appoint a time-keeper and plan an effective 'opening circle' and an appropriate 'closing circle' including a review, appreciations and agreeing a new date and venue. It is best to rotate the facilitator's role. This applies equally to the different roles of facilitating the meeting as a whole and facilitating individuals during the meeting – which everyone can do. Otherwise the group will encourage dependency on one or a few people supposedly good at it. That will ultimately lead to resentment and 'counter-dependency,' ie, rebellious or destructive behavior. And the group will miss the chance to develop *everyone's* facilitating skills. Another job of the facilitator is to be alert to the formation of collusive relationships. It needs to be 'one team,' ie, everyone giving their best to everyone else. I have been in support groups where the leader and another form a collusive pair. I was in another where one person was often left out of being asked to facilitate one-to-one. Ultimately this group didn't work well and broke up as a result. I have been in support groups where everyone seems artificially 'nice' – all hugs and appreciation. This can be a relief from the real world at first but in the end it made me feel sick and angry. Such a group does not survive long because people are not being sincere or authentic. I do not want to be attacked, criticized and abused – I am not a masochist – but I do want that essential balance between encouragement or warmth and challenge. I want 'real' people who are being authentic. Authenticity is fundamental to partnership and trust.

Basic processes for a support group

In some ways a support group meeting is like a teamwork event. Similar processes can be used. Yet of course a support group is not a team. The big difference is that the focus is on *supporting each individual* – not deciding a team's future direction and how each individual will support the team's purpose. The essential role of members of a support group is to give their collective attention, give each other a good listening to and everything in Chapter 9 applies.

First meeting

If the group has not met before, a good process for the first meeting may be for members simply to tell their life stories. For this purpose it may be helpful to suggest some headings (such as those given for introductions at the start of a real time management development workshop, see Chapter 6), or it may be better to leave it open. Then people may be invited to share their highest expectations of the support group; its purpose; their exciting vision for what it will be; what they want from it; the work they want to do; the kind of support they benefit from; and how often they want to meet. This can lead to defining its purpose and agreeing a charter or ground rules. Someone needs to record and distribute this. It is easy to forget purpose and ground rules. If trust is to develop, it is essential to contract on confidentiality.

Second meeting

At a second meeting it may be useful for each person to do the work of the Empowerment Model. This will enable each person to think through the situation they want to transform and decide the action they want to take. It also enables everyone to understand what each person is trying to do and the support they need (see Figure 11.3).

My experience is that it is better not to 'speak to the group' but instead to invite one person to facilitate you through this agenda. This empowers that person to help you through it in their own

- Major environmental forces my organization faces.
- How my organization is responding and its fundamental issues.
- My vision and purpose.
- My strategy.
- Key issues I need to tackle.
- Actions and support.

Figure 11.3 Developing vision and strategy

unique way; prompt you; encourage you; and help you with your blocks. They can't do that if everyone is 'pitching in.' I have often seen that happen and it can be very off-putting to the 'helper.' Though well intentioned it may arise from unaware competition. There needs to be agreement that others will not interrupt while this work is going on and that everyone will give their *complete* but silent attention. Silent attention is powerful. You can invite feedback from each person when you have finished your work. I think it needs to be stressed that a support group is *not* a discussion group. One way people can collude with each other and avoid real work is by having interesting academic discussions. That is not the best use of a support group – not its purpose. It is a big time-waster, and often a form of unaware resistance.

Subsequent meetings

Having done this groundwork, the primary purpose of subsequent meetings is to help members triumph over the ups and downs of making changes; celebrate their successes and work through difficulties; feel their feelings; fulfill their dreams and visions; learn and grow; and create new visions for their lives and work.

A useful agenda (based on Useful Questions Model) for each person to work on is given in Figure 11.4.

- Celebrate my successes.
- Talk about my difficulties, disappointments and feelings.
- Share information about how my environment has changed.
- Set new goals.
- Work on what will otherwise get in my way out there and especially in me.
- My commitments to action and support.

Figure 11.4 Reviewing progress

Reviewing

At the end of each piece of work it is useful to conduct a brief review of:

- What the helper did that worked.
- What the helper might do differently next time.

First the helper comments, then the 'client.' We talked about this in more detail in Chapter 9, there is no need to repeat it here.

'Opening circles' and 'closing circles'

Whoever is facilitating the meeting needs to propose a way of beginning. Their sense of where people are and their intuition will guide them as to what is appropriate, see Figure 11.5 for one pos-

- Why I am pleased to be here.
- Anything that is getting in the way of my being fully present.
- Two good things that have happened recently.
- What I want from our meeting.

Figure 11.5 Opening circle

sibility. I call it a circle because, the 'talking stick' goes round the circle, each person speaking when they want to without getting interrupted. The agenda of the meeting will emerge from what people say. They may want to follow Figure 11.4, or something else may emerge. It is important to sense how people are feeling during the meeting. Feelings may indicate that the process is working well or that a review is indicated. If the group is a large one, it is always possible to split into pairs or two or more smaller groups to do whatever work people want to do. Not everyone may want to do the same thing.

Endings are important. Figure 11.6 gives one possibility that focuses on what people have gained, what has helped the meet-

- What I have gained or learned today.
- What has worked.
- What I suggest we do or do differently next time.

Figure 11.6 Closing circle

- What I appreciate about (the person on the left).
- What I appreciate about myself.
- What I have appreciated about the way you have facilitated this event.

Figure 11.7 Appreciations

ing work and possible changes that are needed. It is useful to consciously keep improving and learning in this way. It will send everyone away feeling good if they not only encapsulate what they have gained but also give and receive appreciation – appreciate each other, themselves and the facilitator (see Figure 11.7).

It is rare to receive high quality appreciation. It can make such a difference to our work and our lives. We can learn more about our uniqueness in this way, also it is useful for us to 'own up to' what we appreciate about ourselves. It enhances our sense of ourselves and it is important that we really value our unique gifts – gifts we were given, gifts we offer the world. This can be difficult for many people.

It is funny how people often argue about any appreciation they are given just as much as they defend themselves against any criticism. It is best to receive both graciously, be open to it and reflect upon it. Difficulties in receiving either appreciation or criticism are forms of blockage which work against fulfilling our potential to achieve all we are capable of. It helps perhaps to see these difficulties as forms of resistance, ways in which we block ourselves.

Self-love, self-esteem

Self-love or, if you prefer, self-esteem is a crucial issue. I know that when I feel good about myself I function better in every way. I am more able to recover from set-backs, learn from difficulties, mistakes or criticism. I make wiser decisions; I am more relaxed; more generous, more flexible, more humorous and I am more my true self. I am more likely to achieve a good balance between my responsibilities and my own needs. I choose braver, bolder, more interesting options. I am less likely to think small or act on resentment. In short I am a more attractive and loving human being.

Yet most people I know struggle to maintain their self-esteem and sense of self-worth through the ups and downs of their lives. If we really loved ourselves, would our sense of well-being be so dependent on what other people thought about us, how successful we were, our status? For many people their sense of self-worth seems quite fragile. We painfully compare ourselves with others and measure our worth by the outward trappings of position, power, achievements. I know this sometimes applies to me. It is as if I am not really worth anything aside from my successes and achievements – a painful state of mind. I catch myself feeling bad as I compare myself with someone else, their successes, their skills, their car, their house, etc. How can I be so silly? I am unique and so is my contribution and my journey through life. This sort of comparison is pointless. Is the fragility of our egos at the root of greed, competitiveness, the desire to be right, dominate and control, to win the argument, know the answers, and our difficulty in admitting mistakes? Do we sometimes surround ourselves with elegant possessions to compensate for inner emptiness? I am sure I do. Do we try to make ourselves feel good by trying to be better than others? If so our security is extremely precarious. I suspect this is at the root of much of the adversarial, competitive and territorial behavior that bedevils real teamwork. There must be a better way. It is to find our security and sense of well-being within ourselves rather than outside. Then we may be able to be good stewards and better able to make responsible decisions.

It helps to belong to a support group in which people express their appreciation of you and love you for who you are, not for what you are, what you know or what you have achieved. You can learn to value yourself unconditionally. It helped me when one member of a support group said to me: 'Bruce, you don't have to do another damn thing to prove your worth.'

Trust your thinking – the principle of the first thought

We know a lot more than we think we know. Some of what we know is intuitive. There is a tendency to discount it because we cannot easily explain it or give reasons. Similarly, our dreams (our vision) are hard to explain and sometimes difficult to justify. Yet they are extremely important. Life is partly about fulfilling our dreams and this can be the most generous and responsible thing to do. It usually leads to giving our gifts. Why we want passionately to do these things and their importance may only become apparent in time. Often doubts set in either about our intuitive thinking or about what we deeply want to do. I have a constant doubter and critic in my head that I have to silence firmly. I need *believing* not *doubting* friends. I find I need good friends who will tell me: 'Trust your thinking – don't doubt it'; similarly: 'Trust your original vision – go for it.' Much the same applies to feelings. Often your feelings are telling you something extremely important. At the beginning you may not know what it is. I used to say to myself 'Stop being so unreasonable. Pull yourself together. Be like other people. Look at them, they all seem fine'. Now I ask myself 'What are my feelings telling me?' 'Why am I feeling so bored?' 'Why am I feeling low, not excited?' 'Why don't I want to do this?' It is no good arguing yourself out of your feelings. If you think 'Why do I feel so uncomfortable with this decision?' 'What deeply held values are being contradicted here?' perhaps your heart is telling you something. Again you need friends who will encourage you to accept the messages of your heart. You may need 'a good listening to' or 'morning pages' (Cameron, 1995) to find the answers.

If you are facilitating another member of your support group, questions like these are helpful:

- 'If you decide to trust your thinking completely what conclusion do you come to?'
- 'What would you do if you fully trusted your thinking?'
- 'If you decided to trust your vision completely, what would you do?'
- 'If you did not have to earn a living, what work would you do?'
- 'If you followed your heart, where would it take you?'

There is another technique I find useful. I will call it *the principle of the first thought*. You ask your client a key question and then you add: 'First thought?' The first thought is extremely important if you can catch it in that instant when it comes. It is the thought before self-doubt censors it. It can be censored so quickly you do not even notice it so you have to be quick! It is the intuitive thought; the most creative thought; the boldest idea; the gem; the ridiculous, outrageous, brilliant idea – before you block it.

Another helpful question is: 'What is the win–win solution?' or 'What is that elegant solution, whereby everyone gains?' I know I would want people in my support group who asked me questions like these. I would want wise friends. There is so much wisdom in Deepak Chopra's *The Seven Spiritual Laws of Success* and Julia Cameron's *The Artist's Way – A Spiritual Path to Higher Creativity.* I would encourage my support group to read both books.

You will remember from Chapter 7 that many of the support groups which started during Real Time Management Development programs or training in facilitation skills went on and on for years. I was in a support group for several years which we called the 'Golden Circle.' This group helped me take bold action as an internal consultant, later they helped me through the transition of starting my own business. It also helped me become a father who was better able to express my affection towards my children. As a person who had been taught not to talk about my feelings, not to share my most intimate concerns, especially not with men, and whose men friends and colleagues were similarly conditioned, the Golden Circle was a revelation to me. It lifted great burdens from my shoulders, also, I discovered I was normal – just like other men inside! What a relief! It was friends like these who for ten or more years kept telling me 'Bruce, you should write a book.' Finally, I believed them.

Networking – creating one team

One of the strategies I suggested in Chapter 5 is to develop widespread friendships in the organization and to network. Here I am suggesting that you build one-to-one relationships for a wide variety of purposes and encourage others to do so. Building relationships in this way promotes trust, awareness of other people's situations and needs, and understanding. Today, teams are constantly changing, and hence need to quickly re-form. If people have been networking extensively this happens more easily. The whole organization needs to be *one team*. Networking is a key way of bringing this about and helping people appreciate how interdependent they are. Networking is important to:

- Build a 'one team,' 'we are all interdependent partners' philosophy.
- Gain a better understanding of the organization and its key issues (whole system).
- Give support to people you respect and admire.
- Gain knowledge and expertise you need.
- Test out and gain support for initiatives you are trying to take.
- Get feedback you can trust.
- Influence, get things done, achieve your dreams and goals.
- Form partnerships with people in joint initiatives.
- Provide each other with mutual support for the changes you are making.

Some of these relationships have the potential to be in effect one-to-one support groups. All of them will be enhanced if they are of mutual benefit. To varying degrees you may be able to use your facilitating skills, the skills of the support group, to make these relationships more rewarding and to assist leaders who are trying to flourish in an uncertain environment and bring about beneficial change. It is an important way of exercising your choice and your leadership. By networking like this you can quietly teach people the skills of giving and getting a good listening to. Also, through your networking the benign universe will deliver your dreams.

References and suggested further reading

Cameron, J. (1995) *The Artist's Way – A Spiritual Path to Higher Creativity*, Pan Books, London, UK.

Chopra, D. (1994) *The Seven Spiritual Laws of Success*, Amber-Allen/New World Library, San Rafael, USA.

Chopra, D. (1993) *Ageless Body, Timeless Mind*, Rider, London, UK.

Egan, G. (1975) *The Skilled Helper*, Brooks/Cole Publishing, Pacific Grove, USA.

Handy, C. (1994) *The Empty Raincoat – Making Sense of the Future*, Hutchinson, London, UK.

Jackins, H. (1973) *The Human Situation*, Rational Island Publishers, Seattle, USA.

Oshry, B. (1995) *Seeing Systems – Unlocking the Mysteries of Organizational Life*, Berrett-Koehler, San Francisco, USA.

I wish to acknowledge how much I benefited and learned from being a member of Chris Bull's support group, the Golden Circle, at a critical point in my life.

12

Developing Widespread Facilitation Skills

The need for facilitation skills

There are many good reasons for developing widespread facilitation skills in today's organizations. The main ones are to bring out everyone's full potential, to help them work well together and to support people through change and uncertainty. One of the key tasks of today's managers is to support and facilitate their people. This strategy will equip them to fulfill this important role.

One of my clients told me that teams in her organization are changing so often that conventional team building is not appropriate. An organization that is as fluid as hers needs to be one team. People need to fully appreciate how interconnected they are and instinctively think about who they need to involve. They also need to be able to rapidly re-form into new teams, absorb new members or quickly form effective ad hoc project groups. It helps if good working connections between many people already exist.

Teaching people one-to-one facilitation skills can promote the sort of relationships my client wants to see. (This also argues the case for large-scale events.) It encourages widespread networking, breaks down barriers and builds trust between people in different parts of the organization. It helps them see how beneficial this can be and gives them an appetite for it. (The discredited 'old boy network' that oiled the wheels of commerce in by-gone times takes on a new meaning today.)

Teaching group facilitation skills can help members of teams or project groups more rapidly to bring new people in or establish themselves as a new group. It gives members the skills to do this. These are skills needed by managers and team members. Rotating the role of facilitator amongst team members can help develop their group facilitation skills. They should not usually have to call in experts to facilitate them. The job of 'experts' is to transfer their skills, coach their clients in doing it for themselves and help them when they are 'stuck' and really need someone from outside the system.

Another client, in the engineering business, wants to build a 'development culture.' Top management want people development to be seen as central to achieving their goal of gaining 'competitive advantage through people.' He believes that facilitation skills need to be part of every manager's toolkit. This has long been the philosophy of many well run companies.

People in the company live in a world of uncertainty and upheaval. This increases their need for support so they can respond positively to change. Yet flatter, more complex, less hierarchical structures make it harder for managers to meet this need amongst their people. There are simply too many of them. Thus peer mentoring or co-facilitating becomes important. There is a growing need for people to learn, not only to facilitate their staff but also each other. This can free up the time of managers for less frequent, strategically focused meetings and for 'walking the job.'

This company has substantial growth plans in Europe. Managers are already under enormous pressure and the fear is that they may get to breaking point unless they adopt new ways of coping. There is a need to grow people for more responsible and bigger roles. They have found that facilitating or helping is the core skill required for the effective mentoring and coaching that will help grow such people. For all these reasons, facilitating skills are increasingly important. They believe the better networking and good relationships that can result will also help people influence across boundaries, break down barriers and competition, create seamless manufacturing and build an organization in which people work together in partnership.

Using all the opportunities to develop one-to-one helping skills

There are all kinds of opportunities to develop people's one-to-one facilitation or helping skills. (Let's call a spade a spade. You may find it judicious to use a different word in your organization, especially at first, but 'helping' is a simple, unpretentious word and I like it for that reason.) I list some of them in Figure 12.1.

- Modeling good helping skills in your contacts with people in your organization.
- Encouraging people to pair up and listen to each other in turn as part of the process in meetings.
- Teaching, demonstrating and using helping skills in RTMD programs.
- Incorporating one-to-one listening into the processes of away days, retreats, team meetings and large group events.
- Using one-to-one helping in support groups and in networking.
- Including it as a key part of training for mentoring and coaching.
- Workshops to develop helping skills.

Figure 12.1 Using all the opportunities to develop one-to-one helping skills

Part of the task is to demonstrate to people just how valuable 'getting a good listening to' can be and how rewarding it is to give it. In my experience, most people readily appreciate the benefits if they get the experience of *doing it*. It requires someone to be bold enough to propose it and push through the initial embarrassment or resistance to a new or 'soft' idea. People discover that 'co-listening' in pairs can be an enlivening way of starting a meeting, can raise energy levels, help people process new information, deal with feelings of fear or resistance, decide what they really think and what they want to do. It can be a useful part of reviewing and ending a meeting as described in Chapter 10. It is a question of introducing people to a new practice and enabling them to discover its benefits. You can give them a simple briefing on how to do it and they will learn by doing, *real time*, in all these different situations.

Successfully introducing workshops to develop one-to-one helping skills

However, at some stage, people will benefit from training in greater depth. Real time workshops to develop helping skills could be an important part of your strategy to transform your company.

One successful workshop can be the start of an evolving program to develop widespread helping skills in your organization. Astutely introduced, this training is likely to prove extremely popular with managers. A demand for training in mentoring or coaching (words that are widely understood and accepted in organizations) may provide you with an entry point because helping is the underlying skill in both cases. Alternatively a successful RTMD program may lead to a demand for training in facilitation skills (both one-to-one and group) for managers.

In my experience there are certain requirements for successfully introducing workshops to develop one-to-one helping skills (see Figure 12.2). Starting with a pilot workshop enables you to gather together a group of potential champions and future workshop tutors who may well help to 'spread the good word' and initiate training in their own part of the organization. They usually appreciate being asked to collaborate with you in devel-

- Establish a clear link between developing helping skills and achieving business goals.
- Start with a pilot workshop for carefully selected participants.
- Involve influential managers in designing and delivering practical workshops.
- Use a *practical real time* approach, ie, ask the participants to bring their real issues and opportunities to work on in the workshops – do not use role playing.
- Give only short inputs and concentrate on learning by doing and reviewing.
- Work in small groups of three or four with a tutor.
- Enable people to learn by working in three roles in turn: helper; client and observer. Each role offers different learning opportunities.

Figure 12.2   Essentials for successful workshops in one-to-one helping

oping something that will be beneficial to their colleagues. In my experience, although most managers are intensely busy, they will still make the time for this work and they greatly value the opportunity to take some time out to stand back and take a look at some of the key issues. Involving one or two respected managers in designing and delivering the workshops helps make sure the design is appropriate to managers' needs, demonstrates the practicality and relevance of one-to-one helping, starts to create a cadre of tutors and equips managers to deliver workshops in their own part of the organization.

Using managers' own real issues and opportunities for the practical work in the workshops demonstrates the value of helping skills far better than contrived role plays. Managers go away from the workshop not only having developed their skills, they have also been *helped with their real problems and issues*. This convinces them of the value of one-to-one helping. Also there is far more to be learned from real, live situations that matter – as compared with imaginary, contrived role plays (trainers retain control!).

In my experience the absolute minimum length for an effective workshop for managers is about one and a half days. An outline of such a design is shown in Figure 12.3. In a workshop like this the priority is to teach Model B: The Facilitating Model described in Chapter 9. There may be time to briefly introduce other models such as Model C: The Empowering Model and Model E: The Reviewing Progress Model. In training consultants, a four- or five-day workshop may be justified in which case all the models offered in Chapter 9 can be introduced and practised.

The bulk of the workshop is best spent doing practical work in small groups of three or four, working with a tutor. Almost the whole of the second day is used in this way. The previous half day is spent putting the workshop in context, establishing the importance of facilitating skills in achieving company goals, agreeing objectives for the workshop, building a climate of trust and safety in which people can work on important and, often, sensitive personal issues, presenting and discussing Model B: The Facilitating Model and enabling people to get to know each other and form small groups of their own choice. Although participants will have been previously briefed, they may need some help to get used to the idea that they will be working on their own real issues and opportunities. They will also need an explanation of how the practical work in small groups will be con-

DAY 1		
4.00	Session 1	**Introduction and contracting**
		• Objectives, approach and agenda.
		• Very brief introductions or 'opening circle.'
		• Building the climate and behavior to work and learn effectively.
4.30	Session 2	**The importance of helping skills**
		• Why these skills are so important. Relevance to business goals.
		• Hopes and vision for the strategy that will emerge from this first workshop.
4.45	Session 3	**The facilitating model**
		• Explanation of the five-stage Model B.
		• Briefing on small-group work.
5.30	Session 4	**Getting to know each other and forming small groups**
		• Self-introductions, sharing issues people want to work on.
		• Forming small groups.
		• Planning preparation for tomorrow.
6.30		**Finish followed by dinner**
DAY 2		
8.30	Session 5	**Practical work in small groups**
		• Opening review in whole group.
		• Work in small groups: stages 1–3 of Model B.
		• Review of learning and discussion of issues in whole group.
		• Presentation of further models.
12.30		**Lunch**
1.15	Session 6	**Further practical work**
		• Work in small groups: stages 4–5 of Model B.
		• Planning individual action to continue learning and promote one-to-one helping.
3.45	Session 7	**Review of workshop**
		• Sharing plans. Reviewing workshop.
4.00	Session 8	**Thinking about strategy**
		• Planning an emerging strategy to develop widespread one-to-one helping skills.
4.30		**Finish**

Figure 12.3   Generic design for a one-and-a-half-day workshop

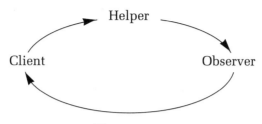

Figure 12.4

ducted and the three roles everyone will experience in turn. Starting on the previous day will give people the opportunity to assimilate Model B: The Facilitating Model and prepare themselves for the practical work on day two.

The second day will be largely devoted to practical work and learning from it. The members of each small group will take turns as helper, client and observer (see Figure 12.4). This is probably the best sequence as helper is the most demanding role and being an observer provides a relative break before taking a turn as client. Each role provides rich and different opportunities for learning. Also, as I have said before, learning to be a good client is as important as learning to be a good helper. A group of three is probably ideal – in a day everyone gets two good chunks of time in each role. After each practice session a review is held and another review of learning takes place at the end of the morning. Learning is then shared in the plenary or large group. One option is for people to work through the first three stages of Model B: The Facilitating Model in the morning and the final two in the afternoon. It is important to have the morning and afternoon sessions, ie, 'two bites at the cherry.' If everyone has a second turn as helper in the afternoon, they can incorporate what they learned from the first attempt in the morning. It is important to give people the satisfaction of doing better the second time, otherwise they have not had an opportunity to put their learning into practice. This is one reason why I regard a one-and-a-half day workshop as absolute minimum.

After the second session of practical work, it is important to give participants time to make and share individual action plans and to contribute to planning a strategy for the further development of one-to-one helping skills in the organization. Their individual plans are likely to include arranging regular support meetings or networking with other participants or colleagues;

and taking the initiative to tutor on or lead similar workshops in their part of the organization or for their teams. They are likely to recommend further workshops and many of the participants will offer themselves as tutors. For these things to happen requires gentle pushing from the workshop leaders.

I have found that this strategy for introducing workshops in one-to-one helping almost invariably works as long as whoever is responsible for training and development or internal consulting *keeps up the momentum*. This requires gentle pushing, ie, *leadership* from the internal consultant. Without that it won't just happen. This means matching the growing enthusiasm of managers with the necessary overall leadership and support (including budget). An important part of such an emerging strategy is to let go of central control and encourage managers to own the work and develop it in the business in their own way.

Developing group facilitation skills

Group facilitation skills are needed just as much as one-to-one facilitating skills. As with one-to-one skills, it is smart to recognize and use all the opportunities to develop these skills (see Figure 12.5).

There is a natural progression which can be used in training people for any kind of facilitation (one-to-one, group or to facilitate RTMD programs) (see Figure 12.6). Astute judgments need to be made as to whether and when people are ready to move to the last two stages.

- Modeling good practice when facilitating groups and explaining what you are doing.
- Gradually handing over the facilitator role when working with small groups on RTMD or other workshops.
- Using participants as facilitators in small groups in all kinds of events and workshops. Rotating the role.
- Having participants at large-scale events take turns to facilitate, record, keep time and report back from their small groups.
- Involving participants in the design of events.

Figure 12.5 Using all the opportunities to develop group facilitation skills

- Experience as a participant.
- Experience in small group facilitation.
- Co-facilitating a medium or large group with an experienced leader.
- Working as leading facilitator* with less or more experienced facilitators.

*The leading facilitator has overall responsibility for the event and leading, supporting and coaching other facilitators.

Figure 12.6   Four-stage training for facilitators

Notice that all these ways of developing group facilitation skills are *learning by doing.* Can there be any real learning without it? If learning by doing is to be effective, regular reviews of what is working, what is difficult and what needs to be done differently are essential. Also experienced support and coaching need to be available. 'Shadow consulting' can be provided too, ie, someone who is not actually present at the event but who can provide support before it takes place, is available on a phone line during breaks and can help in reviewing it afterwards.

Workshops in group facilitation skills

There is also likely to be a place for practical workshops in group facilitation. This can be in the form of 'mini' workshops as part of the preparation for an actual event, or full scale workshops of two or more days can be arranged if there are enough people needing this training. It will work best if participants are preparing to do facilitating work in their organizations, ie, the workshops are a stage in a strategy. They can then use the workshops to plan, design, prepare and skill themselves for work they are about to do. They will bring this work into the workshops as real material.

A useful design for a workshop in group facilitation skills will, as far as possible, model or demonstrate good group work in terms of its structure and processes; demonstrate good facilitation; provide experience of group processes; provide opportunities for participants to facilitate the group; and opportunities for them to plan, work on and prepare themselves for group work they will actually do or are doing out there in the business. This may mean practicing or rehearsing and getting advice and feedback. Chapter 10 provides material for 'inputs' that may be required, however, additional information follows that may be useful to potential group facilitators:

Some additional models for group work

Following the model given in Figure 12.7 will enable a facilitator to be clear about the stages a group (new or existing) will go through and what the tasks of each stage are. This will help the facilitator plan and respond appropriately. She/he will also know

Stages	Focus
1. *Forming*	• orientation. • dealing with anxiety, trust and safety issues. • relationships with leader(s) and other members. • ground rules and behavior. • purpose, structure and boundaries.
2. *Storming*	• conflict between individual needs and group cohesion. • testing the leader's capability often expressed in rebellion, inter-group conflicts and resistance.
3. *Norming*	• group cohesion develops. • ways of working, shared norms and values are developed and mutual support is expressed.
4. *Performing*	• conflict between individual needs and group cohesion is resolved. • the group functions well and the task is performed.
5. *Mourning*	• the focus is on ending, expressing grief and transition to a new environment.

Figure 12.7   The stages of group development

that the group's behaviour is not a personal reaction to her/him but part of what any group needs to do. This will help to *not take reactions personally* – an essential part of a facilitator's repertoire.

Petrushka Clarkson's article 'Group Imago and the Stages of Group Development' in *Group Relations,* provides useful guidance about what facilitator behavior will be destructive and constructive at each stage (Clarkson, 1991). In general terms it will help if the facilitator is aware of what the stages are and allows them to happen; provides clear and appropriate guidance or direction to the group; is relaxed and confident; is not defensive or blaming; and does not take the group's behavior personally. 'I'm okay, you're okay' as a life position gets severely tested at stage 2. Sometimes it may help to explain what the stages are so that the group is more aware. Eric Berne's writing provides further insights (Berne, 1963).

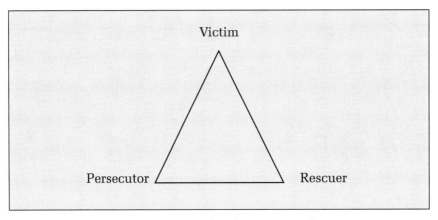

Figure 12.8   The drama triangle

Another useful model (see Figure 12.8) was introduced by S. B. Karpman (Berne, 1975). It is particularly useful for a facilitator to bear in mind at stage 2 – Storming! This describes the three 'reactive' positions. Rather than responding in an 'adult' (Harris, 1973) or appropriate way, we get 'hooked' into behavior that is counterproductive and based on habitual patterns from the past. For example at stage 2, a facilitator may get frustrated, lose her/his 'cool' and bully, criticize or blame the group. This is stepping into the persecutor role which will soon lead to the facilitator becoming the victim. Or the facilitator may step into the rescuing mode. This will not help to empower participants. The facilitator is then

1. **Pseudo-community** Most groups spend most of their time here having low energy, pretending differences do not exist, getting on with the task in polite and amicable ways, and avoiding underlying issues.

2. **Chaos** The frustrations of stage 1 can take the group into this more energetic state. At this stage people attempt to obliterate differences by trying to persuade others to their point of view. There is no space for people to be themselves. Awareness of group processes is lost in a competitive struggle to come out on top.

3. **Emptiness** There are two ways out of chaos – either by going back to stage 1 or by emptying, ie, giving up the belief that we know what is best, letting go of control and instead being authentic and open and respecting difference. If enough people decide to let go in this way, a high level of trust and acceptance can lead the group into stage 4.

4. **Community** This stage is characterized by a high level of authenticity. Conflict can be dealt with effectively and it is easier to manage task and process simultaneously. Differences are welcomed and learnt from and healing takes place. In other words the group functions well and becomes fully effective.

Note: This figure is based on notes provided by the Foundation for Community Encouragement.

Figure 12.9   Stages in community building

likely to become exasperated, step into the persecutor role and end up as victim. All three roles are unhealthy positions. They are ways of *avoiding* honest contact, taking responsibility and making changes. Being aware of these traps helps us avoid them. Scott Peck (1987) offers another model (see Figure 12.9) which bears some similarity to The Stages of Group Development.

I found this model useful in helping me understand that chaos may be a necessary stage before really effective functioning can take place – not to be afraid of it but to facilitate the group through it, being confident that it can lead to group effectiveness. Trying to push the group back into pseudo-community will not help. I found I was able to use this wisdom with some clients just two days after attending the Foundation for Community Encouragement workshop!

Bill Thatcher of the Foundation for Community Encouragement has pointed out to me that movement through these stages is not linear; nor is it a one-time process. Groups may start at stage 2; move from 4 back into 2. A 'normal' group will move between the stages over and over again. Identification of the stages can help a group decide where it is and whether it wants to stay at a particular stage or move on. That certainly fits my experience.

So much of group facilitation is simply being a presence, representing confidence that the group will work through the appropriate stages. It is also the facilitator's task to provide useful broad structures and, sometimes, well-judged direction and to share what she/he observes (without judgment) to heighten awareness. To do this well requires you to be relaxed and confident, firm yet flexible and perhaps most of all, to have sufficient self-esteem not to get 'hooked' into persecutor, victim or rescuer behavior. You need to be able to contain your feelings and use them as interesting data.

References, suggested further reading and resources

Berne, E. (1963) *The Structure and Dynamics of Organizations and Groups*, Grove Press, New York, USA.

Berne, E. (1975) *What Do You Say After You Say Hello?* Corgi, London, UK.

Clarkson, P. (1991) 'Group Image and the Stages of Group Development,' *Group Relations*, the Journal of the Group Relation Training Association, Vol. 2, No. 3, March.

Harris, T. A. (1973) *I'm OK – You're OK*, Pan, London, UK.

Peck, Scott M., (1987) *The Different Drum*, Rider, London, UK.

The Foundation for Community Encouragement, USA. 001–206/784–9000 and Community Building in Britain, 44(0)1635–47377.

13

Using the External Consultant Wisely
A fruitful partnership

'Marriage seems like a useful metaphor for what we are trying to create at work. Imagine a long, successful marriage in which two strong people choose to spend their lives together, working through their common issues towards some shared higher goals. It is not always peaceful because the two are so different. There are peaks and valleys, pain and progress, all accompanied by individual growth because of the relationship. Each finds the other's perspective alternately crazy or mystifying, unreasonable or principled, ignorant or enlightened. Through time the bond between the two grows, the respect grows, the trust and openness grow. A successful marriage holds out the possibility that two people with quite different interests can deal with each other on an equal basis, in an interdependent way, choosing to depend on each other. Many of us can learn something from the work we are doing within our marriage, take that learning to work, and apply it to our relationships with our management, our customers, and other key players.' Geoffrey Bellman.

Why use an external consultant?

The relationship between an insider who is facilitating organizational transformation and an external consultant can be an empowering and rewarding one. It can make all the difference. But how can you justify the time and cost involved?

- Facilitating you in making a bold organizational diagnosis and in developing a challenging strategy.
- Giving you the skills and confidence to deliver the strategy.
- Giving you long-term support to think wisely and persist.
- Providing the perspective of someone outside the system.
- Doing work which really demands someone from outside the system.

Figure 13.1   The difference the external consultant can make

Remember, there are always powerful forces within an organization resisting change and socializing you into conformity. Also, whilst structural changes can be made rapidly, making changes in the culture of an organization and the attitudes and behavior of people may take much longer. People may want to do things differently but they also have a lot of resistance. For all these reasons it is extremely hard for someone inside the system to change it without support from outside.

My experience, first as an internal consultant for many years, and later as an external consultant, is that there are essentially five ways in which a good external consultant can help (see Figure 13.1). Having external support when you are making your diagnosis and developing your strategy will help you fully trust your thinking, break free of the conforming influence of the organization and take bold (and yet astute) decisions about strategy. An outsider can also challenge you where you need to be challenged. Often they can see things clearly which you are too close to see. When I worked with my last employer, I had difficulty fully trusting my thinking and summoning the courage to take the bold action that was required. I was not unique in this respect! Yet I did take that bold action, partly because I had solid external support over a long period.

You may not yet have the skills or experience to do some of the things required (such as real time management development or large group interventions) and it will help to work alongside and in partnership with an external consultant in developing such interventions. I believe much better work will be done if the external consultant does the work *with* you rather than *for* you. Each of you has something unique to contribute which will make for a far better outcome. You, the internal consultant, have a unique understanding of the organization, a wide network of contacts, trust and credibility and you provide leadership. The external consultant's experience and confidence gained from having done these things before may give you and your organization that degree of safety needed to successfully take a step into the unknown. But I believe the job of the external consultant is to work with you, hand over these skills to you and then step aside, make way for you to do it yourself. She/he needs the confidence and maturity to know when to withdraw.

However there may be some work that really demands someone from outside the system. Top management may feel it needs an outsider. Sometimes you may simply not be able to help your clients with issues that need the help of someone from outside. You may be too close to the problems, too much part of the system to see the issues clearly, too easily seduced into colluding with your clients. This is a judgment which you and they need to make wisely. It may be a good solution for you and the external consultant to facilitate together.

Although the external consultant has withdrawn from working alongside you directly with your clients, you may still benefit from long-term support or 'shadow consulting,' ie, someone who helps you review your work, work through blockages (your own and the organization's) and decide what new directions need to be taken. My experience is that in the early, exciting phases of organizational transformation, things often go well. There is a great deal of optimism, energy and enthusiasm. Gradually, dependence and resistance can take their toll on you. Often the internal facilitator grows weary, stale and gets 'stuck.' There may be problems in transferring ownership to the clients. Mistakes are bound to have been made, difficulties and setbacks experienced. Wise advice may not have been taken (people need to do things in their own way and find out for themselves). Perhaps at this point the organization is confronted with some of its most fundamental difficulties yet may be unaware that this is happening. Often at this stage there may be a desire to avoid issues and try something different, offload the external consultant and try someone else – to look for another way, a better magician who will do a better job and rescue us. Or the organization may decide to continue without outside help. It questions whether the outsider is adding value and believes it *should* do it without outside help. Perhaps that will be another way of avoiding. You may collude with that and believe they should manage without support. That may be your blockage. All this will be happening without awareness. It is a critical point in the transformation work – a crossroads. One road can lead to avoidance and ultimately cynicism. The other can lead to a deeper relationship with the external consultant, deeper learning for the organization and ultimately success. It takes wisdom and maturity to decide astutely that you need to bring back the external consultant to help overcome the blocks.

Phases in the relationship

Another process is going on which affects the relationship with the external consultant. Geoffrey Bellman reminded me of a model (Bellman, 1992) which illuminates what tends to happen in the relationship between client and consultant (see Figure 13.2). It also casts light on family relationships and relationships between leaders and their teams.

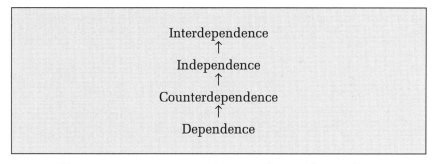

Figure 13.2   Four stages in consulting relationships

The client/consultant relationship begins with the client in a relationship of dependence on the consultant to provide expertise and support. The relationship is not as simple as that of course because the consultant is heavily dependent on the client to provide her/him with work, income and opportunity for fulfillment and learning. And the client always has the upper hand. So both parties are in fact dependent on each other. The wise consultant will work from the position of empowering the client and handing over her/his skills and expertise, thus enabling the client to do the work for her/himself with a view to ultimate interdependence and partnership. This first phase is usually very rewarding and enjoyable. The next stage is the prelude to moving out of dependence and it may be characterized by conflicts and what might be described as 'irrational' behavior. This can be painful for the consultant who is highly dedicated to the work and has enjoyed a constructive and rewarding relationship. It seems strange how two people who got on well now seem to have difficulties which can only be explained by something going on at an unaware, unconscious level.

The next stage is when the client in one way or another breaks loose and declares independence. They no longer feel they need your help. This is where 'shadow consulting' or support role may be appropriate but the client may decide to have none of it. It is quite possible that the work may actually suffer as a result of the client's independence. But this stage is in the nature of things. The client may well do the work extremely successfully. Or the client may look for a different 'mentor,' putting her/himself back into the dependent stage but with someone else. This may be painful for the first consultant. Finally, the client/consultant relationship may mature into interdependence – the strongest and most constructive position for relationships at work and in the home.

> *'This is where we choose, out of strength and trust, to rely on others as we do our joint work. Interdependence means choosing to depend on another not because you cannot stand on your own but because you see it as more effective to undertake this part of your work and your life in partnership with someone else.'* G. Bellman (1992).

If you can achieve it, this is a mature relationship of equals, where there is real honesty, sharing of responsibility, lack of pretense, admission of difficulties and not knowing what to do, not expecting perfection or putting the external consultant on a pedestal, ready forgiveness of mistakes and learning from each other. It is joint exploration, a journey together. Often the relationship does not reach this stage or does so only after a break. This is a pity because I really believe that successful consulting work benefits greatly from a long-term partnership between the internal and external consultant. The work benefits from a relationship with someone who has a growing understanding of the organization and its difficulties. As in any relationship, there is much to be gained and much to be learned from working through, rather than avoiding, difficulties.

With the benefit of past experiences, I now often think to myself: 'Will this client let me stay with them long enough to achieve a successful outcome? Or will they unintentionally sabotage the work by dropping me too soon? What can I do to prevent this without seeming to be clinging to the work?'

As we have said before, awareness helps considerably. At the beginning of a long-term piece of work it is a wise investment for the internal and external consultant to share their expectations and vision for the relationship – how they want it to evolve, their respective roles and how they can best support each other. This can create a kind of charter. This discussion can be informed by the four-stage model, then both will be aware of the phases the relationship is likely to go through and better able to talk openly about any difficulties that may emerge and manage it constructively. They will be able to agree the best role for the external consultant at each stage. It will also be wise to plan regular reviews of how the relationship is working and what constructive steps they want to take. It may be difficult to spend time and money doing this but, considering how much is at stake in a long-term intervention, it is a wise investment. It may also be wise for the external consultant to arrange for external support or supervision to be available for her or himself. The external consultant can get stuck too!

When I started thinking about this chapter, a number of themes entered my mind:

Congruence

If we want to influence our clients in the organization for the better, then how we (the external and internal consultant) behave with each other – our relationship – matters greatly. Our clients will be more influenced by our actions than our words. They will be watching to see whether what we do matches what we say. This will be fundamental to our credibility and the trust people put in us. That became a problem in the work described in Case study 2 in Chapter 7. It was not a problem at first but it became one when the consulting team changed its membership.

- In the way we work we will involve our clients and seek to win their hearts and minds.
- We will empower and enable each other, model partnership and work for the same relationship with our clients.
- We will demonstrate the benefits of valuing difference in the way we work together and with our clients.
- We will rejoice in unpredictability and uncertainty, respond with creative flexibility and help our clients do the same.
- We will demonstrate being passionate about our work and loving each other and our clients.
- We will take a long-term perspective towards our work and demonstrate an attitude of stewardship.

Figure 13.3 Draft charter for a transforming partnership

Principles

If the principles for business set out in Chapter 2 are valid and I intend to be congruent, then they need to govern my relationships with my clients. They may need to be adapted to fit this kind of relationship but they should still stand. Perhaps they could be modified to form a draft charter for the relationship between internal and external consultants and their clients (see Figure 13.3).

Love

This is a difficult word to use in the context of business and I notice my embarrassment. It sounds soft and sentimental, but that is nonsense. Basically, it just means caring a great deal and acting accordingly – cherishing the work we are doing as a precious opportunity and cherishing each other. When I reflect on the best work I have done with clients, we have done it with passion and, yes, loving support for each other. People doing transformation work are undertaking something so difficult they need a special kind of support. Cold professionalism is not enough to enable people to do great things. We have been both supportive and nurturing *and* rigorous and challenging. It goes back to Mary's balance of gentle encouragement and the loving boot! This is not easy. Being authentic may feel very risky for the consultant. It may end the partnership. Because of the four phases, the relationship may enter a stormy time before interdependence is achieved. The consultant has to hang in there, as we do with our teenage children, being authentic without interfering too much – a delicate judgment. Children don't usually break with their parents. Clients do sack their consultants – sometimes just when the work is entering its most critical phase. It will help if both parties are aware, as I suggested earlier.

A long-term relationship

I must admit I prefer long-term partnerships. I do not particularly enjoy doing short-term pieces of work. That is both a strength and a limitation. I do not really believe skill development workshops make much of a difference to transforming an organization, except as part of a long-term strategy, although they may help individuals. So I declare my personal bias.

On the whole, transformation work takes a sustained effort over a long time. It is facilitated by a long-term relationship with an external consultant who helps you develop a long-term strategy and supports you through the ups and downs of seeing it through. That consultant becomes increasing valuable as she/he gains a deepening understanding of the organization and of you, the leader or internal consultant, and can lightly and humorously help you deal with your blockages.

You may learn a lot about different approaches and add to your repertoire of skills by working with a succession of external consultants. But that will not necessarily help with the hard work of transforming an organization. Acquiring knowledge and skills is interesting but what makes a difference is using them. You need to ask yourself whether there is something you are avoiding by having a succession of partners or constantly searching for different approaches.

Because of all the hazards along the way, and the danger of getting too close and too involved in the system and its difficulties, the external consultant may need supervision. The best consultant has to be completely there and present for the client and yet, at the same time, able to stand outside the situation. This can be difficult to do over a long period of time, especially when we are deeply involved and committed and our living, our reputation for competence and our self-esteem are on the line. It is hard to detach yourself if you care a lot about what you are doing. And yet, if you do care passionately, detaching yourself and letting go may be precisely what you have to do.

Finally, can I put in a perspective here from the view point of the external consultant? It seems to me that more and more success-ful organizations are valuing their suppliers as important stake-holders – as important as customers, employees and other stake-holders. They invest in their suppliers, aim for long-term relationships with them and treat them fairly and well. It is not an exploitative relationship because, in the long term, that will not work or produce value and quality. Shall I say I have not al-ways felt treated as a valued and highly esteemed supplier, par-ticularly after a specific piece of work has come to an end? Simple things make a big difference to the relationship and do much for the image of the organization (suppliers are usually customers too). For example: being paid on time or early; re-sponding to phone messages (after the work is ended); investing the time to review a piece of work when it is finished and rigor-ously decide whether the goals were achieved, what can be learned and what further steps need to be taken; keeping in touch to brief the consultant on progress and review further opportunities for collaboration; and jointly reviewing the fee rate, rather than bargaining it down as low as possible. Remember, the external consultant's 'huge' fees have to cover pension, vacations, sick pay, frequent unpaid work, office ser-vices and a car – all usually covered by your package. A partner-ship that feels exploitative or instrumental is a contradiction in terms. You need win–win relationships with suppliers as excel-lent companies have discovered.

I have tried to describe a fruitful partnership between an inter-nal and external consultant from both their perspectives. Awareness always seems to help us make sensible choices. Also, awareness may help two partners develop a vision of how they want their relationship to be and, if difficulties arise, explore them frankly and openly, without blame. That will require being really honest first with ourselves and then with each other.

References and suggested further reading

Bellman, G. (1992) *Getting Things Done When You Are Not in Charge*, Berrett-Koehler, San Francisco, USA.

14

❖

How to Avoid Avoiding

'Why would you expect that to be a smooth and predictable process? You have created flux, instability. In that instability lies hope – the hope of creating new patterns that will be more satisfactory for all. Don't run away from flux. Work with it. It is the sound of the old dance shaking.' Barry Oshry.

'You can't create light without casting a shadow.' Anon.

'Destructive forces will prevail unless you bring them into the light.' Anon.

Resistance is part of being human

When I started out as a consultant, one of my friends told me:

'The one thing you can be sure of is that there will be resistance. It's just a question of what form it will take and when it will happen.'

Sometimes I think, if it were not for resistance, our work as leaders or facilitators of change would be a joy. There is nothing like a client who knows how to use you well and gets on with whatever needs to be done – or a team who enjoy and respond to good leadership. And yet if it were like this all the time, how boring and unreal it would be. Also it might be dangerous if people did not resist – I am thinking of Europe in the 1930s and 1940s.

'For the triumph of evil, it is only necessary that good men do nothing.' Edmund Burke.

Resistance is inevitable and probably essential. It serves a function. Without it people and organizations would lack stability.
They would rush first in one direction and then in another, chas-
ing one fad or fashion and then another – precisely what some
people and organizations do! Habits (which are a component of
resistance because changing involves developing new habits)
serve a purpose as long as they continue to be appropriate and
functional. They help embed changes. Because we don't have to
think about what is habitual, it gives us space to think about
those other things that do require our attention. It is when they
cease to be functional and block desirable or essential changes
that habits become a problem. Perhaps when we talk about 'resistance' what we really mean is 'avoidance' or the way in which
we 'block' ourselves, get in our own way.

None of us is immune to resistance in the sense of avoidance.
We can perhaps more easily spot resistance that is blocking other
people rather than our own. Yet I know I am resistant in many
ways. Sometimes this has saved me from doing things I did not
want to do, that were not in my best interest, but, equally I find it
hard to give up my various addictions (such as far too many cap-
puccinos and croissants) although I know it would be good for
me to do so. And I still have not made that appointment for a fitness assessment at my local sports center. I know it would be
good for me.

Healthy and dysfunctional resistance

On the one hand there is *healthy*, functional resistance and on the
other resistance that is *dysfunctional*. For example it is *healthy*
when people want to critically assess whether a proposed change
will actually lead to improvement; explore the consequences for
them; and look at other options. It is healthy not to want to be
controlled or made to do something. It is natural to be un-
enthusiastic about change which may adversely affect you or decisions in which you have played no part. It is entirely human
and natural to need to deal with feelings of regret, anxiety or fear.
Suspicion and distrust are natural if there has been a history of
not disclosing all the information or probable consequences.

Resistance is usually *dysfunctional* when people: avoid dealing
with issues that confront them (unless they do not feel safe

enough to do so); decline to work on inevitable changes; engage in sabotage when offered opportunities to be involved in deciding what should be done; decline to work collaboratively with others to find ways forward; and blame and criticize others but decline to make alternative proposals themselves or take initiatives. There may be a history which readily explains why they are doing this. When people resist in these ways, the role of the leader or facilitator is not an easy one. Resistance of this kind – which can be extremely frustrating and sometimes unpleasant to deal with because it can involve attacking the leader or consultant – is often unintentional. People are not always fully aware of what they are doing or that their behavior results from something going on at a deeper level. Often the underlying causes are fear, panic, distrust, hopelessness or feelings of powerlessness. They are doing what they are doing because they would prefer to avoid facing these painful feelings. Yet avoidance is ultimately more painful because it prolongs the pain. Avoidance is not usually a healthy strategy for coping with change, but it can be a wise decision if the person is not yet ready to work on the issue. The choice must always be with the client. It is not helpful to pressure the client and it will not work. It may help, though, to point out the choice.

Planning and designing to work with resistance

I nearly headed this section 'Avoiding resistance,' then I thought again. That would not be a healthy stance. So much of this book has been about planning change and designing our work in ways that take account of resistance and avoid creating it unnecessarily. I try to design unnecessary resistance out of the system, not create it. But the principle of unpredictability will ensure you never succeed completely! It is still worth attempting and Figure 14.1 gives some ways of doing so.

To elaborate the first two points: I believe that as internal or external consultants it does not make sense to expend our energies with people who do not use our skills to advantage. It is exhausting and unproductive. There are always others who will use us well. Similarly, a leader needs a well chosen team. It is no good battling on with people who are destructive. I do not mean avoiding healthy difference and conflict.

- If you are a consultant, choosing clients who are not chronically resistant to change.
- If you are a leader, choosing team members most of whom are not resistant to change (perhaps you need some).
- Involving people fully at every stage of planning and implementing change and gaining their willing commitment.
- Enabling people to express their diverse views and find common ground.
- Using processes that empower people, give them choice and do not bring out 'dependency' or 'counter-dependency.'
- Transferring ownership to your clients or workforce.
- Building in opportunities for people to express their feelings, eg, anger, fear, anxiety, distrust, grief and powerlessness.
- Building trust and creating safety for people to express their thoughts and feelings with impunity.
- Building awareness about how human beings typically react to change.
- Providing opportunities for people undergoing change to give each other support.
- Being completely honest and trustworthy.
- Being firm about vision, values, purpose and direction but flexible and creative about strategy and actions.
- Modeling an attitude of welcoming change and upheaval!

Figure 14.1   Designing resistance out of the system

Handling resistance when it happens

'With awareness comes choice.' Barry Oshry.

So what can you do when resistance occurs? Typical forms of resistance are where people are:

- Declining to do the work that needs to be done.
- Expressing complacency.
- Colluding with each other in avoiding things.

- Rejecting constructive leadership that is offered.
- Blaming, criticizing or attacking the leader or facilitator.
- Fighting or competing with each other rather than agreeing on a way forward.

These are all ways of avoiding things. Bion's classic writings about his experiences in groups in the 1940s and 1950s make fascinating if somewhat difficult reading (Bion, 1992). He talks of 'fight' or 'flight' as two basic ways of avoiding responsibility or learning. I found it reassuring to read about how difficult he found this very same situation. There are a number of possible ways of facilitating the situation constructively – see Figure 14.2.

Russ Vince and Linda Martin offer an illuminating model (Vince, and Martin, 1993) which I have slightly modified in Figure 14.3. This model demonstrates the emotional, as opposed to rational, aspects of transforming or learning. Underlying resistance is our anxiety – our clients' and our own.

- Not intervening – just confidently staying with them while they express or act out their resistance and move through it.
- Stating what you observe without judgment or criticism.
- Offering an interpretation without judgment or criticism.
- Saying what you think is the choice facing the group.
- Making a proposal, accepting that while people may initially resist it, they may accept it in time.
- Not giving people cause to feel you are trying to make them do anything.
- Being humorous, relaxed and confident in the ultimate wisdom of your clients.
- Not getting angry, taking it personally, becoming victim, persecutor or rescuer.
- Proposing a break.
- Give yourself a good listening to.
- In a break work on the situation with your co-facilitator or call a trusted friend.

Figure 14.2   Constructive ways of facilitating resistance

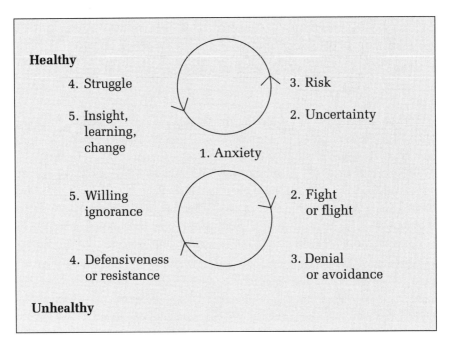

Figure 14.3   The choice we have

It shows the choice participants will almost certainly face more than once in an event or process of transformation. There is likely to be a 'strategic moment' when our clients can choose between going with uncertainty, risk, struggle and ultimately learning or changing *and* fight or flight, denial or avoidance, defensiveness or resistance and not learning or changing. Our job is to intervene in the best way we can at that strategic moment when this choice presents itself and, to quote Russ, 'hold them on that ground.' It may help if, at a cooler moment, you have prepared them for this situation. You can use the model to build greater awareness of what is likely to happen. The model will also inform you about what is happening at an emotional level at that crucial moment when resistance is the big issue in the room. Russ comments that he is not sure that willing ignorance is always an 'unhealthy' choice. Sometimes ignorance is bliss in organizations (and life). I wonder whether this is true in the case of organizations. Yet no matter what you or I think, the choice will always be the client's. It is our job to draw their attention to that choice – no more.

I think you have to be prepared for *any* observation, interpretation or proposal you make to be resisted – at least initially. (Much will depend on how much trust they have in you and they may be testing you.) If so, perhaps you just have to stay with the situation, confident and relaxed (despite how you feel inside!) and wait for wisdom to prevail, perhaps in the form of constructive interventions from a few participants. But maybe that will not happen and the group will just get into a very messy situation which they may or may not come out of. It has to be their choice. 'You win some and you lose some' as they say. After what I thought at the time was a 'disaster,' I have had people come up and say how much they learned. Sometimes benign and constructive forces are not the most vociferous!

Being authentic is recommended, yet so is containing feelings. A fine judgment needs to be made about when to express or describe your feelings (without blaming or judging) and when this will be constructive and when it will not. If you do it, you need to be extremely honest and look beneath the anger which almost certainly covers fear, anxiety or some other emotion. I have often seen participants transform a situation for the better by saying how they feel – particularly when they do so with authenticity and without blaming the other person. When the facilitator does so, it is more likely to be interpreted as blaming or judging, more likely to create a situation that undermines safety and trust. It is often constructive when the facilitator accurately picks up and expresses feelings that are in the room – felt but not yet orally expressed by others. It has helped others be more aware of and express how they feel. It is not constructive when it has been essentially an angry outburst from the facilitator. Then you lose your ability both to be present and yet stand outside the situation. You are no longer working from a position of compassion. You lose your credibility or authority as a facilitator – you have 'blown it' as they say.

Sometimes there are people who are bent on being destructive. Hopefully others will deal with them, but maybe not. In that event firm action is needed. I am reminded of the skills a good teacher exercises in a classroom. However, it is not the same as dealing with disruptive pupils when company politics and 'face' are involved. There is no simple answer. One falls back on one's inner strength and authority.

The inner work we need to do

One of the great benefits of resistant clients is that they confront you with the work you have to do on yourself – better than almost anything else I can think of! For me this means learning to be fully empathetic with my clients, particularly in what seems to be the most difficult (ie, interesting) situation, perhaps when I am tired too, and not falling into the trap of putting my attention on my own feelings of anxiety or inadequacy. To avoid this, I particularly need my humor. 'Well, here we have an interesting situation,' I say to myself or out loud. At that moment, I most need to love myself in order to love my clients.

Avoiding our own avoiding

If we are going to help our clients to the fullest extent, we need to avoid our own avoiding. When I think about my own avoiding, there seem to be perhaps four or five things I can do. In Figure 14.4 Julia Cameron (1995) has many more wise things to say on this subject. For example I am aware that I often go into

---

- Become aware of how I avoid. Means being very honest.
- Make a decision – choose.
- Throw myself into the situation I find difficult again and again until I master it.
- Be gentle with myself.
- Get support from a 'believing' friend.

Figure 14.4

the garden to avoid the 'discomfort' of sitting at my desk and writing. Sometimes I go there for inspiration. That is fine. But I also go there to avoid. I know the difference. All I have to do is choose. This is relatively easy for me. I am minded of one of Julia Cameron's 'rules of the road': 'Remember that it is far harder and more painful to be a blocked artist than to do the work.' The same is true about the blocked consultant. I find it useful to ask myself 'What is your investment in being blocked?' or 'What is the pay-off in staying blocked?' When I answer these questions, I laugh because the answers usually don't make any sense. But I still have to make the decision.

Then there are those situations I find difficult like dealing well with resistant clients (or people I think are driving irresponsibly). Sometimes I get angry especially when I am tired. I am aware of this. I understand what is underneath my anger (fear that they will not overcome their resistance). But it feels very difficult to *decide*, or exercise the *choice*. I know I have the choice. I can choose to be relaxed and confident. I can also choose to see the situation with compassion and empathy instead of anger. But somehow the situation keeps catching me out – the way I phrase that reveals how I don't take responsibility and deny my choice. My conclusion is that I need to keep throwing myself into that situation until I master it. I notice the Universe has a way of throwing me into all the situations I need to work on again and again. Luckily I have some friends who believe in me and they make sure I am gentle with myself and *do not struggle* with these situations but work with them with humor and lightness.

I am going to talk a bit more about our own avoiding in the next chapter too. In particular I want to draw attention to how we avoid the challenge of doing the work in the world and with our clients that will make the biggest difference and choose blander, safer things instead.

References and suggested further reading

Bion, W. R. (1992) *Experiences in Groups*, Routledge, London and New York.

Cameron, J. (1995) *The Artist's Way – A Spiritual Path to Higher Creativity*, Pan Books, London, UK.

Oshry, B. (1995) *Seeing Systems – Unlocking the Mysteries of Organizational Life*, Berrett-Koehler, San Francisco, USA.

Vince, R. and Martin, L. (1993) 'Inside Action Learning: An Exploration of the Psychology and Politics of the Action Learning Model,' *Management Education and Development*, Vol. 24, Part 3, 1993, pp. 205–15.

15
❖
Ending
Including how our own development is the key to it all

'We cannot wait for great visions from great people, for they are in short supply at the end of history. It is up to us to light our own small fires in the darkness.' Charles Handy.

'Western man has one foot in the past, one foot in the future and pisses on the present.' Mahatma Ghandi.

For some time now I have been thinking about what to include in this final chapter. What does one put in a final chapter? How does one end a book? I have had quite a long relationship with you, the reader, and an even longer one with the book. (When the writing is done will it leave another 'fertile void'?) Perhaps this chapter is best seen as an opportunity to draw threads together and my last chance in this book to share with you things I have not yet shared.

Themes revisited

I began the book by outlining several themes. Amongst these was the idea that we are perhaps moving towards a world in which we are more aware of how interconnected everyone and every-thing is. Perhaps this is leading us towards a greater respect for each other and valuing the ways in which we are different. Perhaps our prospering (not just in a material sense but emotionally and spiritually, too) and even our survival depends on finding more inclusive and respectful ways of working together, reaching decisions and achieving common goals. I sense a move away from the old, adversarial and competitive ways in which some or a few impose their will on others because they have the power to do so – whether this is in our companies, our communities, in local or national politics, in the global market or in international relations. I sense a mood in which many people are tired of the 'I'm right and you are wrong' or 'We are superior and you are inferior' culture. I hope my judgment is not clouded by the aftermath of a General Election as a result of which we may, in the UK, be on the threshold of constitutional reform; we have the first Muslim MP; a woman MP in a wheelchair; over 100 women members of Parliament; an openly gay Cabinet Minister and another who is blind.

I have also argued that what we do in organizations matters greatly. This is where we can shape what it is to be successful and fully human at the same time.

Another theme has been that we can all *make a difference*. It really does not matter how big or how small our contribution appears to be; it is important, nonetheless. This is partly because the essence of the world is that it is a huge creative intelligence. We are all involved in this extraordinary creative evolution. Even an act of courtesy on the road can have multiple beneficial effects or repercussions that we cannot possibly know about. Everything we do matters if we see ourselves in a world that is immensely creative and interconnected. The little things we do with the people around us perhaps have more effect than grand gestures. This particularly applies to how we are with our children.

We also have much more power than we think we have (and much less if we have egotistical illusions about formal power). For example our purchasing choices have tremendous power to influence what happens in the Third World, how our food is produced and the health of the environment. Similarly the lobbying we do, the NGOs or charities we support can have profound effects. Big shifts are made up of millions of small actions.

Another theme has been the presence we bring to what we do. This can make all the difference, too. We are more likely to have a beneficial influence when we bring humor, relaxed confidence and high expectations. In many situations, simply how we are matters far more than what we do or say. Sometimes, if we have that quality in our presence, we may need to say or do much less. Presence is about being fully present, neither in the future nor in the past. A good way to learn about this is to meditate (see Amaravati, Self Realization or Mandala on pages 257–8).

This brings me back to another theme – *our own development is the key* (stage 5 of the Empowerment Model will invariably take us to that point if we allow it. So will stage 7 of the Internal Consultant's Model). That has certainly been my experience. The difficulties I have with clients (or colleagues), I mean in facilitating them, are essentially *my* difficulties. I am constantly brought back to this realization. Since I started working for myself, that realization has been brought into even sharper focus. If you work for yourself, you have absolutely no one you can hold responsible but yourself. This is dramatically good for your development. You succeed or fail through your own efforts. You are forced to learn if you wish to survive and prosper. It seems that it is not my experience, not my knowledge or skills but the quality of my presence in almost every situation I am in that matters most. This realization confronts us with some of the most difficult things we have to learn.

I find my family is one of the best laboratories in which to learn these things. It is a place where a ten-year-old has as much as anyone to teach a sixty-year-old and will say it with unerring accuracy and simplicity. It is a place where emotions often run high, your shell is broken and you are stripped of any pretensions. Almost all you learn here can be applied in the workplace. You are the same person in both arenas but perhaps in the family you are exposed in all your nakedness. As I have said earlier, sometimes leaders 'act out' in their organizations the 'pathology' they acquired in childhood and have not yet learned to leave behind.

I have also argued the case for dispensing with didactic or contrived learning or at least using it much less. I have tried to make a strong case for the richness and potential of learning from the real opportunities and issues we are confronted with; learning from doing rather than separating the two. I have called this Real Time Development. I hope I have not been dogmatic or doctrinaire about this. The truth is complicated, many sided and there are always interesting exceptions.

This brings me to two things I wish to share with you that I have so far left out.

Creativity and uncertainty

Being self-employed confronts one with the issue of uncertainty better than anything else I know. Employment creates an illusion of security, at least until it is shattered. Self-employment creates no such illusion. It has therefore helped me empathize with my clients who face uncertainty and unpredictability in abundance. It has helped me towards a more spiritual perspective and some principles that seem essential to succeeding (see Figure 15.1). Julia Cameron says: 'Our creative dreams and yearnings come from a divine source' and 'As we open our creative channel to the creator, many gentle but powerful changes are to be expected.'

- The universe will support us in fulfilling our vision.
- The people and circumstances we need will come into our lives.
- Have intentions, essences rather than specific form.
- Whatever we focus on, we create more of.
- Fear and anxiety are the greatest dampeners of vision fulfillment.
- Gratitude for our blessings is the key to unlocking abundance.
- Whatever happens is just exactly what I need for my development.
- Let go of the old to make room for the new.
- Live in the present for we can do nothing about the past and cannot control the future.

Figure 15.1   Useful principles

I was reminded of many of these principles when I went to a weekend workshop led by Nick Williams of Alternatives, based at St James's Church, Piccadilly, London. I also learned a simple three-stage process:

- Visualize – vision and intention.
- Energize – action.
- Detach – be available and willing to receive.

My life in organizations had taught me to visualize, create a vision and to energize and take action. It had also taught me to persist, sometimes appropriately and sometimes not. What it had not taught me was to *detach and be willing to receive* what I most desire, not necessarily in the form in which I envisaged it. That is for me a most valuable piece of learning. When I reflect, almost everything I desire has come into my life, but most often not in the form or the manner I expected. And my inability to detach exhausted me and probably delayed what I desired coming into my life. I was used to struggling. That seems to me to be a most empowering lesson for all leaders, especially those of the more traditional, controlling kind! Detaching gives other people more freedom to contribute creatively and willingly to a leader's vision. I am also learning that if I meditate for 20 minutes every day I shall enhance my chances of succeeding in everything I desire, enhance my ability to offer a benign 'presence' in those critical situations I find difficult and give my immune and healing systems a better chance of working.

Resolving conflict without violence

Much of this book has been about finding ways of working together more constructively, but I have realized that it offers little about how to resolve conflict constructively when it happens as it most certainly will. It dawned on me that I was somewhat ill-equipped when a client recently asked me if I would help with two key members of his team who often got into severe conflict with one another. He wanted them to learn to sort things out for themselves, rather than come to him. About that time I got the chance to attend a one-day workshop called **Non-Violent Communication** led by Dr. Marshall Rosenberg. I cannot do justice to the richness of his model here or even the basic elements of his thinking but I hope that my brief summary may interest you. Details of where you can find out more are given at the end of this chapter.

Marshall Rosenberg argues that we each have enormous power to make life more wonderful for other people. It is natural for us to want to give. We delight in meeting the needs of others if we can do so willingly. We resist being controlled or made to do things however.

'Never give unless you give from the heart.'

Part of the problem is that we have learned what Marshall calls 'Jackal Language':

> *'I'm right; you are wrong.'*
>
> *'There is something wrong with you if you don't agree with me.'*

It is the language of attack, blame, criticism, trying to make people do things because they would otherwise feel guilty. It is the language of ought and should, of manipulation and punishment. This is the language of power *over* people and we can make people do things because we can hurt them if they don't. It is the enemy of compassion and of learning. (It is also the language of the British House of Commons.)

What he advocates instead is 'Giraffe Language' (giraffes are the mammals with the biggest hearts). This is the language of compassion. It connects us at heart level and enables us to see the human in the other person, to 'see their beauty.' Communicating at that level enables us to discover other people's needs and forces us to be creative in finding ways of meeting everyone's needs. It keeps our attention on human needs and gives us power *with* people. Giraffe Language enables us to acknowledge that our feelings are never caused by what other people do. Their behavior is never the cause of our feelings; only the stimulus. Our feelings are caused by how we choose to *hear* what they say. We can choose to feel bad, guilty, that there is something wrong with us, or we can choose to see instead the hurt of the other person, their beauty, the disappointed visionary beneath their anger. Anger tells us that we are disconnected from our needs. Usually below anger there is fear or powerlessness. 'Whenever there is anger in your heart there's a should in your head.' 'Thinking wrongness creates anger [your own].' Jackal Language greatly reduces our chances of getting our needs met.

At the heart of Marshall's teaching is a simple model (see Figure 15.2) which offers a way of resolving conflict without violence – verbal or otherwise. It is a model which can be used by two people in turn or simply by one person to invite a response to meet their needs. It can all be said concisely in about 40 words, for example: 'When I see (hear) you .... I feel .... because I am needing .... and I would like you to ....'

1.	**Observation**	An accurate, factual statement of what I see or hear. No interpretation, evaluation or diagnosis. Separate observation from evaluation.
2.	**Feeling**	This is how I feel when this happens. No blame, judgment or attempt to imply the feeling is caused by the other. Do not confuse feeling and thinking or interpretation. Take responsibility for your feelings.
3.	**Need**	The need, not the stimulus. This is the need I have which is not being met.
4.	**Request**	This is what I request you do – not refrain from doing. Positive, not negative. A specific request that will meet the need. And no implied threat if you choose not. Not a demand.

Figure 15.2   Four-stage model for non-violent communication

It is important that there are no words that criticize, judge, diagnose, interpret or insult. This leaves the other person free to respond positively to your request or creatively find an even better way to meet your need – the win-win solution.

Again, how we choose to hear what the other person says depends on what ears we are wearing. Whether we hear blame, our own inadequacy or simply the needs of another human being. It is our choice whether we decide to feel good or bad about ourselves when other people are being authentic.

I have been introducing this model to my family and practicing it, partly to get ready to help my client – partly because it is so central to good family relationships. These are organizational relationships in microcosm. It is simple but not easy! I have found it a very rigorous discipline.

I wanted to include it because the model and the thinking behind it are so central to the themes in this book: moving from adversarial to collaborative relationships; from coercion to willing partnership; from verbal violence to respect; humility instead of arrogance; taking responsibility for our behavior and our feelings; doing things from the heart and head rather than only from the head. It also gives the facilitator valuable insights including how to be 'present' rather than to judge.

Staying in the real world

In our efforts to develop ourselves and do the best possible work for our clients, we can detach ourselves from the real world of ordinary working and living. This is the world of the overwhelming majority of human beings on the planet. We run the risk of doing this when we: focus on professionalism and higher qualifications as if they were what most mattered; pride ourselves in being at the leading edge and informed of all the latest developments; become captivated by methodologies – means rather than ends; are seduced by the prestigious, clever and ingenious; develop a passion for one methodology which we begin to believe is the answer to everything (I call this 'worshipping at altars,' and that can easily lead to organizations that take on the characteristics of sects or cults); start talking a language that others cannot understand; sit at the feet of or become devotees of 'gurus'; focus our attention on top managers rather than the whole workforce and never set foot in a factory or talk to working people. And when did you last listen to or learn from someone of a different race, culture or color? Can you explain what you do to 'ordinary' people?

Perhaps at the root of these ways of limiting ourselves is the desire for certainty or security in a bewildering world. Also, in Great Britain, they may reflect the lingering class system, élitism and intellectual snobbery. I think I may say these things because I have been guilty of falling into all these traps. There is a paradox here. Not all of these activities are harmful in themselves. It is only when we get them out of balance, forget what our purpose is, what we are here to do, what matters most and get out of touch with the majority of other human beings that there is a problem. Then we limit our potential to *make a difference* in our workplace and in the wide world.

Whether we are fully aware of it or not, we are all part of a long march towards a more equitable and respectful global society in which it is possible for everyone to be more truly human. And what we do in our organizations is an important part of this. Seen in this light, our work and learning together become part of something very inspiring and exciting.

Something that Harrison Owen (see Chapter 8 and read his books and articles) wrote to me recently seems very apt here:

'Somehow I think we are just working too hard. So for me, transformation is happening, it is not something you do. Certainly we have to figure out appropriate responses, but my learning recently is that the total organism of the Homo sapiens in its several parts (countries, companies, what have you) seems to be engaged in an evolutionary process which is enabling us to cope with the emerging reality. All of this is occurring (I think) not because we have figured things out, but in spite of the fact we haven't. We do have a choice, but it is rather more about accepting the emerging organizational (life) form – or not, and if not, we, like the dinosaurs, will simply disappear.

I am not the sort to throw my hands in the air in defeat, but neither do I feel the necessity to work overly hard at something which seems to be doing pretty well by itself. No guarantees of course, but I think we are going to make it. If there is a key it is all about self-organizing systems. I think that is what we are essentially. We just like to pretend we have done all this good work. Could be.'

Perhaps I should have called this book *Tools for Muddling Through* – but would anyone have bought it?

I want to end with two poems; the first by Benjamin Zephaniah (Zephaniah, 1996) and the second by Adisa.

GOOD HOPE

I believe
There is enough food
On this planet
For everyone.

I believe
That it is possible
For all people
To live in peace.

I believe
We can live
Without guns,
I believe everyone
Is important.

I believe
there are good Christians
and good Muslims,
Good Jews
And good not sures,
I believe
There is good in everyone
I believe in people.

If I did not believe
I would stop writing.

I know
Every day
Children cry for water,
And every day
Racists attack,
Still every day
Children play
With no care for colour.
So I believe *there is hope*
And I hope
That there are many believers
Believing
There is hope,
That is what I hope
And this is what I believe,
I believe in you,
Believe me.

REAL REVOLUTIONARIES MOVE IN SILENCE

Real Revolutionaries move in silence
Real Revolutionaries move in silence
Real Revolutionaries move in silence

You can say what you want but it don't mean a thing
It's the turning of that thought into action that carries the swing
Nobody is scared of a bee's buzz but they are scared of a bee's sting
It's not the bark it's the bite
It's not the talk it's the fight

If you spend all your time talking you will never get anything done
It's like you're in the starters block waiting for the starters gun
But if you were blind, deaf and dumb
You wouldn't know, the race had already begun
You wouldn't know you're a dog under a table being fed the
masters crumbs
You wouldn't know that your people were homeless and living
in the slums
Maybe we would know if we stopped jigging around and showing
each other our gums

In this line of work there is no pay
You will have to think for yourself 24/7 each and every day
You will have to become the attacker and no longer the prey
Knowledge is power and will keep ignorance at bay
We are all actors on stage what part do you play?
You should be one rung higher on the ladder than you
were yesterday
Read and listen to what our ancestors had to say
This will help to wipe the plaque from your brain and stop
the decay
Keep a picture in your mind of what it is you have to do
And each and every day make sure it's that you pursue
Use your mouth to speak, your ears to hear and your eyes to view
Know the difference between a lie and what is true
Know the difference between who and what has been here since
time in memorial

And who and what is brand spanking new
Become a detective hunting, searching for your next vital clue
But!!! stay alert and fresh like the morning dew
Or the next dead revolutionary could be you, or you or you!!!

Real Revolutionaries move in silence
If you are still confused as to what that statement means
I will now throw a little more light on the scene

To be real means to be real to yourself and real to your people
You're not Malcolm X or Harriet Tubman but you can be
their equal
Revolution means the movement, the turning of something
upside down
Revolution means going against the crowd
Revolutionary means being able to perceive

If you can't go through the wall go over or around

Silence – when you're under pressure will keep you calm
Silence – when there is danger all around will keep you from harm
Listen to your inner voice let that be your alarm

When you think before you talk you are in silence
When you fight before you think now that's meaningless violence
I hope in this poem I have been of some constructive guidance
As to why
Real Revolutionaries
Must always
move in
Silence.

References, suggested further reading and resources

Adisa, Dais Productions, Providing a Platform for the Speakers of Tomorrow, PO Box 12101, London N5 2RQ. (Tel: +44–(0)171–503–3889).

Alternatives, St James's Church, Piccadilly, London W1V 0CC (Tel: +44–(0)171–287–6711).

Amaravati Buddhist Monastery, Great Gaddesden, Hemel Hempstead, Hertfordshire HP1 3BZ, England (Tel: +44–(0)1442–842455). There are introductory classes in meditation on Saturday afternoons.

Cameron, J. (1995) *The Artist's Way – A Spiritual Path to Higher Creativity*, Pan Books, London, UK.

Centre for Creation Spirituality, St James's Church, Piccadilly, London W1V 0CC. (Tel: +44–(0)171–287–2741).

The Findhorn Foundation, The Park, Forres IU36 0TZ, Scotland. (Tel: +44–(0)1309–690311; Fax: +44–(0)1309–691301). The Findhorn Foundation offers a variety of workshops and programmes for people interested in their own spiritual and personal development.

Handy, C. (1994) *The Empty Raincoat – Making Sense of the Future*, Hutchinson, London, UK.

Handy, C. (1997) *The Hungry Spirit Beyond Capitalism – A Quest for Purpose in the Modern World*, Hutchinson, London, UK.

Mandala Yoga Ashram, Pantypistyll, Llansadwrn, Llandeilo, Dyfed SA19 8NR, Wales. (Tel/Fax: +44–(0)1558–685358).
Rosenberg, Dr. The Centre for Non-violent Communication, PO Box 2662, Sherman, TX 75091, USA (Tel: 001–903–893–3886) and Wasserfallenhof, Postfach 232, 4418 Reigoldswil, Switzerland (Tel: +41–61–941–2060).
Roth, G. (1995) *Maps to Ecstasy: Teachings of an Urban Shaman*, Thorsons, London, UK.
Self Realization Meditation Healing Centre, Laurel Lane, Queen Camel, Yeovil, Somerset BA22 7NU, UK. (Tel: +44–(0)1935–850266, Fax: +44–(0)1935–850234).
Zephaniah, B. (1996) *Funky Chickens*, Viking, London, UK.

Appendices
❖
Tools for Transformation

Appendix 1
Empowerment Model

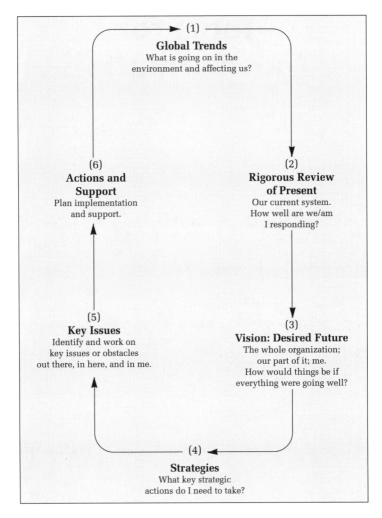

This is the basic model you can use for Real Time Management Development (Chapter 6). Getting the Whole System into the Room (Chapter 8), Working with Individuals (Chapter 9), or with Teams (Chapter 10), and in Support Groups (Chapter 11).

Appendix 2
Internal Consultant's Model

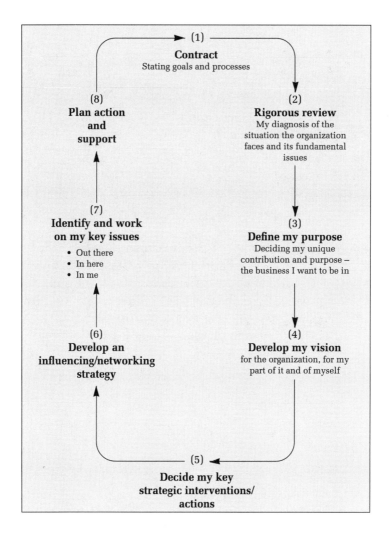

This is a model that you can use to develop your strategy if you are an internal consultant. Based on the Empowerment Model, its use is fully explained in Chapter 5.

Appendix 3
Useful Questions Model

* What is going well?
* What is difficult?
* What is your thinking about the current situation?
* How do you want to change things? How would things be if everything were going well?
* What will get in the way if you don't tackle it?
* What will you do?
* How can I help?

This is another variant of the Empowerment Model. You can use it to get out into the business and develop widespread friendships, collect data and build readiness for change (see Chapters 5, 6 and 10) or in networking (Chapter 11). These are empowering questions that help people clarify their thinking, build a vision and plan effective action to change things for the better.

Appendix 4
Helping Model

- **Contracting**

  Agreeing on the ground rules; initial definition of purpose or desired outcome.

- **Building a relationship**

  Getting to know the person and building trust.

- **Exploring the issue**

  Getting to know the problem exploring the data and the feelings and issues underlying it.

- **Understanding the problem and setting goals**

  Identifying underlying causes; grasping the pattern; making sense of it all; setting change goals.

- **Planning and acting**

  Turning identified need for change into practical strategies for action. Including the support needed to succeed.

This is a simple version of the Facilitating Model in Chapter 9. It is a basic model for one-to-one helping and teaching one-to-one facilitation.

Appendix 5
Consulting Model

- Gaining entry.
- Developing a clear agreement.
- Collecting data.
- Making a diagnosis.
- Planning change.
- Implementing change.
- Evaluating, monitoring, reviewing.
- Withdrawing.

Note: Ownership will be strongest when the key stages of bringing about change are carried out by the client with the support of the consultant.

This is a basic model for planning and implementing transformation in an organization whether it be managing a change or a piece of consulting work. See Chapter 5.

Appendix 6
Support Group Agenda

'Opening Circle' to get people here and express
desired outcomes.

●●●●●●

- Celebrate successes.
- Talk about what has been difficult and your feelings. What have you learned from this?
- Your thinking about the current situation.
- How you now want to change things for the better and what you will do.
- Identify what will get in the way and work on it.
- Make commitments.

●●●●●●

'Closing circle' to review what helped, what to do
differently next time and express appreciation.

This is a model you can use as an agenda for a support group, or a follow-up meeting with an individual, group or team or for the second part of a Real Time Management Development program.

Appendix 7
The Sunflower or Spider's Web

Present state – rigorous review

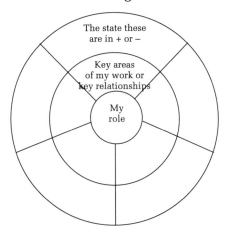

The desired state – my vision

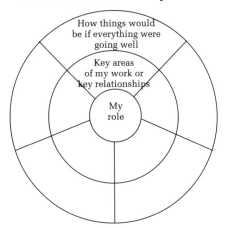

How to use the sunflower

You can use the sunflower to help people review the current situation rigorously and then decide how they want to change it. First they plot in the center circle their role, their job, their team, their department or their business. In the next circle they plot the key areas (domains) or relationships they want to look at. Finally in the outer circle, they briefly note what is going well (+) and what they are not happy with or that needs to be changed (-).

The next stage is to plot their vision or the desired state they want to bring about. They can use the same areas or domains or focus on those they regard as a priority for changing.

Either they can prepare their own charts and then share them with colleagues or they can talk through their thinking and their vision while a facilitator or colleague writes it up on two flip charts for them.

I have found many people really like this method. It is a useful way of working on stages 2 and 3 of the Empowerment Model in small groups in a real time management development program. It can also be used for an initial support group meeting or in facilitating an individual. It works well in a small (or support) group on a real time management development program because each member can gain a good understanding of her/his colleagues' situation and can offer feedback and suggestions. Managers generally highly value learning from each other.

The technical term for this tool is 'domainal analysis.'

Appendix 8
Developing Your Network

This is an exercise we developed at Sun Alliance and later used on our open program and other places in which we worked as independent consultants. Both managers and internal consultants found it extremely useful. I think we may have borrowed the basic idea from British Airways.

Networking: building your credibility and influence

The first and most important step in bringing about change is building relationships or, putting it more simply, making friendships with people in the organization. It is also a key way of bringing about change.

By establishing trust, asking questions and listening you can build up an accurate and comprehensive picture of the key issues of the organization. Paradoxically asking questions and listening are key ways of exercising leadership. People find it refreshing and empowering to be listened to. Gradually you will find there are a lot of people with similar views to your own and a similar vision of how they want things to be.

In my experience, useful questions to ask are:

- What is going well?
- What is difficult?
- What is your thinking about the situation?
- How do you want to change things?
- What will get in the way if you don't tackle it?
- How can I help?

These are empowering questions. They give people the chance to think about what they want to change, form a vision of the future and make decisions. By asking these questions you are providing valuable support and you may be invited to help them more actively if you do this well. As trust develops, it may become appropriate to share your vision with them. Gradually in this way you are building a network of people who want to change things and you are building a support network for yourself. Some will be enthusiastic. Others will come along more slowly. Yet others will not wish to be involved actively. However by making contact with them and showing respect, you will minimize the chances of opposition and maximize the chances of constructive relationships.

Analyzing your network

The following is a useful practical exercise for analyzing your network and deciding what action you want to take to develop it. I suggest you do the work on your own first and then share it with a close colleague and get their feedback and suggestions.

Kinds of contacts

There are three kinds of contacts:

Formal ('F')	In a formal position to help or we need to work with them because of their position in the organization.
Experts ('E')	They have information or experience we need.
Carriers/Influencers ('C')	Really carry the message, bring about change and influence others.

Action

1. List your network: above, around and below you. Make a long list.
2. Label them 'F,' 'E' or 'C' – whatever they are predominantly.
3. Who do you really trust? Who trusts you? Mark them 'T.'

4. Make notes on the action you want to take – those who are priorities to bring into the 'trust' category; those with whom it is important you take some action.

5. Finally, it may be helpful to plot people in three circles – the key people you target.

Inner circle   Those who are or will be your closest allies, perhaps 6-9; you will regularly spend time with them.

Middle circle   Those you aim to make allies but not spend large amounts of time with. Not major sources of support or allies but perhaps important clients.

Outer circle   Those you will have a long-term goal of bringing in closer or you need to keep in touch with – possibly in non time-consuming ways.

The network I have

Names	F, E, C	T	Actions

The network I want

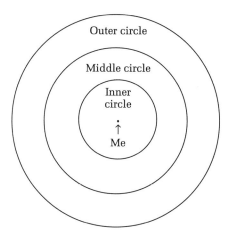

With the help of new technology, I now have an enormous network all over the world. I have discovered that is how I make it possible for the Universe to support me in my evolution and in making my difference.

Index